Torah (The Law) for
Modern Messiah Believers

By

Michel Robillard

Prayer:

Blessed are you, Heavenly Father, King of the universe. You are the Mighty One of Abraham, Isaac, and Jacob, the One who resurrected the Messiah from the dead; blessed is your Set-Apart Name forever and ever.

It has been placed in my heart to share this information, so I pray that it is done in a way that best represents who You are. Please protect the information in this book. I pray that You give me the tools, knowledge, and anointing to present this information correctly and that Your Set-Apart Spirit guides me throughout this project.

I write this book for those who seek to follow You, those who seek to understand who You are, and those who are dedicated to walking in Your ways like Yeshua Messiah demonstrated and taught throughout the letters of Matthew, Mark, Luke, and John. For those who read this book, I pray that you give them eyes to see, ears to hear, and a heart that seeks to know You and Your truth. May those who seek and need this information find it, and may You guide them to Your righteousness.

I say all this in the name of Yeshua, our King and Messiah, Amen.

About Jeff Clarke:

I presented this project to Jeffrey Clarke about 10 years ago with the idea that we would write this book together. At the time, Jeff was already an established author and leader in the Messianic community, and I was excited to begin this project with him. Little did we know at the time that life had other plans. Shortly after starting this project, Jeff moved to another country, while I was dealing with major changes in my own life, and we drifted apart (not on bad terms). We lost contact for a time, and that was it for this project for years.

During the summer of 2024, a fire was lit within me to complete this book and have it published. Since I lost all the previous documents that Jeff and I had worked on, along with new revelations, I rolled up my sleeves and started over from scratch. As I was finishing this book, Jeff and I reunited, and I couldn't be happier!

Jeff played a huge part in the conception of this book. Thanks to Jeff, this evolved from an idea to a project, and ultimately to a completed book. I am ecstatic and honored that he has written the foreword.

In the 2+ decades I've known Jeff, he has always had a big heart for the Messianic community, along with anyone who believes in Yeshua. Today, Jeff Clarke is a Messianic leader actively serving the faithful wholeheartedly. His accolades are:

- Founder of Messianic Discipleship Institute (www.mymdi.org)
- Host of "The Daily Torah" podcast, YouTube channel
- Director of the American Judeo-Christian Charities
- Author of the book series "The Daily Torah" and the book "The Set Feasts of the LORD"

Thank you, Jeff, for your friendship over the years, for everything you've done for me, and for everything you continue to do.

Foreword:

It is both an honor and a joy to pen this foreword for Michel Robillard's new and vital work, Torah for Modern Messiah Believers. Over the past two decades, I have had the privilege of journeying alongside Mike—not only as a friend, but also as a fellow worshipper and seeker of truth within our Messianic community. Our paths first crossed at Beit Yisrael in Orlando, where we learned and grew together, and later, we continued our fellowship at Eitz Chaim in Dallas, Texas. Through the seasons of joy and the trials that inevitably arise, I have witnessed Mike's steadfast devotion, his hunger for authentic understanding, and his unwavering commitment to serving others.

This book is the culmination of years of study, reflection, and spiritual wrestling. Torah for Modern Messiah Believers is not simply a scholarly commentary or a compilation of ancient wisdom; it is the heart-cry of one who both cherishes tradition and seeks to apply it meaningfully in the present age. Michel thoughtfully bridges the timeless truths of the Torah with the vibrant and ever-evolving journey of Messianic believers today.

Among the many strengths of this work, I would like to highlight a few areas that stand out to me:

- Practical Application: Michel does not leave the Torah as an abstract concept. He challenges readers to embody its principles —compassion, justice, and humility — within the reality of modern life, addressing questions and struggles unique to our time.
- Insightful Connections: This book draws insightful parallels between the ancient text and the teachings of Messiah, inviting readers to discover the unity and

continuity of God's revelation. Michel's ability to weave together the voices of Moses and Yeshua is both sensitive and illuminating.
- Community Relevance: Perhaps most importantly, Torah for Modern Messiah Believers is written as a gift to the Messianic community. It provides both a foundation for newcomers and fresh perspectives for seasoned believers, encouraging greater unity and understanding within our diverse movement.

Having witnessed Mike's journey—his perseverance through challenges, his deep love for Adonai, and his heart for people—I am profoundly proud of what he has accomplished here. This project is not only a testament to his scholarship and faithfulness but also a much-needed resource for all who seek to walk in the footsteps of Messiah with integrity and devotion.

To those who pick up this book: I encourage you to approach it not only as a study guide but as a companion for your spiritual journey. May the words within these pages inspire you, challenge you, and draw you closer to the One who gave us Torah and revealed Himself through Messiah Yeshua.

With gratitude and anticipation for the fruit this work will bear,

Jeffrey Clarke
Messianic Discipleship Institute
www.myMDI.org

- *Deeply rooted in scripture.*
- *Nothing that goes against scripture or is taken out of context.*
- *The target audience is the Hebrew roots/Torah positive community.*
- *Bold statements that challenge biblical assumptions*
- *Inviting the reader to dig deeper into scripture*
- *Great job connecting the entire bible*
- *Very well organized and easy to reference back to scripture*
- *Sincere and full of conviction*
- *Great introduction for those new to Torah-observance but still challenging for long-time believers.*
- *Thought-provoking questions encourage self-examination and scriptural deep digging.*
- *Teaches important Hebraic concepts like Torah, covenant, and obedience without overwhelming the reader.*

-Sabrina McCain

"I truly believe that Torah for Modern Messiah Believers will be a wonderful tool for any serious student of The Holy Scriptures. Not only does it show each command as it appears in Scripture, but it shows how they are interconnected and repeated. There is some commentary, but for the most part Scripture is allowed to stand on its own."

-Ruth Williams

Thank You:

- To Rabbi Steve Berkson. Your teachings and approach to the scriptures were the missing links I didn't realize I needed for this project. Your leadership, wisdom, love, and knowledge are priceless. Every time I've listened to you teach, you provided me with the fuel required to complete this book.
- To the Pavlik family, thank you for helping me discover my passion for teaching Torah and for providing a solid Messianic foundation for my understanding of the Torah.
- To Rabbi David Schiller, thank you for showing me how to search for the heart of Elohim and for showing me love in my greatest time of need.
- To Dan "best-bro-in-the-universe" Woodruff, I am so glad that we met. Thank you for your encouragement, support, and for providing an ear when I needed someone to listen to me as I worked through this book.
- To Brian Heilig, without your advice about this book creation process, I would not have finished this in a reasonable timeframe. Thank you, and many blessings to you and your beautiful family!
- Thank you, Pastor Ural Williams and Minister Robert Durst, for believing in me when I couldn't believe in myself.
- Thank you, Ruth Williams and Sabrina McCain, for your valuable feedback!
- To my extended Balboa family: You all are my inspiration to press forward and succeed. I love you all! This includes Jesse Riley and his beautiful family.
- Special thank you to my kids, Jordan, Michael, Noah, Francis, and Joelle, for your encouragement and support!
- Last, thank you, Joanna! You encouraged me when I was discouraged, helped me refocus when I lost my way, were my best cheerleader, my sounding board, and the greatest wife I could ever hope for! Thank you for everything, my love!

Preface:

Over eighteen years ago, I embarked on a journey to submit to the Law written by Moses. I did this because the words of the Messiah, as seen in Matthew, Mark, Luke, and John, led me there. This journey sent me on a personal mission to study and identify the commands of Elohim (GOD) found throughout the first five books of the Bible. I thought this was an easy goal; I had no idea what challenges I would face.

When it comes to the commands of the Law, Christianity's contributions leave much to be desired. Driven to achieve my goal, I was drawn to the Jewish scholars for the information I sought. Through Jewish commentaries, I discovered a treasured trove of spiritual wisdom, sound knowledge, and profound insights into the teachings from a Jewish perspective. With the Jewish insights, I was drawn into a deeper understanding of loving, fearing, and being in awe of Elohim. However, mixed in with this incredible knowledge came information that made no sense and did not align with the words I read in the scriptures. Some of the information even made me question my faith at times. One of the biggest problems with studying Jewish commentary is that you run into some anti-missionary (anti-Christian) views sprinkled throughout the information. Based on the horrific history between Judaism and Christianity, I get it.

At first, I thought my confusion was a simple lack of understanding, but as time passed, I began to realize something. Communication evolves, world systems change, and idiomatic phrases come and go. Many commentaries I ran across are hundreds, even thousands, of years old. Had I lived when they were first presented, it is possible that I would have had a better understanding of what the sages were communicating. It is not enough to identify the instructions of the Heavenly Father; His teachings should also be presented in a way that makes sense for people today.

Regarding Torah, there is no shortage of controversy and confusion in the religious world. The Heavenly Father is the Mighty One of order, not confusion, and the entire Bible is inspired through the One true Set-Apart Spirit. The problem is not with how He communicates the information; the problem is a combination of information displaced in time, the progression of how the written language has evolved, and some flawed men with flawed interpretations of what we read in the Bible.

This book has three primary goals:

1. To identify the commands of the All-Mighty.
2. To present the commands so they make practical sense for today's audience.
3. To show continuity between the Bible, the biography books of Yeshua, and the letters written by Yeshua's Disciples.

Approach this book as a comprehensive introduction to Torah. Yeshua sought the purity of Torah as Moses wrote, and I try to follow that example in this book. Focusing on the proper perspective and how to view the commands in today's world is important. I also wanted to ensure that our Heavenly Father's Set-Apart Spirit has room to do what it does best. With that said, not every command will have commentary. Many commands are straightforward and speak for themselves.

Knowing Torah is essential for having a proper relationship with the Heavenly Father. I've written this book to help people get the information they need and avoid the pitfalls, nonsense, and rabbit trails leading nowhere that I ran into while seeking this information. I hope you find value in this book and allow the Heavenly Father to guide you in all truths. To His Set-Apart Name be all the glory!

About This Book:

This book is written for anyone interested in understanding Torah, regardless of religious affiliation or background. Although this book is written for everyone, it is a Messianic book. The information found within this book is foundational upon the idea that Yeshua is the Messiah we follow, and Torah is the way we should live. Torah is what Yeshua taught, and it is how he lives.

This "About" section is mainly for those who know nothing, or very little, about the Messianic faith or Judaism. This is not a Messianic apologetics book (Command #812 is the only exception to this statement). It is not my job to convince anyone to keep the instructions of the Heavenly Father. I started this journey because the Heavenly Father chose to pop my bubble in a Sunday church service. Almost everyone I know who has joined this walk shares different but similar origins in this faith.

The Torah lifestyle is rooted in the Hebrew culture and language. You do not need to speak or read Hebrew fluently to live according to Torah. However, there are some Hebrew words you should get accustomed to. The Hebrew language and the English language do not translate smoothly. At times, it is better to stick with the original Hebrew word to maintain proper focus on what the Heavenly Father is trying to communicate to us. In this book, I will be utilizing the Strong's Dictionary system because, at times, it is necessary to explore a word from its original language for clarity and, most importantly, to avoid taking those words out of context.

In this book, we refer to our Messiah by his Hebrew name, Yeshua, which means salvation in Hebrew. Messiah means anointed one, and within Judaism, there is a list of people recognized as Messiahs. In this book, we will acknowledge Yeshua primarily as the Messiah we follow. I say this because Moses can also be considered a Messiah, an anointed one, and all others who contributed to the Bible.

In this book, we honor Yeshua as our Savior, King, and Messiah, but we will not worship Yeshua. Throughout the books of Matthew, Mark, Luke, and John, Yeshua never sought people to worship him; he always pointed to the Father for worship alone (See John 4:23-24, Matthew 4:10, John 14:6, John 17:3, and Luke 18:19).

When we refer to the One that Yeshua identifies as greater than himself, the only One we should fear, who can destroy both the body and the soul (See Luke 12:4-5), we can call Him:

- Adonai (Lord or Master)
- The Heavenly Father/The Father/Abba
- The One who freed Israel from Egypt
- The All-Mighty

For simplicity, we will refer to Him as the Heavenly Father most throughout the book. He does have a name, it is YHWH (commonly pronounced as Yahweh), but one of the commandments tells us not to make His name common, so we will not commonly use His name in this book. To distinguish the Heavenly Father further, when speaking of false gods, we will use "god," (with or without capital G) but when referring to the One True Heavenly Father as our Mighty One, we will use Elohim.

In this book, the word "holy" will be replaced by "set-apart." This is done because "holy" has been diluted by religion, while "set-apart" is more defined in terms of what the Hebrew word means. When I speak of the Sabbath, I often use Shabbat. I'm more accustomed to that word. And when it comes to the Law, I mainly use the word Torah. Torah means teachings or instructions. Those words can intertwine throughout this book. Every Bible verse shown in this book will come from the World English Bible (WEB) version. It is in the public domain and honors the name of Adonai. The verses you see will be slightly modified to honor Yeshua and the Father, along with minor clarifications in punctuation and so on.

Finally, this book employs the PaRDeS system for the scriptures. Our Jewish brothers recognized four levels or approaches to the written voice of our Heavenly Father. These levels are used as a tether for studying the scriptures. The word PaRDeS is a Jewish acronym formed from the initials of the following four Hebrew approaches/levels:

- **Peshat** (פְּשַׁט): "surface" or "straight": the literal and direct meaning of the Scriptures.
- **Remez** (רֶמֶז): "hints": the deeper, allegorical, hidden, or symbolic meaning that goes beyond the literal sense; revelations of the Scriptures.
- **Derash** (דְּרַשׁ): from the Hebrew darash, meaning "to inquire" or "to seek": the comparative (midrashic) meaning, derived through similar occurrences-insights gained through discussion on the Scriptures.
- **Sod** (סוֹד pronounced with a long "O" as in 'lore'): "secret" or "mystery"—the esoteric or mystical meaning, as given through inspiration or revelation from the Set-Apart Spirit. The spiritual meaning of the Scriptures.

The PaRDeS system is a great approach to understanding the Scriptures. It is effective because when all four levels flow together perfectly, you are on a safe path to understanding the scriptures as He intended them to be understood. The inspired words of the Heavenly Father come from one source that does not contradict.

The Peshat level serves as the foundation for every command in this book. Although this approach has pros and cons, it offers a strong starting point. Torah has parables, idioms, and cultural phrases lost in time. Nonetheless, the Peshat level is the safest way to approach Torah because when the Heavenly Father speaks, every word is fully maximized; once again, without contradictions. Using the Peshat level as our main understanding is imperfect; however, it will provide the safest approach.

Last, this book is written in a way that encourages you to have your copy of the Bible in hand as you go through it. This book is a helper for those studying Torah for the purpose of knowing who our Heavenly Father is. This book, along with all others like it, should never be a replacement for the inspired Word of Elohim. Be Bereans and check this book against the Bible.

Table of Contents

Introduction:

613?

Categories:

#1. Genesis 1:28 ~ To Be Fruitful

#2. Genesis 1:28 ~ To Have Dominion Over the Earth

#3. Genesis 2:24 ~ To Marry

#4. Genesis 4:7 ~ To Master Sin

#5. Genesis 9:4 ~ Not to Consume Blood

#6. Genesis 17:10 ~ Circumcision of Men

#7. Genesis 17:12 ~ Circumcision of 8-Day-Old Boys

#8. Exodus 12:2 ~ Beginning of New Moons (Observing Rosh Chodesh)

#9. Exodus 12:3-5 ~ To Observe the Passover Lamb for 4 Days Starting on the 10th of Nisan

#10. Exodus 12:6 ~ To Slaughter the Passover Lamb

#11. Exodus 12:8 ~ To Eat the Passover Meal

#12. Exodus 12:9 ~ To Eat it Whole, Do Not Break the Bone

#13. Exodus 12:14 ~ To Observe Passover Every Year

#14. Exodus 12:15 ~ To Observe the Week of Unleavened Bread

#15. Exodus 12:16 ~ The First and Last Day of Unleavened Bread is a Shabbat

#16. Exodus 12:17 ~ To Guard the Feast of Unleavened Bread

#17. Exodus 12:18 ~ To Eat Unleavened Bread Every Day for the Feast of Unleavened Bread

#18. Exodus 12:19 ~ No Leaven in the House During the Week of Unleavened Bread

#19. Exodus 12:20 ~ Do Not Eat Anything with Leaven During the Week of Unleavened Bread

#20. Exodus 12:24 ~ To Remember Passover Forever

#21. Exodus 12:26-27 ~ To Teach Children About Passover

#22. Exodus 12:43 ~ Uncovenanted People Cannot Eat the Passover Meal

#23. Exodus 12:44 ~ Servants That Are Covenanted May Eat the Passover Meal

#24. Exodus 12:45 ~ Uncovenanted People and Uncovenanted Servants, cannot eat the Passover Meal

#25-26. Exodus 12:46 ~ To Eat the Passover Meal in One House/Not to Take Any of the Flesh Outside

#27. Exodus 12:46 ~ Do Not Break the Bone

#28. Exodus 12:47 ~ All of Israel is to Observe the Passover

#29. Exodus 12:48 ~ Only Circumcised Males Can Partake of the Passover Meal

#30. Exodus 12:49 ~ One Torah for All

#31. Exodus 13:2 ~ To Sanctify the First-Born Males

#32. Exodus 13:3 ~ To Remember the First Day of Unleavened Bread as the Day Israel Left Egypt

#33. Exodus 13:6 ~ To Eat Unleavened Bread for 7 Days

#34. Exodus 13:6 ~ The Seventh Day of Unleavened Bread is a Shabbat

#35. Exodus 13:7 ~ To Eat Unleavened Bread for 7 Days

#36. Exodus 13:7 ~ Nothing with Leaven is to be Seen on Your Property During Unleavened Bread

#37. Exodus 13:8 ~ To Teach Children About the Feast of Unleavened Bread

#38. Exodus 13:9 ~ To Remember That the Heavenly Father Freed Israel from Egypt

#39. Exodus 13:10 ~ To Guard the Feast of Unleavened Bread Every Year

#40. Exodus 13:11-12 ~ All Firstborn Males Belong to the Heavenly Father

#41. Exodus 13:13 ~ To Ransom the First-Born Donkey with a Lamb

#42. Exodus 13:13 ~ To Ransom All First-Born Males

#43. Exodus 13:14-16 ~ Teach Children About How the Heavenly Father Freed Israel from Egypt

#44. Exodus 15:26 ~ To Carefully Obey the Voice of the Heavenly Father

#45. Exodus 19:5-6 ~ The Covenant of Relationship

#46. Exodus 20:2 ~ To Acknowledge the Heavenly Father Who Freed Israel

#47. Exodus 20:3 ~ Do Not Worship Other Gods

#48. Exodus 20:4-5 ~ Not to Make Statues, Idols, or Figures to Worship

#49. Exodus 20:7 ~ Not to Shame the Name of the Heavenly Father

#50. Exodus 20:8 ~ To Keep the Weekly Shabbat

#51. Exodus 20:9-10 ~ To Work 6 Days of the Week

#52. Jeremiah 17:21-22 ~ To Do No Work on Shabbat

#53. Nehemiah 13:15-18 ~ Do Not Conduct Business on Shabbat

#54. Amos 8:4-7 ~ Do Not Desire Shabbat to End so You Can Do Business

#55. Exodus 20:12 ~ Respect Your Father and Mother

#56. Exodus 20:13 ~ Do Not Murder

#57. Exodus 20:14 ~ Not to Commit Adultery

#58. Exodus 20:15 ~ Do Not Steal

#59. Exodus 20:16 ~ Do Not Lie About Others

#60. Exodus 20:17 ~ Do Not Desire What Belongs to Other People

#61. Exodus 20:23 ~ Not to Make Idols Out of Silver or Gold

#62. Exodus 20:24 ~ To Make a Slaughter Place for Sacrifices

#63. Exodus 20:25 ~ To Make the Slaughter Place with Natural Stones

#64. Exodus 20:26 ~ Not to Make Steps Leading to the Slaughtering Place

#65. Exodus 21:2 ~ Male Hebrew Slaves Can Go Free After 7 Years

#66. Exodus 21:3 ~ Male Hebrew Slaves Who Become Slaves While Single Leave Single; Those Married Before Being Slaves Leave with Their Spouse/Family.

#67. Exodus 21:4 ~ Single Male Hebrew Slaves Who Are Given a Wife to Marry by The Master; The Slave Can Leave Without His Family; They Belong to The Master.

#68. Exodus 21:5-6 ~ Option for Male Slaves Who Want to Stay with Family

#69. Exodus 21:7 ~ Female Hebrew Slaves Do Not Go Out Like Male Slaves After 7 Years

#70. Exodus 21:8 ~ To Ransom Displeasing Female Hebrew Slaves

#71. Exodus 21:8 ~ Not to Sell Female Hebrew Slaves to Foreigners

#72. Exodus 21:9 ~ If the Master Gives a Female Hebrew Slave to His Son for Marriage (1st wife), She is No Longer a Slave.

#73. Exodus 21:10 ~ If the Son of the Master Marries Another, the First Wife (Former Slave) is Still to be Honored as the First Wife

#74. Exodus 21:11 ~ If the Son Neglects 1st Wife (Former Slave), She is Free to Leave Him Without Obligations (Possibly for All 1st Wives' Situations)

#75. Exodus 21:12 ~ He Who Murders on Purpose Must be Executed

#76. Exodus 21:13 ~ He Who Murders by Mistake May Flee (To a City of Refuge)

#77. Exodus 21:14 ~ Those Who Plot Murder Must Be Executed

#78. Exodus 21:15 ~ Those Who Strike Their Parents Must be Executed

#79. Exodus 21:16 ~ Those Who Kidnap Must Be Executed

#80. Exodus 21:17 ~ Those Who Curse Their Parents Must be Executed

#81. Exodus 21:18-19 ~ Those Who Injure Another in a Fight Must Cover Wages Lost and Medical Expenses

#82. Exodus 21:20 ~ Those Who Murder a Slave Must be Punished

#83. Exodus 21:21 ~ No Restitution for Slaves Injured (Minor injuries) by Slave Masters

#84. Exodus 21:22 ~ If a Man Strikes a Pregnant Woman and there is no Injury, the Husband Can Seek Justice Through a Judge.

#85. Exodus 21:22-25 ~ Eye for Eye, Tooth for Tooth

#86. Exodus 21:26-27 ~ Slaves Are Free to Leave Their Master if Their Master Causes Them Permanent Physical Injuries

#87. Exodus 21:28 ~ If an Ox Kills Someone, it Must be Stoned; No One is to Benefit from it. The Owner is Innocent.

#88. Exodus 21:29 ~ If an Ox Has Been Known to Injure People Before, and it Kills Someone

#89. Exodus 21:30-31 ~ In case of a Sin Covering (If the Owner is Redeemed) Then He Shall Pay a Ransom Determined by a Judge.

#90. Exodus 21:32 ~ If an Ox Injures a Slave, They Give the Master 30 Shekels, and the Ox is Stoned to Death.

#91. Exodus 21:33-34 ~ If an Animal Dies Due to an Uncovered Pit

#92. Exodus 21:35-36 ~ If a Person's Animal Kills an Animal That Belongs to Another.

#93. Exodus 22:1 ~ When Someone Steals an Ox or Sheep to Slaughter or Sell

#94. Exodus 22:2 ~ If a Thief is Caught in the Act of Breaking in and is Killed

#95. Exodus 22:3 ~ Do Not Hold a Thief Hostage to Kill Later

#96. Exodus 22:4 ~ If a Stolen Ox, Sheep, or Donkey is Found Alive in the Hand of a Thief

#97. Exodus 22:5 ~ If Livestock is Feeding on Another Man's Property Without Permission

#98. Exodus 22:6 ~ The One Who Starts a Fire Must Pay for Damages

#99. Exodus 22:7-8 ~ If You Hold onto a Neighbor's Possession and it Gets Stolen

#100. Exodus 22:9 ~ For Unresolved Disputed Civil Matters

#101. Exodus 22:10-15 ~ If Something Happens to What is Borrowed

#102. Exodus 22:16-17 ~ If a Man Sleeps with a Virgin Out of Wedlock

#103. Exodus 22:18 ~ To Execute Those Who Practice Witchcraft

#104. Exodus 22:19 ~ To Execute Those Who Have Sexual Relations with Animals

#105. Exodus 22:20 ~ To Execute Those Who Sacrifice to Other Gods

#106. Exodus 22:21 ~ Not to Oppress Those Uncovenanted Within Israel

#107. Exodus 22:22 ~ Do No Wrong to Widows and Orphans

#108. Exodus 22:25 ~ When Lending to the Poor Within the Body, Do Not Add Interest

#109. Exodus 22:26-27 ~ If You Borrow Your Neighbor's Garment, Return It Before Sundown

#110. Exodus 22:28 ~ Do Not Disrespect Leaders

#111. Exodus 22:29-30 ~ To Sanctify the Firstborn Animals on the Eighth Day.

#112. Exodus 22:31 ~ Do Not Eat Animals Torn in the Fields

#113. Exodus 23:1 ~ Do Not Provide False Testimony

#114. Exodus 23:2 ~ Do Not Follow a Crowd into Evil

#115. Exodus 23:3 ~ Do Not Favor the Poor in Legal Judgments

#116. Exodus 23:4-5 ~ Do Not Neglect Your Enemy's Animal in Distress; Return it to Its Owner.

#117. Exodus 23:6 ~ Do Not Neglect the Right Rulings of the Poor

#118. Exodus 23:7 ~ Stay Away from False Matters

#119. Exodus 23:8 ~ Do Not Take Bribes

#120. Exodus 23:9 ~ Do Not Oppress Those Uncovenanted Within the Body

#121. Exodus 23:10-11 ~ The 7th Year Rest of the Land

#122. Exodus 23:12 ~ To Work 6 Days and Rest on Shabbat

#123. Exodus 23:13 ~ Do Not Mention the Names of False Gods

#124. Exodus 23:13 ~ Be Careful to Do as the Heavenly Father Says

#125. Exodus 23:14-17 ~ To Appear 3 Times a Year Before the Heavenly Father

#126. Exodus 23:18 ~ Not to Sacrifice Animals with Leavened Bread

#127. Exodus 23:18 ~ No Leftovers for the Feasts

#128. Exodus 23:19~ Bring the First Fruits to the House of the Heavenly Father

#129. Exodus 23:19 ~ Not to Cook a Goat in its Mother's Milk

#130. Exodus 23:21 ~ Do Not Rebel Against the Heavenly Father's Anointed Appointed People

#131. Exodus 23:24 ~ Do Not Submit to the Gods of Other Nations

#132. Exodus 23:25 ~ To Serve the Heavenly Father

#133. Exodus 31:13 ~ To Guard the Shabbats of the Heavenly Father

#134. Exodus 31:14 ~ To Not Work on Shabbat

#135. Exodus 31:15 ~ Work 6 Days and Rest on Shabbat

#136. Exodus 31:16 ~ Guard the 7th Day Shabbat

#137. Exodus 34:18 ~ To Guard the Feast of Unleavened Bread

#138. Exodus 34:20 ~ To Ransom the Firstborn Donkey with a Lamb

#139. Exodus 34:20 ~ To Break the Neck of a Firstborn Donkey Not Being Redeemed

#140. Exodus 34:20 ~ To Ransom All Firstborn Sons

#141. Exodus 34:20 ~ Ransomed Firstborn Sons Will Not Appear Before the Heavenly Father Empty-Handed

#142. Exodus 34:21 ~ Work 6 Days and Rest on Shabbat

#143. Exodus 34:22 ~ To Observe Sukkot

#144. Exodus 34:23 ~ To Gather 3 Times a Year Before the Heavenly Father

#145. Exodus 34:25 ~ The Passover Lamb is Not to be Eaten with Leavened Bread

#146. Exodus 34:25 ~ No Leftovers for Passover Meal

#147. Exodus 34:26 ~ To Bring the First Fruits to the House of the Heavenly Father

#148. Exodus 34:26 ~ Not to Boil a Young Goat in its Mother's Milk

#149. Exodus 35:2 ~ Work 6 Days and Rest on the Shabbat

#150. Exodus 35:3 ~ To Not Kindle Fire on Shabbat

#151. Leviticus 1:1-9 ~ Ascending Offering of the Herd (Ox, Bulls, Cows)

#152. Leviticus 1:10-13 ~ Ascending Offering from the Flock (Sheep or Goat)

#153. Leviticus 1:14-17 ~ Ascending Offering of Birds

#154. Leviticus 2:1-3 & Leviticus 2:8-10 ~ Grain Offering

#155. Leviticus 2:4 & Leviticus 2:8-10 ~ Baked Grain Offering

#156. Leviticus 2:5-6 & Leviticus 2:8-10 ~ Griddled Grain Offering

#157. Leviticus 2:7-10 ~ Stewing-Pot Grain Offering

#158. Leviticus 2:11 ~ Not to Burn Leaven with the Grain Offering

#159. Leviticus 2:11 ~ Not to Burn Honey with the Grain Offering

#160. Leviticus 2:11-12 ~ To Bring Honey and Leaven to First Fruits

#161. Leviticus 2:13 ~ To Season the Grain Offerings with Salt (Salt Covenant)

#162. Leviticus 2:14 ~ Grain Offerings for First Fruits

#163. Leviticus 2:15 ~ To Add Oil and Frankincense to the First Fruits Grain Offering

#164. Leviticus 2:16 ~ Burning the Remembrance Portion

#165. Leviticus 3:1-5 ~ Peace Offering from the Herd

#166. Leviticus 3:6 ~ Male or Female from the Flock is Permissible for Peace Offering

#167. Leviticus 3:7-11 ~ Peace Offering of a Lamb

#168. Leviticus 3:12-16 ~ Peace Offering of Goat

#169. Leviticus 3:17 ~ Not to Eat the Blood or Fat of the Sacrifices

#170. Leviticus 4:1-12 ~ Sin Offerings for Anointed Priests

#171. Leviticus 4:13-21 ~ Sin Offerings for Israel

#172. Leviticus 4:22-26 ~ Sin Offerings for Rulers

#173. Leviticus 4:27-31 ~ Sin Offerings for Individuals of Israel with a Goat

#174. Leviticus 4:32-35 ~ Sin Offerings for Individuals of Israel with a Lamb

#175. Leviticus 5:1 ~ To Truthfully Testify to an Oath Made

#196. Leviticus 7:24 ~ Not to Consume the Fat of a Dead Animal Torn

#197. Leviticus 7:26-27 ~ Not to Consume Blood

#198. Leviticus 7:29-36 ~ Bringing the slaughtering of the peace offering

#199. Leviticus 10:9-11 ~ Priesthood is Not to Drink Strong Drink Before Going into the Tent of Appointment

#200. Leviticus 11:2-3 ~ Animals That Are Good for Food

#201. Leviticus 11:4-7, 26-27 ~ Animals of the Earth You Do Not Eat

#202. Leviticus 11:8 ~ Do Not Touch the Carcasses of Animals You Do Not Eat

#203. Leviticus 11:9 ~ Creatures of the Water That Can Be Eaten

#204. Leviticus 11:10-12 ~ Creatures of the Water That Are Not for Food Are an Abomination

#205. Leviticus 11:13-19 ~ Birds That Should Not Be Eaten Are Abominations

#206. Leviticus 11:20 & 23 ~ Flying Insects That Creep on All Fours Are Abominations

#207. Leviticus 11:21-22 ~ Insects That Can Be Eaten

#208. Leviticus 11:24-25 ~ Touching Insects Not for Food Makes You Unclean

#209. Leviticus 11:26-28 ~ Touching the Carcasses of Animals Not to Eat Makes You Unclean

#210. Leviticus 11:29-30 ~ Creeping Creatures That Are Not for Food

#211. Leviticus 11:31 ~ Touching Creeping Creatures Not for Food Makes You Unclean

#212. Leviticus 11:32-38 ~ Instructions of Unclean Creeping Creatures Dying on Objects

#213. Leviticus 11:39-40 ~ Touching the Carcass of a Clean Animal Makes You Unclean Until Evening

#214. Leviticus 11:41-42 ~ Swarming Creatures Are Not to be Eaten

#215. Leviticus 11:41-42 ~ Swarming Creatures Are Abominations

#239. Leviticus 16:2 ~ The High Priest Is Not Allowed to Enter the Set Apart Place Except for Yom Kippur

#240. Leviticus 16:3-34 ~ Instructions for Yom Kippur

#241. Leviticus 17:2-6 ~ The Heavenly Father Accepts Sacrifices in One Place

#242. Leviticus 17:7 ~ Not to Sacrifice to Any False Gods

#243. Leviticus 17:8-9 ~ Sacrifices Are Only Allowed at the Door of the Tent of Appointment

#244. Leviticus 17:10-12 ~ No One is Allowed to Consume Blood, Not Israel nor the People with Israel

#245. Leviticus 17:13-14 ~ When Hunting, You Must Drain and Bury the Blood

#246. Leviticus 17:15-16 ~ If You Eat Animals Torn by a Beast or That Died Naturally

#247. Leviticus 18:4 ~ To Guard and Follow Torah

#248. Leviticus 18:5 ~ To Live by Torah

#249. Leviticus 18:6 ~ Do Not Have Sexual Relations with Family Members

#250. Leviticus 18:7 ~ Do Not Have Sexual Relations with Father or Mother

#251. Leviticus 18:8 ~ Do Not Have Sexual Relations with Your Father's Wife

#252. Leviticus 18:9 ~ Do Not Have Sexual Relations with Your Sister Born of Your Father or Mother

#253. Leviticus 18:10 ~ Do Not Have Sexual Relations with a Daughter Born from Your Son or Daughter

#254. Leviticus 18:11 ~ Do Not Have Sexual Relations with the Daughter of Your Father's Wife

#255. Leviticus 18:12 ~ Do Not Have Sexual Relations with Your Father's Sister

#256. Leviticus 18:13 ~ Do Not Have Sexual Relations with Your Mother's Sister

#257. Leviticus 18:14 ~ Do Not Have Sexual Relations with Your Father's Brother or His Wife

#258. Leviticus 18:15 ~ Do Not Have Sexual Relations with Your Daughter-in-Law

#259. Leviticus 18:16 ~ Do Not Have Sexual Relations with Your Brother's Wife

#260. Leviticus 18:17 ~ Do Not Have Sexual Relations with a Woman and Her Daughter, Her Son's Daughter or Daughter's Daughter

#261. Leviticus 18:18 ~ Do Not Marry Your Wife's Sister While Your Wife is Still Alive

#262. Leviticus 18:19 ~ Do Not Have Sexual Relations with a Woman During Her Monthly Uncleanness

#263. Leviticus 18:20 ~ Do Not Have Sexual Intercourse with Your Neighbor's Wife

#264. Leviticus 18:21 ~ To Not Give Your Children to Molek (or Molech)

#265. Leviticus 18:21 ~ Not to Profane the Name YHWH

#266. Leviticus 18:22 ~ Men Are Not to Have Sexual Relations with Other Men

#267. Leviticus 18:23 ~ Men and Women Do Not Have Sexual Intercourse with Animals

#268. Leviticus 18:26 ~ To Guard Torah, All Israel, and Those with Israel

#269. Leviticus 18:30 ~ To Guard Torah

#270. Leviticus 19:2 ~ To Be Set Apart

#271. Leviticus 19:3 ~ To Fear Your Mother and Father

#272. Leviticus 19:3 ~ To Guard the Shabbats

#273. Leviticus 19:4 ~ Do Not Turn to Idols

#274. Leviticus 19:4 ~ Do Not Make Figures to Worship

#275. Leviticus 19:5 ~ Sacrifices of Peace Offering are For Your Acceptance

#276. Leviticus 19:5-8 ~ To Eat the Sacrifice of a Peace Offering Within 3 Days

#277. Leviticus 19:5-8 ~ Burn the Remainder of the Sacrifice of the Peace Offering on the 3rd Day

#278. Leviticus 19:9-10 ~ Do Not Reap the Corners or Gleaning of Your Harvest for the Poor

#279-281. Leviticus 19:11 ~ Do Not Lie to Gain Deceitfully and Steal

#282. Leviticus 19:12 ~ Do Not Swear Falsely in the Name of YHWH

#283. Leviticus 19:13 ~ Do Not Oppress Your Neighbor

#284. Leviticus 19:13 ~ Do Not Rob Your Neighbor

#285. Leviticus 19:13 ~ Do Not Delay in Paying Wages

#286. Leviticus 19:14 ~ Do Not Hate or Cause Hardship to the Handicapped

#287. Leviticus 19:14 ~ To Fear the Heavenly Father

#288. Leviticus 19:15 ~ For Leaders to be Righteous in Right-Rulings

#289. Leviticus 19:15 ~ Leaders Should Not Be Partial to the Poor nor Favor the Great

#290. Leviticus 19:15 ~ For Leaders to Rightly Rule the People

#291. Leviticus 19:16 ~ Do Not Slander

#292. Leviticus 19:16 ~ Do Not Stand Against the Blood of Your Neighbor

#293-294. Leviticus 19:17 ~ Do Not Be Bitter Towards Others/To Correct Others When They Sin

#295. Leviticus 19:18 ~ To Not Seek Vengeance

#296. Leviticus 19:18 ~ To Love Your Neighbor as Yourself

#297. Leviticus 19:19 ~ To Guard Torah

#298. Leviticus 19:19 ~ To Not Let Livestock Mate with Other Kinds

#299. Leviticus 19:19 ~ Not to Sow Fields with Mixed Seeds

#300. Leviticus 19:19 ~ Do Not Wear a Garment with Two Different Types of Threads

#301. Leviticus 19:20-22 ~ When a Man Sleeps with a Servant Engaged or Ransomed

#302. Leviticus 19:26 ~ Do Not Consume Blood

#303. Leviticus 19:26 ~ Do Not Practice Fortune-Telling or Magic

#304. Leviticus 19:27 ~ Do Not Round the Corners of Your Beard

#305. Leviticus 19:27 ~ Do Not Destroy the Corners of Your Beard

#306. Leviticus 19:28 ~ Not to Cut Yourself for the Dead

#307. Leviticus 19:28 ~ Not to Put on Tattoos for the Dead

#308. Leviticus 19:29 ~ Do Not Turn Daughters into Whores

#309. Leviticus 19:30 ~ To Keep the Shabbats

#310. Leviticus 19:30 ~ To Respect the Set Apart Place

#311. Leviticus 19:31 ~ Do Not Turn to Mediums, Spiritists, and Magic

#312. Leviticus 19:32 ~ To Respect the Elders

#313. Leviticus 19:33 ~ Do Not Oppress the Uncovenanted Among Israel

#314. Leviticus 19:34 ~ To Love the Uncovenanted Among Israel as Israelites

#315. Leviticus 19:35-36 ~ To Be Honorable in Business

#316. Leviticus 19:37 ~ To Guard Torah

#317. Leviticus 19:37 ~ To Live by Torah

#318. Leviticus 20:1-5 ~ To Not Give Children to Molek

#319. Leviticus 20:6 ~ Do Not Turn to Fortune Tellers and Spiritists

#320. Leviticus 20:7 ~ To Be Set Apart

#321. Leviticus 20:8 ~ To Guard Torah and Live by It

#322. Leviticus 20:9 ~ Do Not Curse Your Parents

#323. Leviticus 20:10 ~ To Execute Adulterers, Both the Man and Woman

#324. Leviticus 20:11 ~ To Execute Both the Man and the Mother-in-Law Who Has Sexual Relations

#325. Leviticus 20:12 ~ To Execute Both the Man and the Daughter-in-Law Who Have Sexual Relations

#326. Leviticus 20:13 ~ Both Men Who Have Sexual Relations with Each Other Are to Be Executed

#327. Leviticus 20:14 ~ To Execute a Man Who Marries a Woman and Her Mother

#328. Leviticus 20:15 ~ To Execute a Man and an Animal Who Has Sexual Relations

#329. Leviticus 20:16 ~ To Execute a Woman and an Animal Who Has Sexual Relations

#330. Leviticus 20:17 ~ To Cut Off Siblings Who Have Sexual Relations

#331. Leviticus 20:18 ~ Cut Off Couples Who Have Sexual Relations During a Woman's Monthly Uncleanse

#332. Leviticus 20:19 ~ Do Not Sleep with Your Aunt

#333. Leviticus 20:20 ~ A Man Should Not Have Sexual Relations with His Uncle's Wife

#334. Leviticus 20:21 ~ Man Should Not Have Sexual Relations with His Brother's Wife

#335. Leviticus 20:22 ~ To Guard and Live by Torah

#336. Leviticus 20:25 ~ To Distinguish Between Clean and Unclean Animals

#337. Leviticus 20:26 ~ To Be Set Apart

#338. Leviticus 20:27 ~ To Stone Those Who Practice Fortune Telling, Magic, and Spiritism

#339. Leviticus 21:1-3 ~ Rule of Defilement from the Dead for the Priesthood

#340. Leviticus 21:4-5 ~ The Priesthood is Not Allowed to Make Any Bald Places on Their Heads

#341. Leviticus 21:4-5 ~ The Priests Are Not Allowed to Shave the Corners of Their Beards

#360. Leviticus 22:4-7 ~ An Unclean Levite Is Not to Eat the Set-Apart Offerings

#361. Leviticus 22:8 ~ A Levite Does Not Eat What Dies of Natural Causes or Is Torn by Beasts

#362. Leviticus 22:9 ~ A Levite Must Guard Torah

#363. Leviticus 22:10 ~ Those Uncovenanted Are Not Allowed to Have the Set-Apart Offering

#364. Leviticus 22:11 ~ A Levite Priest and His Family Can Eat What He Bought with Silver

#365. Leviticus 22:12 ~ If a Levite's Daughter Marries an Uncovenanted Man, That Daughter Can't Eat of the Set-Apart Offering

#366. Leviticus 22:13 ~ A Priest's Daughter Who Has Left and Returned

#367. Leviticus 22:14 ~ When a Man Eats the Set-Apart Offering by Mistake

#368. Leviticus 22:15-16 ~ The Levite Priesthood is Not to Profane the Set-Apart Offerings

#369. Leviticus 22:17-20 ~ Do Not Bring Offerings with Blemishes

#370. Leviticus 22:21-25 ~ Identifying Blemished Animals

#371. Leviticus 22:27 ~ Animals Are Acceptable for Sacrifice After 8 Days Old

#372. Leviticus 22:28 ~ Do Not Kill a Cow or Sheep with Their Offspring on the Same Day

#373. Leviticus 22:29 ~ A Sacrifice of Thanksgiving is For Your Acceptance

#374. Leviticus 22:30 ~ A Sacrifice of Thanksgiving is to be Eaten on the Same Day Only

#375. Leviticus 22:31 ~ To Guard Torah

#376. Leviticus 22:32 ~ Not to Profane What is Set-Apart

#377. Leviticus 22:32-33 ~ The Heavenly Father is Set Apart

#378. Leviticus 23:3 ~ To Work 6 Days

#379. Leviticus 23:3 ~ To Rest on Shabbat

#380. Leviticus 23:5 ~ To Observe Passover at Its Appointed Time

#381. Leviticus 23:6 ~ To Observe the Feast of Unleavened Bread for 7 Days

#382. Leviticus 23:7 ~ The First Day of Unleavened Bread is a Shabbat

#383. Leviticus 23:8 ~ To Bring Sacrifices Every Day for Unleavened Bread

#384. Leviticus 23:8 ~ The 7th Day of Unleavened Bread is a Shabbat

#385. Leviticus 23:10 ~ To Observe the Feast of First Fruits

#386. Leviticus 23:11 ~ To Wave the Sheaf on the Day After Shabbat for the Feast of First Fruits

#387. Leviticus 23:12 ~ An Ascending Offering for the Feast of First Fruits

#388. Leviticus 23:13 ~ The Grain Offering for the Feast of First Fruits

#389. Leviticus 23:14 ~ To Not Eat Bread, Roasted Grain, or Fresh Grain

#390. Leviticus 23:15 ~ To Count the Weeks from the First to Shavuot (Feast of Weeks)

#391. Leviticus 23:16 ~ To Count 50 Days from the First Shabbat of Unleavened Bread to Shavuot

#392. Leviticus 23:16 ~ To Bring New Grain Offerings to Shavuot

#393. Leviticus 23:17 ~ To Bring Two Wave Loaves for Shavuot

#394. Leviticus 23:18 ~ To Bring 7 Lambs for Shavuot

#395. Leviticus 23:19 ~ To Do Sacrifices on Shavuot

#396. Leviticus 23:20 ~ For the Priest to Wave the Bread of the First Fruits for Shavuot

#397. Leviticus 23:21 ~ Shavuot is a Shabbat

#398. Leviticus 23:22 ~ Do Not Reap the Corners or Glean Your Harvest for the Poor

#399. Leviticus 23:24 ~ To Observe the Feast of Trumpets

#400. Leviticus 23:25 ~ The Feast of Trumpets is a Shabbat

#401. Leviticus 23:27 ~ To Observe Yom Kippur

#402. Leviticus 23:27 ~ To Fast on Yom Kippur

#403. Leviticus 23:28 ~ Yom Kippur is a Shabbat

#404. Leviticus 23:31 ~ Do No Work at All on Yom Kippur

#405. Leviticus 23:32 ~ To Fast on Yom Kippur

#406. Isaiah 58:13-14 ~ Do Not Do Your Pleasure on Yom Kippur

#407. Isaiah 58:13-14 ~ To Call Yom Kippur a Delight

#408. Isaiah 58:13-14 ~ To Esteem Yom Kippur

#409. Isaiah 58:13-14 ~ To Not Do Your Desires on Yom Kippur

#410. Isaiah 58:13-14 ~ To Not Speak Your Own Words on Yom Kippur

#411. Leviticus 23:34 ~ To Observe the Feast of Sukkot

#412. Leviticus 23:35 ~ The First Day of Sukkot is a Shabbat

#413. Leviticus 23:36 ~ To Sacrifice 7 Days for Sukkot

#414. Leviticus 23:36 ~ The 8th Day of Sukkot is a Shabbat

#415. Leviticus 23:36 ~ To Sacrifice on the 8th Day of Sukkot

#416. Leviticus 23:39 ~ To Gather the Fruit of the Land for Sukkot

#417. Leviticus 23:39 ~ The 1st and 8th Day of Sukkot is a Shabbat

#418. Leviticus 23:40 ~ To Gather Good Trees, Branches, Palm of Trees, Twigs of Leafy Trees, and Willows for Sukkot

#419. Leviticus 23:41 ~ To Celebrate Sukkot for 7 Days

#420. Leviticus 23:42 ~ To Dwell in Booths During Sukkot

#421. Leviticus 24:2-4 ~ The High Priest's Duties with the Lamp Outside the Veil of Witness

#422. Leviticus 24:5-9 ~ Instructions for the Bread of the Tabernacle

#423. Leviticus 24:10-16 ~ Do Not Blaspheme the Name YHWH

#424. Leviticus 24:10-16 ~ To Execute the Ones Who Blaspheme the Name of the Heavenly Father

#425. Leviticus 24:17 ~ A Man Who Commits Murder Must Be Executed

#426. Leviticus 24:18 ~ If a Man Kills a Beast That Belongs to Someone Else, They Must Replace the Animal

#427. Leviticus 24:19-20 ~ If a Man Strikes a Man and Leaves Lasting Bodily Injury, Punishment cannot be beyond the Injury

#428. Leviticus 24:21 If a Man Kills a Beast that Belongs to Someone Else, They Must Replace the Animal

#429. Leviticus 24:21 ~ A man who Murders Another Man Must be executed

#430. Leviticus 25:2-7 ~ The 7th Year Shabbat of the Land

#431. Leviticus 25:8 ~ 7 Times 7 Years is the Year of Jubilee

#432. Leviticus 25:9 ~ To Sound the Trumpet on Yom Kippur for the Year of Jubilee

#433. Leviticus 25:10 ~ The Year of Jubilee is Set Apart

#434. Leviticus 25:10 ~ The Year of Jubilee is the Year Israelite Slaves Are Set Free

#435. Leviticus 25:11-12 ~ Do Not Sow or Reap That Which Grows by Itself or Gather from Untended Vines During the Year of Jubilee

#436. Leviticus 25:13 ~ For Every Hebrew Slave to Return to Their Property

#437. Leviticus 25:14-16 ~ To Be Above Reproach in Buying and Selling Due to the Jubilee Year

#438. Leviticus 25:17 ~ To Not Cheat One Another

#439. Leviticus 25:18-22 ~ To Keep the Commands for the Year of Jubilee

#440. Leviticus 25:23 ~ The Land Belongs to the Heavenly Father and Cannot be Sold

#441. Leviticus 25:24 ~ To Redeem the Land

#442. Leviticus 25:25-28 ~ Instructions to Redeem Land Sold

#443. Leviticus 25:29-30 ~ Instructions to Redeem a House in a Walled City

#444. Leviticus 25:31 ~ Instructions to Redeem Houses of Villages

#445. Leviticus 25:32-34 ~ Instructions for Redeeming Levite Property

#446. Leviticus 25:35 ~ To Help an Israelite Who Has Become Poor

#447. Leviticus 25:36-37 ~ To Not Profit from an Israelite Who Has Become Poor

#448. Leviticus 25:39-41 ~ Instructions for a Hebrew Who Sells Himself as a Servant

#449. Leviticus 25:42 ~ To Not Sell Hebrews as Slaves

#450. Leviticus 25:43 ~ Do Not Rule Harshly Over Hebrew Servants

#451. Leviticus 25:44-46 ~ Instructions for Non-Hebrew Slaves

#452. Leviticus 25:47-55 ~ Instructions to Redeem a Hebrew Sold to a Non-Hebrew

#453. Leviticus 26:1 ~ Do Not Make Idols

#454. Leviticus 26:1 ~ Do Not Set Up Carved Images or Pillars

#455. Leviticus 26:1 ~ Do Not Place Stone Images (For worship)

#456. Leviticus 26:2 ~ To Guard the Shabbats

#457. Leviticus 26:2 ~ To Respect the Set Apart Place

#458. Leviticus 27:1-28 ~ Instructions to Estimate the Value of a Promise

#459. Leviticus 27:29 ~ Those Under the Ban Cannot be Ransomed/Redeemed and Are to be Executed

#460. Leviticus 27:30 ~ Tithe Belongs to the Heavenly Father

#461. Leviticus 27:31 ~ To Add 1/5 to Redeemed Tithe

#462. Leviticus 27:32 ~ The Tithe from Herd or Flock is Set Apart to the Heavenly Father

#463. Leviticus 27:33 ~ To Not Inquire the Condition of the Tithe

#464. Leviticus 27:33 ~ To Not Exchange

#465. Leviticus 27:33 ~ If it is Exchanged

#466. Numbers 3:6-10 ~ The Duties of the Levites

#467. Numbers 3:10 ~ To Execute Those That Should Not Come Near

#468. Numbers 5:6-10 ~ Instructions for Confessing Sins and Paying Restitution

#469. Numbers 5:11-31 ~ Instructions to Test if a Wife Committed Adultery

#492. Numbers 18:22-23 ~ Only Levites Come Near the Tent of Appointment

#493. Numbers 18:26-28 ~ To Tithe 10% (1st Tithe)

#494. Numbers 18:29-32 ~ For the Levites to Give the Best Offerings to the Heavenly Father

#495. Numbers 19:11 ~ Touching a Dead Body Makes You Unclean for 7 Days

#496. Numbers 19:12 ~ To Wash Yourself on the 3rd Day if You Touch the Dead

#497. Numbers 19:13 ~ Not Washing Yourself After Touching the Dead on the 3rd Day is a Sin

#498. Numbers 19:14-15 & 17-19 & 21-22 ~ Instructions for People Who Live in a House Where Someone Dies

#499. Numbers 19:16 ~ Touching the Dead

#500. Numbers 19:20 ~ Not Washing Yourself After Touching the Dead on the 3rd Day is a Sin

#501. Numbers 28:2-8 ~ Instructions for Daily Offerings

#502. Numbers 28:9-10 ~ Instructions for Shabbat Offerings

#503. Numbers 28:11-15 ~ Instructions for Monthly Offerings

#504. Numbers 28:16 ~ To Observe Passover on its Appointed Time

#505. Numbers 28:17 ~ To Observe the Feast of Unleavened Bread on its Appointed Time

#506. Numbers 28:18 ~ The First Day of Unleavened Bread is a Shabbat

#507. Numbers 28:19-24 ~ Instructions for Unleavened Bread Offerings

#508. Numbers 28:25 ~ The 7th Day of Unleavened Bread is a Shabbat

#509. Numbers 28:26-31 ~ Instructions for Shavuot Offerings

#510. Numbers 29:1 ~ To Observe the Feast of Trumpets

#511. Numbers 29:2-6 ~ Instructions for Feast of Trumpets Offerings

#512. Numbers 29:7 ~ To Observe Yom Kippur

#513. Numbers 29:8-11 ~ Instructions for Yom Kippur Offerings

#514. Numbers 29:12 ~ To Observe the Feast of Sukkot

#515. Numbers 29:13-40 ~ Instructions for Sukkot Offerings

#516. Numbers 30:2 ~ For Men to Keep Their Vows to the Heavenly Father

#517. Numbers 30:3-16 ~ Instructions for When a Woman Makes a Vow

#518. Numbers 35:1-8 ~ Cities for Levites

#519. Numbers 35:9-34 ~ Cities of Refuge

#520. Deuteronomy 4:1 ~ To Listen to Moses

#521. Deuteronomy 4:2 ~ To Not Alter the Words of Torah

#522. Deuteronomy 4:6 ~ To Guard Torah

#523. Deuteronomy 4:6 ~ For Torah to be Our Wisdom and Understanding

#524. Deuteronomy 4:9 ~ To Carefully Guard Yourself

#525. Deuteronomy 4:9 ~ Do Not Forget Torah

#526. Deuteronomy 4:9 ~ To Teach Your Children and Grandchildren About Torah

#527. Deuteronomy 4:10 ~ To Fear the Heavenly Father

#528. Deuteronomy 4:15 ~ To Carefully Guard Yourself

#529. Deuteronomy 4:16-19 ~ Do Not Worship Idols

#530. Deuteronomy 4:23 ~ To Guard Yourself from Forgetting Torah

#531. Deuteronomy 4:23 ~ Do Not Forget the Covenant

#532. Deuteronomy 4:35 ~ The Heavenly Father Has No Equal

#533. Deuteronomy 4:40 ~ To Guard Torah

#534. Deuteronomy 4:41-43 ~ Cities of Refuge

#535. Deuteronomy 5:1 ~ To Learn Torah

#536. Deuteronomy 5:1 ~ To Guard and Do Torah

#537. Deuteronomy 5:6 ~ To Acknowledge YHWH Who Brought Israel out of Egypt

#538. Deuteronomy 5:7 ~ To Worship YHWH Alone

#539. Deuteronomy 5:8-9 ~ Do Not Create Carved Images to Worship

#540. Deuteronomy 5:11 ~ Do Not Disgrace the Name of YHWH

#541. Deuteronomy 5:12 ~ To Guard the Weekly Shabbat

#542. Deuteronomy 5:13-14 ~ To Work 6 Days and Rest on Shabbat

#543. Deuteronomy 5:15 ~ To Remember That We Were Slaves in Egypt and the Heavenly Father Freed Us

#544. Deuteronomy 5:16 ~ To Respect Your Parents

#545. Deuteronomy 5:17 ~ Do Not Murder

#546. Deuteronomy 5:18 ~ Do Not Commit Adultery

#547. Deuteronomy 5:19 ~ Do Not Steal

#548. Deuteronomy 5:20 ~ Do not Lie Against Someone

#549. Deuteronomy 5:21 ~ Do Not Covet or Desire What Belongs to Someone Else

#550. Deuteronomy 5:29 ~ To Fear the Heavenly Father

#551. Deuteronomy 5:29 ~ To Guard Torah

#552. Deuteronomy 5:32 ~ To Not Deviate from Torah

#553. Deuteronomy 5:33 ~ To Walk in a Way that Flows Perfectly with Torah

#554. Deuteronomy 6:2 ~ To Fear the Heavenly Father

#555. Deuteronomy 6:2 ~ To Guard Torah

#556. Deuteronomy 6:3 ~ To Hear and Do Torah

#557. Deuteronomy 6:5 ~ To Love the Heavenly Father with Everything You Are

#558. Deuteronomy 6:6 ~ For Torah to be in Your Heart

#559. Deuteronomy 6:7 ~ To Teach Your Children Torah

#560. Deuteronomy 6:7-8 ~ To Always Think About Torah

#561. Deuteronomy 6:9 ~ To Have Torah on Your Doorposts and Gates (Mezuzahs)

#562. Deuteronomy 6:13 ~ To Fear the Heavenly Father

#563. Deuteronomy 6:13 ~ To Serve the Heavenly Father

#564. Deuteronomy 6:13 ~ To Swear by the Name YHWH

#565. Deuteronomy 6:14 ~ Do Not Seek After Other Gods

#566. Deuteronomy 6:16 ~ Do Not Test the Heavenly Father

#567. Deuteronomy 6:17 ~ To Guard the Commands of the Heavenly Father

#568. Deuteronomy 6:18 ~ To Do What is Right in the Eyes of the Heavenly Father

#569. Deuteronomy 6:20-24 ~ To Explain to Children Why We Keep Torah

#570. Deuteronomy 6:25 ~ Torah is Our Righteousness

#571. Deuteronomy 7:6 ~ To Be Set Apart for the Heavenly Father

#572. Deuteronomy 7:11 ~ To Guard Torah

#573. Deuteronomy 8:1 ~ Be Careful to do Everything that the Heavenly Father Commands

#574. Deuteronomy 8:6 ~ To Guard the Commands

#575. Deuteronomy 8:6 ~ To Walk in the Ways of the Heavenly Father

#576. Deuteronomy 8:6 ~ To Fear the Heavenly Father

#577. Deuteronomy 8:11 ~ Be Careful Not to Forget the Heavenly Father's Commands

#578. Deuteronomy 10:12 ~ To Fear the Heavenly Father

#579. Deuteronomy 10:12 ~ To Walk in All the Ways of the Heavenly Father

#580. Deuteronomy 10:12 ~ To Love the Heavenly Father

#581. Deuteronomy 10:12 ~ Serve the Elohim with Everything That You Are

#582. Deuteronomy 10:13 ~ To Guard the Commands of the Heavenly Father

#583. Deuteronomy 10:16 ~ To Circumcise the Foreskin of Your Heart

#584. Deuteronomy 10:19 ~ To Love the Non-Israelite

#585. Deuteronomy 10:20 ~ To Fear the Heavenly Father

#586. Deuteronomy 10:20 ~ To Serve the Heavenly Father

#587. Deuteronomy 10:20 ~ To Cling to the Heavenly Father

#588. Deuteronomy 10:20 ~ To Swear by the Name of YHWH

#589. Deuteronomy 11:1 ~ To Love the Heavenly Father

#590. Deuteronomy 11:8 ~ To Guard All the Commands

#591. Deuteronomy 11:13 ~ To Love Elohim with Everything That You Are

#592. Deuteronomy 11:16 ~ Be Careful Not to Turn Away from the Heavenly Father and Serve Other Gods

#593. Deuteronomy 11:18 ~ To Have Torah in Your Mind and Soul

#594. Deuteronomy 11:19 ~ To Teach Torah to the Children

#595. Deuteronomy 11:20 ~ To Have Torah on Your Doorposts and Gates (Mezuzahs)

#596. Deuteronomy 12:5-7 ~ To Sacrifice at the Place Where the Heavenly Father Chooses

#597. Deuteronomy 12:8 ~ Do Not Do What is Right in Your Own Eyes

#598. Deuteronomy 12:11 ~ To Sacrifice Where the Heavenly Father Chooses

#599. Deuteronomy 12:13-14 ~ Only Sacrifice Where the Heavenly Father Accepts Sacrifices

#600. Deuteronomy 12:15 ~ Those Clean and Unclean May Eat of What is Sacrificed

#601. Deuteronomy 12:16 ~ Do Not Consume Blood

#602. Deuteronomy 12:17-18 ~ To Eat the Sacrifices Vowed Before the Heavenly Father

#603. Deuteronomy 12:19 ~ Do Not Neglect the Levites

#604. Deuteronomy 12:21 ~ Sacrificing Within Israel, When the Place the Heavenly Father Chooses is Too Far

#605. Deuteronomy 12:22 ~ The Clean and Unclean Can Eat When Sacrificing Within the Land

#606. Deuteronomy 12:23-25 ~ Do Not Consume Blood

#607. Deuteronomy 12:26 ~ The Set Apart Gift and Vowed Offering Must Only Go to the Place Where the Heavenly Father Chooses

#608. Deuteronomy 12:27 ~ Make Ascending Offerings at the Slaughter Place of the Heavenly Father

#609. Deuteronomy 12:28 ~ To Guard the Commands of the Heavenly Father

#610. Deuteronomy 12:28 ~ To Obey the Commands of the Heavenly Father

#611. Deuteronomy 12:30 ~ Do Not Seek Other Gods or Learn Their Ways

#612. Deuteronomy 12:32 ~ To Guard What Moses Says

#613. Deuteronomy 12:32 ~ Do Not Add to or Take Away from What Moses Wrote

#614. Deuteronomy 13:1-3 ~ Do Not Listen to Anyone Who Leads You Away from the Heavenly Father's Commands

#615. Deuteronomy 13:4 ~ To Walk After the Heavenly Father

#616. Deuteronomy 13:4 ~ To Fear the Heavenly Father

#617. Deuteronomy 13:4 ~ To Guard the Commands of the Heavenly Father

#618. Deuteronomy 13:4 ~ To Obey the Voice of the Heavenly Father

#619. Deuteronomy 13:4 ~ To Serve the Heavenly Father

#620. Deuteronomy 13:4 ~ To Cling to the Heavenly Father

#621. Deuteronomy 13:5 ~ To Execute the Prophet or Dreamer of Dreams, The One Who Leads You Away from Following the Heavenly Father

#622. Deuteronomy 13:6-8 ~ Do Not Listen to Anyone Who Says to Worship Another God

#623. Deuteronomy 13:9-11 ~ To Execute Those Who Try to Entice You to Worship Other Gods

#624. Deuteronomy 13:12-18 ~ If You Hear a City Has Turned Away from the Heavenly Father

#625. Deuteronomy 14:1 ~ Do Not Cut Yourself for the Dead

#626. Deuteronomy 14:1 ~ Do Not Shave the Front of Your Head for the Dead

#627. Deuteronomy 14:3 ~ Do Not Eat What is Abominable

#628. Deuteronomy 14:4-7 ~ Animals That Are Good for Food and Not Good for Food

#629. Deuteronomy 14:8 ~ Do Not Eat Pig

#630. Deuteronomy 14:8 ~ Do Not Touch the Dead Carcass of a Pig

#631. Deuteronomy 14:9 ~ What Can Be Eaten from the Waters

#632. Deuteronomy 14:10 ~ Whatever does not have fins and scales from the waters is not for food

#633. Deuteronomy 14:11 ~ Clean Birds for Food

#634. Deuteronomy 14:12-18 ~ Birds That Are Not for Food

#635. Deuteronomy 14:19 ~ Insects That Fly Are Not for Food

#636. Deuteronomy 14:20 ~ Clean Birds That Are for Food

#637. Deuteronomy 14:21 ~ Do Not Eat What Dies Naturally

#638. Deuteronomy 14:21 ~ To Sell What Dies Naturally to the Non-Covenanted and Foreigners

#639. Deuteronomy 14:21 ~ Do Not Cook a Young Goat in Its Mother's Milk

#640. Deuteronomy 14:22 ~ To Do the Yearly Tithe (The 2nd Tithe)

#641. Deuteronomy 14:23 ~ To Sacrifice Only Where the Heavenly Father Chooses for Grain Offerings During Sukkot

#642. Deuteronomy 14:24 ~ To Use Up the 2nd Tithe for the Feast of Sukkot

#643. Deuteronomy 14:27 ~ To Give the Remainder of the 2nd Tithes to the Priesthood

#644. Deuteronomy 14:28-29 ~ To Give a 3rd Tithe of Benevolence Every 3 Years

#645. Deuteronomy 15:1-3 ~ To Release Debts Every 7 Years for Those Covenanted

#646. Deuteronomy 15:7-8 ~ To Help the Covenanted Poor

#647. Deuteronomy 15:9-11 ~ Do Not Withhold from Giving to the Poor Due to the Coming of the Sabbatical Year

#648. Deuteronomy 15:12 ~ If a Covenanted Man or Woman Is Sold, They Serve 6 Years and Are Freed on the 7th Year.

#649. Deuteronomy 15:13-14 ~ If a Covenanted Enslaved Man is Freed, Send Them Away with Riches

#650. Deuteronomy 15:15 ~ To Remember That We Were Slaves in Egypt

#651. Deuteronomy 15:16-17 ~ If a Covenanted Slave Chooses to Stay on the Sabbatical Year

#652. Deuteronomy 15:18 ~ To Rejoice When You Set a Covenanted Slave Free

#653. Deuteronomy 15:19 ~ The Firstborn Males of the Herd or Flock are Set Apart

#654. Deuteronomy 15:20 ~ To Eat the Set Apart Firstborn at the Place Where the Heavenly Father Chooses

#655. Deuteronomy 15:21 ~ To Not Sacrifice a Firstborn from the Flock or Herd with a Defect Before the Heavenly Father

#656. Deuteronomy 15:22 ~ To Sacrifice and Eat the Firstborn from the Flock or Herd Within Israel's Borders

#657. Deuteronomy 15:22 ~ Those Clean and Unclean May Eat of the Defected Firstborn of the Flock or Herd

#658. Deuteronomy 15:23 ~ Do Not Consume the Blood of the Defected Firstborn of the Flock or Herd

#659. Deuteronomy 16:1 ~ To Guard the New Moon

#660. Deuteronomy 16:1 ~ To Observe Passover

#661. Deuteronomy 16:2 ~ To Slaughter the Passover Lamb, Where the Heavenly Father Chooses to Place His Name

#662. Deuteronomy 16:3 ~ Do Not Eat Leavened Bread with the Passover Meal

#663. Deuteronomy 16:3 ~ To Eat Unleavened Bread for 7 Days

#664. Deuteronomy 16:4 ~ No Leavened Bread Should Be Seen on Your Property for 7 Days

#665. Deuteronomy 16:4 ~ No Remains of the Passover Meat by the Next Morning

#666. Deuteronomy 16:5-6 ~ To Only Sacrifice the Passover Lamb Where the Heavenly Father Chooses to Make His Name Dwell

#667. Deuteronomy 16:7 ~ To Roast the Passover Lamb

#668. Deuteronomy 16:7 ~ To Return Home the Next Night of Passover

#669. Deuteronomy 16:8 ~ To Eat Unleavened Bread During the Week of Unleavened Bread

#670. Deuteronomy 16:8 ~ The 7th Day of Unleavened Bread is a Shabbat

#671. Deuteronomy 16:9 ~ To Count 7 Weeks to Shavuot

#672. Deuteronomy 16:10-11 ~ To Observe the Feast of First Fruits, Where the Heavenly Father Chooses

#673. Deuteronomy 16:12 ~ To Remember That You Were Slaves in Egypt During the Feast of Shavuot

#674. Deuteronomy 16:13-14 ~ To Observe the Feast of Sukkot with Rejoicing

#675. Deuteronomy 16:15 ~ To Observe Sukkot Where the Heavenly Father Chooses

#676. Deuteronomy 16:16 ~ To Appear Before the Heavenly Father 3 Times a Year at the Location He Chooses

#677. Deuteronomy 16:16-17 ~ To Not Appear Before the Heavenly Father at the 3 Appointed Times Empty-Handed

#678. Deuteronomy 16:18 ~ To Appoint Judges and Officers to Judge Israel

#679. Deuteronomy 16:19 ~ Judges and Officers Are Not Allowed to Distort the Right Rulings of Torah

#680. Deuteronomy 16:19 ~ Judges and Officers Are Not Allowed to Show Partiality

#681. Deuteronomy 16:19 ~ Judges and Officers Are Not Allowed to Take Bribes

#682. Deuteronomy 16:19 ~ Judges and Officers Are to Follow Righteousness Alone

#683. Deuteronomy 16:21 ~ Do Not Plant a Tree (Idol) Near the Slaughter Place of the Heavenly Father

#684. Deuteronomy 16:22 ~ Do Not Erect Pillars for Worship

#685. Deuteronomy 17:1 ~ Do Not Slaughter Defective Animals to the Heavenly Father

#686. Deuteronomy 17:2-5 ~ Instructions for When Someone Is Guilty of Idolatry

#687. Deuteronomy 17:6 ~ Two or More Witnesses Are Needed for the Death Penalty

#688. Deuteronomy 17:7 ~ Witnesses Are the First to Throw Stones

#689. Deuteronomy 17:8-9 ~ Go to the Levites and Judges for Hard Issues

#690. Deuteronomy 17:10-11 ~ To Follow the Judgments of the Levite and the Judge

#691. Deuteronomy 17:12-13 ~ To Publicly Execute the Individual Who Does Not Listen to the Judgment of the Levite and/or the Judge

#692. Deuteronomy 17:15 ~ The Heavenly Father Selects the Kings of Israel

#693. Deuteronomy 17:15 ~ Only an Israelite Can Be King Over Israel

#694. Deuteronomy 17:16 ~ A King of Israel Is Not to Increase Horses for Himself

#695. Deuteronomy 17:16 ~ A King of Israel is Not Allowed to Cause the People of Israel to Return to Egypt to Increase Horses

#696. Deuteronomy 17:17 ~ A King of Israel is Not to Increase Wives for Himself

#697. Deuteronomy 17:17 ~ A King of Israel is Not to Increase Silver and Gold for Himself

#698. Deuteronomy 17:18 ~ A King of Israel Must Write a Copy of Torah for Himself

#699. Deuteronomy 17:19 ~ A King of Israel Must Always Keep His Own Personal Copy of Torah with Him

#700. Deuteronomy 17:19 ~ A King of Israel Must Read His Personally Written Copy of Torah Every Day

#701. Deuteronomy 17:19 ~ A King of Israel Must Fear the Heavenly Father

#702. Deuteronomy 17:19-20 ~ A King of Israel Must Guard Torah

#703. Deuteronomy 18:1 ~ The Levites Can Eat the Offerings Made to the Heavenly Father

#704. Deuteronomy 18:2 ~ The Heavenly Father is the Inheritance of the Levites

#705. Deuteronomy 18:3 ~ Of the Slaughters of the Heavenly Father, The People Are to Give the Levites the Shoulder, Cheeks, and Stomach

#706. Deuteronomy 18:4-5 ~ To Give the First Fruits of the Grain to the Levites

#707. Deuteronomy 18:4-5 ~ To Give Your New Wine to the Levites

#708. Deuteronomy 18:4-5 ~ To Give Your Oil to the Levites

#709. Deuteronomy 18:4-5 ~ To Give the First of the Fleece of Your Sheep to the Levites

#710. Deuteronomy 18:6-8 ~ When a Levite Goes to Where the Heavenly Father Chooses to Serve

#711. Deuteronomy 18:10-11 ~ Do Not Make Your Children Pass Through the Fire

#712. Deuteronomy 18:10-11 ~ Do Not Practice Divination

#713-714. Deuteronomy 18:10-11 ~ Do Not Use Magic/ Do Not Interpret Omens/ Do Not Practice Sorcery

#715. Deuteronomy 18:13-14 ~ To Be Perfect Before the Heavenly Father

#716. Deuteronomy 18:15 & 19 ~ To Follow the Prophet (Anointed one) of the Heavenly Father

#717. Deuteronomy 18:20-22 ~ False Prophets Must be Executed

#718. Deuteronomy 19:2-3 & 7 ~ To Create 3 Cities of Refuge for People Who Murder by Mistake

#719. Deuteronomy 19:4-6 ~ Defining Who the City of Refuge is for and Why

#720. Deuteronomy 19:8-10 ~ To Add More Cities of Refuge as the Borders of Israel Increase

#721. Deuteronomy 19:11-13 ~ A City of Refuge Will Not protect one who murders on purpose

#722. Deuteronomy 19:15 ~ Judgements Cannot Be Made on One Witness Alone

#723. Deuteronomy 19:16-21 ~ How to Deal with False Witnesses

#724. Deuteronomy 20:1 ~ Not to Fear Your Enemies in Battle

#725. Deuteronomy 20:2-4 ~ For the Levite Priesthood to Encourage Israel Before a Battle

#726. Deuteronomy 20:5 ~ A Man Who Built a New House Cannot go out to War

#727. Deuteronomy 20:6 ~ A man who plants a vineyard and has not used it yet, cannot go out to war

#728. Deuteronomy 20:7 ~ A Man Who is Engaged to be Wed Cannot go out to War

#729. Deuteronomy 20:8 ~ The Fearful Cannot go out to War

#730. Deuteronomy 20:9 ~ Officers Appoint Command Divisions for War

#731. Deuteronomy 20:10-11 & 15 ~ To Make a Call for Peace Before War for Cities Far from the Land

#732. Deuteronomy 20:10-11 ~ If Peace is Received, the People Will Become Laborers

#733. Deuteronomy 20:12-14 ~ If Peace is Not Received

#734. Deuteronomy 20:19-20 ~ During Times of War, do not Destroy Trees That Bear Fruit

#735. Deuteronomy 21:1-9 ~ Instructions for Unsolved Murders

#736. Deuteronomy 21:15-17 ~ Rights of the Firstborn

#737. Deuteronomy 21:18-21 ~ To Execute a Rebellious Son

#738. Deuteronomy 21:22-23 ~ Do Not Allow a Body to Hang Overnight

#739. Deuteronomy 22:1 ~ To Return a Straying Sheep or Ox to Your Brother

#740. Deuteronomy 22:2 ~ To Take Care of What is Lost Until the Owner Comes for It

#741. Deuteronomy 22:3 ~ Do Not Hide Lost Items for Yourself

#742. Deuteronomy 22:4 ~ To Help Your Brother with Their Donkey in Need

#743. Deuteronomy 22:5 ~ Men and Women Do Not Cross-Dress

#744. Deuteronomy 22:6-7 ~ When You Find a Nest of Birds with Mother and Eggs or a Mother with Younglings

#745. Deuteronomy 22:8 ~ Build a Parapet on Your Roof

#746. Deuteronomy 22:9 ~ Not to Sow Two Different Kinds of Seeds in a Vineyard

#747. Deuteronomy 22:10 ~ Not to Plow an Ox and Donkey Together

#748. Deuteronomy 22:11 ~ Do Not Put on Garments with Wool and Linen Together

#749. Deuteronomy 22:12 ~ To Make Tassels (Tzitzit) For Your Garments

#750. Deuteronomy 22:13-19 ~ When a Man Wrongfully Accuses His Wife of Not Being a Maiden

#751. Deuteronomy 22:20-21 ~ When a Man Rightfully Accuses His Wife of Not Being a Maiden

#752. Deuteronomy 22:22 ~ Men Having Sexual Relations with Married Women is Adultery; Both Must Be Executed

#753. Deuteronomy 22:23-24 ~ If an Engaged Woman Sleeps with Another Man, Both Must Be Executed

#754. Deuteronomy 22:25-27 ~ A Man Who Rapes an Engaged Woman Must Be Executed

#755. Deuteronomy 22:28-29 ~ Instructions for a Man Who Sleeps with a Maiden Who Is Not Engaged

#756. Deuteronomy 22:30 ~ Men Do Not Sleep with Their Father's Wife

#757. Deuteronomy 22:30 ~ Not to Uncover Your Father's Skirt

#758. Deuteronomy 23:1 ~People Born Because of an Abominable Union Cannot Enter the Community of Israel

#759. Deuteronomy 23:3-4 ~ Ammonites and Moabites Shall Not Enter the Assembly of Israel

#760. Deuteronomy 23:6 ~ Do Not Seek Peace nor Goodwill with Ammonites and Moabites

#761. Deuteronomy 23:7 ~ Do Not Hate the Edomite or the Egyptians

#762. Deuteronomy 23:9-14 ~ Instructions on How to Keep the Camp Clean During War

#763. Deuteronomy 23:15-16 ~ Instructions for When a Slave Flees to You

#764. Deuteronomy 23:17 ~ Prostitution is Not Allowed in Israel

#765. Deuteronomy 23:18 ~ Do Not Give a Vowed Offering from Sinful Profits

#766. Deuteronomy 23:19 ~ Do Not Lend to Your Brother with Interest

#767. Deuteronomy 23:20 ~ Can Lend to Foreigners with Interest

#768. Deuteronomy 23:21 ~ To Quickly Pay a Vow to the Heavenly Father

#769. Deuteronomy 23:22 ~ Vowing to the Heavenly Father is Optional

#770. Deuteronomy 23:23 ~ To Do What You Say You Will Do

#771. Deuteronomy 23:24 ~ Instructions When Eating in a Vineyard

#772. Deuteronomy 23:25 ~ Instructions to Eat Grain in a Field

#773. Deuteronomy 24:1-4 ~ Instructions on Divorce

#774. Deuteronomy 24:5 ~ Men Are Exempt from War in the First Year of Marriage

#775. Deuteronomy 24:6 ~ Do Not Take a Life in a Pledge

#776. Deuteronomy 24:7 ~ Kidnappers Should Be Executed

#777. Deuteronomy 24:8 ~ To Carefully Follow the Priests in an Outbreak of Leprosy

#778. Deuteronomy 24:9 ~ Remember What the Heavenly Father Did to the Egyptians When We Came out of Egypt

#779. Deuteronomy 24:10-11 ~ When You Lend to Your Brother, Do Not Be Aggressive to Get Back

#780. Deuteronomy 24:12-13 ~ To Return a Poor Man's Pledge Right Away

#781. Deuteronomy 24:14 ~ To Pay the Poor Promptly

#782. Deuteronomy 24:15 ~ Do Not Delay in Giving the Poor Their Wages

#783. Deuteronomy 24:16 ~ Fathers Are Not Responsible for the Sins of Their Sons

#784. Deuteronomy 24:16 ~ Sons Are Not Responsible for the Sins of Their Fathers

#785. Deuteronomy 24:17 ~ Do Not Distort Justice for the Stranger

#786. Deuteronomy 24:17 ~ Do Not Distort Justice for the Fatherless

#787. Deuteronomy 24:17 ~ Do Not Take the Garment of a Widow

#788. Deuteronomy 24:18 ~ To Remember That the People of Israel Were Slaves in Egypt

#789. Deuteronomy 24:18 ~ To Remember That the Heavenly Father Ransomed Israel from Egypt

#790. Deuteronomy 24:19 ~ To Leave Some Produce in Your Fields for Strangers, the Fatherless, and Widows

#791. Deuteronomy 24:20 ~ To Leave Some Olives for the Stranger, the Fatherless, and the Widows

#792. Deuteronomy 24:21 ~ To Leave Some Grapes in Your Vineyard for Strangers, the Fatherless, and the Widow

#793. Deuteronomy 24:22 ~ To Remember That We Were Slaves in Egypt

#794. Deuteronomy 25:1 ~ For Men to go to a Judge for Disputes

#795. Deuteronomy 25:2-3 ~ Instructions for Wrongdoers to be Struck According to the Judge's Ruling

#796. Deuteronomy 25:4 ~ To Not Muzzle an Ox While it's Threshing

#797. Deuteronomy 25:5-6 ~ Duties of a Husband's Brother

#798. Deuteronomy 25:7-10 ~ If the Husband's Brother Refuses His Duties

#799. Deuteronomy 25:11-12 ~ Women Are Not Allowed to Damage Men's Genitals

#800. Deuteronomy 25:13-15 ~ To Have Perfect and Right Weights for Business Transactions

#801. Deuteronomy 25:14-15 ~ To Have Perfect and Right Measures for Business Transactions

#802. Deuteronomy 25:17-19 ~ To Remember What Amalek Did While Israel Was Coming Out of Egypt

#803. Deuteronomy 26:12-19 ~ When Giving the 3rd Tithe

#804. Deuteronomy 27:1 ~ To Guard all of Torah

#805. Deuteronomy 27:10 ~ To Obey the Voice of the Heavenly Father

#806. Deuteronomy 29:9 ~ To Guard the Words of the Covenant

#807. Deuteronomy 29:9 ~ To Do the Words of the Covenant

#808. Deuteronomy 30:16 ~ To Love the Heavenly Father

#809. Deuteronomy 30:16 ~ To Walk in the Ways of the Heavenly Father

#810. Deuteronomy 30:16 ~ To Guard the Commands of the Heavenly Father

#811. Deuteronomy 30:16 ~ To Guard the Right Rulings of the Heavenly Father

#812. Deuteronomy 30:19 ~ To Choose Life

#813. Deuteronomy 30:20 ~ To Love the Heavenly Father

#814. Deuteronomy 30:20 ~ To Obey the Voice of the Heavenly Father

#815. Deuteronomy 30:20 ~ To Cling to the Heavenly Father

#816. Deuteronomy 31:10-13 ~ To Read All of Torah to the Congregation of Israel Every 7 Years

#817. Deuteronomy 32:46-47 ~ To Know the Final Song of Moses

#818. 2nd Chronicles 15:2 ~ To Seek Adonai

#819. Psalms 119:142 ~ Torah is Righteousness and Truth Forever

#820. Proverbs 6:16-19 ~ 7 Things the Heavenly Father Hates

#821. Proverbs 10:4 ~ Do Not Be Lazy

#822. Proverbs 14:30 ~ Do Not Envy

#823. Proverbs 28:25 ~ Do Not Be Greedy

#824. Ecclesiastes 12:13 ~ To Obey the Commands of Adonai

#825. Isaiah 8:20 ~ To Teach Torah and the Testimony

#826. Isaiah 51:7 ~ To Not Fear Man

#827. Jeremiah 9:23-24 ~ Do Not Be Prideful

#828. Matthew 5:19 ~ To Teach and Do Torah

#829. Matthew 5:21-26 ~ To Avoid Anger

#830. Matthew 5:27-28 ~ Do Not Lust After Other People

#831. Matthew 5:29-30 ~ To Fight Against Your Weaknesses

#832. Matthew 5:31-32 ~ To Only Divorce for Sexual Immorality

#833. Matthew 5:33-37 ~ How to Approach Oaths

#834. Matthew 5:38-39 ~ Not to Retaliate

#835. Matthew 5:40-41 ~ To Go Above Court-Ordered Restitution if You Lose a Trial

#836. Matthew 5:42 ~ To Lend When Asked

#837. Matthew 5:43-48 ~ To Love Your Enemies

#838. Matthew 6:1-4 ~ To Not Give for Vanity

#839. Matthew 6:5-15 ~ How to Pray

#840. Matthew 6:16-18 ~ Do Not Fast for Vanity

#841. Matthew 6:19-21 ~ To Lay Up Treasures in Heaven

#842. Matthew 6:22-23 ~ Be Careful of What You Expose Yourself To

#843. Matthew 6:24 ~ Avoid Personification of Wealth

#844. Matthew 6:25-34 ~ Do Not Be Anxious

#845. Matthew 7:1-5 ~ Not to Judge

#846. Matthew 7:6 ~ Do Not Waste Time with People Who Will Not Listen

#847. Matthew 7:7-11 ~ To Ask the Heavenly Father What You Want

#848. Matthew 7:12 ~ Treat Others as You'd Like to be Treated

#849. Matthew 7:13-14 ~ Enter the Narrow Gate

#850. Matthew 7:15-20 ~ To Be Aware of False Prophets

#851. Matthew 11:25-26 ~ To Forgive

#852. Matthew 7:24-27 ~ To Hear and Do What Yeshua Says in the Sermon on the Mount

#853. Luke 6:42 ~ Avoid Hypocrisy

#854. Luke 9:35 ~ To listen to Yeshua (Also see John 3:36)

#855. John 13:34 ~ To Love One Another as Yeshua Loves

#856. John 14:12 ~ To Imitate Yeshua

#857. John 14:15 ~ To Guard the Commands of Yeshua

#858. Romans 12:19 ~ Do Not Seek Revenge

#859. 1st Corinthians 5:7-8 ~ To Keep the Passover Feast

#860. 2nd Corinthians 6:14 ~ Avoid Being Unequally Yoked with Non-Covenanted People

#861. 2nd Corinthians 10:3-5 ~ To Fight Thoughts That Are Against Torah

#862. Ephesians 4:1-6 ~ For the Body of Believers to be Unified

#863. Colossians 3:5-9 ~ Do Not Do as Those in the Flesh

#864. Colossians 3:17 ~ To Work as if Unto Yeshua

#865. 1st Timothy 4:16 ~ To Watch What You Say and Do Carefully

#866. 1st Timothy 5:8 ~ To Provide for Your Family

#867. 1st Timothy 6:9-10 ~ Do Not Love Money

#868. 2nd Timothy 2:22 ~ To Avoid Lust

#869. 2nd Timothy 2:22 ~ To Seek Righteousness

#870. 1ˢᵗ John 2:6 ~ To Walk as Messiah Walks

#871. James 1:19-20 ~ Seek Understanding More Than to be Understood

#872. James 2:10 ~ To Live by All of Torah

#873. 1ˢᵗ John 4:1 ~ To Test Every Spirit

#874. Revelation 12:17 ~ To Believe in Yeshua and Keep Torah

#875. Revelation 14:12 ~ To keep the Torah of the Heavenly Father and Believe in Yeshua

Conclusion:

To The Messianic/Hebrew Roots Community:

Choose Life

Introduction:

What is Torah? Many people believe it refers solely to the famous 10 Commandments of Moses. Those who take the time to study the subject will find that it is the first five books of the Tanach (Bible): Genesis, Exodus, Leviticus, Numbers, and Deuteronomy. People who dig deeper will tell you that Torah is a series of 613 commands: Torah encompasses all these things and more. When it comes to understanding what Torah is, there could be various answers to that question, but at the root of it all, Torah is the voice of the Heavenly Father.

Because Torah is the voice of our Heavenly Father, it is more than just the 10 commandments. The voice of our Heavenly Father extends beyond the book of Deuteronomy. The Heavenly Father guide us through His Set-Apart Spirit, anointed people, the rest of the Bible/the scriptures, and in various ways, even today. Everything that He communicates to us is foundational upon His inspired voice written in the Bible.

Torah is not just the voice of our Heavenly Father; it is also a binding universal covenant between the All-Mighty and Israel. A covenant that is based on us hearing His voice and simply obeying what He says because of who He is and what He has done for us (See Exodus 19:4-6). The voice of our Heavenly Father is the foundation of the entire Bible. It establishes the proper relationship between the Heavenly Father and mankind (Ecclesiastes 12:13). The voice of our Heavenly Father also connects us to Yeshua—our Messiah, Lord, Savior, and King!

Throughout the four gospel books of Matthew, Mark, Luke, and John, Yeshua demonstrates complete submission to the voice of the Heavenly Father, setting an example of how his true followers should also submit to the Father. Yeshua kept Torah perfectly. Torah is who

Yeshua is; it is deeply ingrained in his character. When we examine what Yeshua said and how he lives, you cannot separate Torah from Yeshua.

Everything that Yeshua did and said aligns with the voice of Abba. This is how we know beyond a shadow of a doubt that Yeshua is the son of our Heavenly Father. It is also how we can identify those who are anointed today. Even though all of us struggle with something and/or have character flaws we need to overcome, the anointed and appointed people of our Elohim will demonstrate that they are doing everything possible to imitate Yeshua. Most importantly, the anointed and appointed people of Elohim will not say things to lead Israel, His people, astray from the voice of our Heavenly Father as presented by Moses, the prophets, and Yeshua.

Yeshua showed us the blueprint of what anointed from above looks like, and it is the bullseye that we all must strive towards in our walk. We can be confident in the knowledge that this bullseye target will never move or change because Abba never changes. People who do not demonstrate that they are aiming for that goal are on a different path from the narrow road that Yeshua talks about in Matthew 7:13-14. I do not say that as if you need to prove to people anything, but what you truly believe in your heart comes out in your actions *and* the words you speak. You can say you believe in something or someone until you are blue in the face, but if the actions and words do not line up... In other words, what you say and do matters (1st Timothy 4:16).

People who do not act like or strive to act like the Messiah we see in the four biography books cannot be people of the Heavenly Father or anointed from above. People who speak contrary to what Yeshua has said throughout the four biography books cannot be people of the kingdom or anointed from above! In Matthew 7:21-23, Yeshua makes it very clear that He does not even have a relationship with people who do not submit to the voice of the Heavenly Father! In Matthew 12:46-50 and Luke 8:20-21, Yeshua goes so far as to say that only those who listen to the voice of the Heavenly Father **and** do His will are His family. Those who follow Yeshua believe in him by guarding his words (See John 14:15-24), which leads us to obey the voice of the Heavenly Father just like he does! Yeshua without Torah is a false Yeshua!

For Yeshua's believers, to live by Torah is evident in every word he spoke, every letter written by Paul, and the rest of the apostles. In Revelation 12:17 and Revelation 14:9-12, we see that the opponents of the beast, the enemy of the Heavenly Father, are described as individuals who believe in Yeshua **and** follow the instructions of the Heavenly Father. The more we understand Torah as the voice of the Heavenly Father, the closer we come to know Yeshua and ultimately transform more like him. The Heavenly Father would love to see all humanity behave like Yeshua because He wants us all to be saved (1st Timothy 2:1-6). With all that said, let us address some things about Torah and how this book differs from others like it.

613?

Where do we get the idea that there are 613 commands within Torah? According to the Babylonian Talmud, in Tractate Makkot 23b, a man named Rabbi Simlai, around 200-300 AD, first proposed the idea. Rabbi Simlai stated that there were 365 negative commands that represent the number of days in the solar calendar. He also stated that 248 positive commands represent the number of members in the human body, referring to the number of bones in the human body known at that time. For a long time, Judaism blindly accepted Rabbi Simlai's idea that there are 365 negative and 248 positive commands within Torah until a man named Moses Ben Maimon, aka Maimonides, aka the Rambam, came onto the scene.

Torah for Modern Messiah Believers

The Rambam, who lived from 1135 AD to 1204 AD, wrote the Mishnah Torah with the primary purpose of identifying the 365 negative commands and the 248 positive commands that Rabbi Simlai stated before him; that is how we get the 613 commands or Mitzvot in Hebrew today. Initially, the Mishnah Torah faced strong opposition from the Jewish community; however, over time, Judaism embraced it. Soon, other Jewish philosophers began challenging the content of the Mishnah Torah, which inspired them to create lists of 613 commands of their own. Various Torah lists can be found today, each slightly different from the next, but the Rambam's list is still the most popular.

For this book, I decided to start from scratch. I didn't do this to undo the idea that there are 613 commands; that number has been an arbitrary concept from the very beginning. When I began this project, I expected maybe 50 to 100 more commands because I wanted to identify the commands written in the first five books and key commands found beyond Deuteronomy. The list in this book has a total of 875 commands. Should this number be taken as an official number? I'm not sure. When I constructed this list, I had a few simple rules.

- Did the Heavenly Father say it?
- Was it reaffirmed?
- Does it support another command?
- Is there something we can learn from it today?

Not every command found in Torah is in this list because some commands were specific to one person like what we see for Abram in Genesis chapter 15. The instructions on how to build a tabernacle is not on this list because that was a one-time thing. If someone else from the Messianic or Hebrew Roots faith follows behind me and does what I've done in this book, it is possible that they can receive information and inspiration from above on verses I did not. My 5th and biggest rule for this book was to make sure that I provided information on what the Heavenly Father wants me to share.

Why are there so many commands in this list? Unlike my predecessors, I was not tethered to the idea of finding 365 negative commands and 248 positive commands. I focused on identifying all of Abba's commands to the best of my ability. I do not doubt that the Rambam and everyone else who has gone down this path saw everything that I saw. You can kind of see it from their commentaries that attempt to squeeze a bunch of command understandings together.

Another reason this list of commands is 875 long is that this list honors the instructions that our Heavenly Father repeats; there will be some redundancy. There are many repeated commandments found within Torah. At one point, I was going to consolidate all the repeated commands, but it fell upon me not to do that. I believe that the Heavenly Father repeating Himself is a strategy to emphasize what is essential for His people, much like when parents repeat themselves to their children. I suspect it also serves as a safety measure from human interference and/or scriptural translation errors.

Look at the Masoretic Text and the Septuagint. Has man tampered with the scriptures? Some people are afraid to entertain such an idea, but if we are seeking truth, it is a subject that should be tackled. As a "glass half full" type of person, I believe some flaws were made by mistake, but it is also hard to ignore clear patterns focused on Yeshua's credibility.

The Septuagint (LXX—literally 70) was written before Yeshua, a project that began around 250 BC, while the Masoretic text was written between the 7th and 10th centuries AD. You can see videos of the differences between the two texts by searching online. The subject provides information that cannot be ignored.

Torah for Modern Messiah Believers

The Catholic church maintained tight control of the Disciples' manuscripts for over 1000 years. Some information, such as the Didache (The Way of Life), a series of teachings that the 12 apostles gave to gentile believers, didn't even see the light of day until 1873. The Catholics saw them as too Jewish! Had those letters been made public from the beginning, they could have easily reshaped the way Christianity looks today and erased many of the atrocities Christianity has done to the Jewish people in the past.

It would be naive to believe the Catholics would not have tampered with Yeshua's biographical books and the disciples' letters. Anything that the Catholics have established is highly suspect since they proudly take ownership of changing Adonai's day from Saturday to Sunday because they believe that they have the authority to do so (search Codex Justinianus 3.12.3, Council of Laodicea, and Constantine's Sunday law). The Bible is still trustworthy, despite human shenanigans, it still has all the information we need to have a proper relationship with Abba. Despite the flaws and arrogance of man, the Heavenly Father is light years ahead of us and repeats things not only because we are stiff-necked but also to help us stay focused on His voice and what is important to Him! The repeated commands of the Heavenly Father help us identify things that may not be of His Spirit when reading religious books, listening to people preach, or even reading the scriptures.

The last reason there are 875 commands in this book is that this is a Messianic book. Every instruction Yeshua gives us in the "Sermon on the Mount" in Matthew chapters 5-7 are included in this list. These commands are the foundations of his ministry. Almost everything he says past Matthew chapter 7, along with the books of Mark, Luke, and John, can point back to something he says in the Sermon on the Mount.

The commands that Yeshua gives us are not his own but the commands of the Heavenly Father! In John 14:24, he says, *"He who doesn't love me doesn't keep my words. The word which you hear isn't mine, but the Father's who sent me."* This makes Yeshua's words a continuation of the voice of the Heavenly Father, in other words, Torah. Nothing that Yeshua spoke contradicts the Torah as written by Moses and the prophets because it all came from the same source: The Heavenly Father. We know that He does not change (Malachi 3:6), His words do not return void (Isaiah 55:11), and He does not contradict Himself (Proverbs 30:5).

Categories:

Thanks to mainstream religion (Christianity of all kinds), many people believe that Torah is a list of ceremonial and moral commands. When we test this concept, it doesn't take long to realize that the categories of ceremonial and moral commands don't work. Not all commands fit within those two categories. Commands such as Exodus 12:49, Leviticus 25:8, Numbers 35:1-8, and Deuteronomy 5:29 are just a small sampling of commands that have nothing to do with ceremonies or morality. Some commands are about faith alone, and faith-based commands do not fit within ceremony or morality—you either believe or don't!

We will be placing each command in 3 categories.

1. Positive or Negative
2. Loving Abba or Loving People
3. Conditional or Unconditional

Positive or negative commands do not mean good or bad commands. All the commands of our Elohim are good. A positive command is a call to action, something you should do. A negative command is something you should avoid. Our Jewish brothers have used this system for a long time. When it comes to negative commands, we all should strive to identify them to know what we should not do. Positive commands can be a bit more complicated because we can do some and not others. Positive instructions depend on the situations and conditions tied to those commands.

Loving Adonai or loving people is a set of categories first presented by Yeshua when someone asked, "Which commandment is the greatest?" His response was:

> *"You shall love YHWH your Elohim with all your heart, with all your soul, and with all your mind. This is the first and great commandment. A second is likewise this: 'You shall love your neighbor as yourself.' The whole of Torah and the prophets depend on these two commandments."* – Matthew 22:37-40 (also cited in Mark 12:28-34)

Yeshua's answer directs us to Deuteronomy 6:5 and Leviticus 19:18. When you examine these two commands, Messiah is teaching us that every instruction within Torah shows us the details of how to meet the expectations of loving the Heavenly Father and/or loving each other; all according to the Heavenly Father's point of view. As followers of Yeshua, we should follow his lead and identify these categories when focusing on the commands.

When it comes to identifying which commands are about loving the Heavenly Father and which ones are about loving people, it can be a bit tricky. When you think about it, anytime we obey a command simply because "the Heavenly Father says..." you are loving Him. With that logic, all obeyed commands show love to the Heavenly Father directly and indirectly.

A practical approach was needed to distinguish between loving the Heavenly Father and loving people. I began looking at whether commands benefit people directly or only provide spiritual benefits, for example, commands on sacrifices and offerings. The Levites were the primary beneficiaries of these things, followed by the poor who depended on them for benevolence. Once this was identified, it was easy to see that those commands were about loving people. The Levites lived off the sacrifices and offerings that allowed them to serve the Heavenly Father full-time and ultimately serve Israel full-time. This shows a clear practical sign of loving people. Commands such as not eating a beast torn by animals do not reveal a clear benefit for mankind, since they could be sold to foreigners for consumption. For such commands, I identified them as loving the Heavenly Father. Although we don't fully understand it, doing them has spiritual benefits for the people of Israel.

Identifying conditional or unconditional commands is about understanding what commands we can or cannot obey and why. Unconditional commands are without restrictions; they apply to anyone who believes in the Heavenly Father, regardless of gender, age, or where they live. Conditional commands are tied to specific requirements that determine if they can be done. The command to stone people requires an official Israel government with judges submitted to Torah that controls the land; a condition we do not have today. Knowing whether a command is conditional or unconditional will be the most practical category in this book.

Some people misquote James and say, "If you are going to keep the law, you better do it all!" Such people reveal their lack of understanding when it comes to Torah. For example, I am not a Levite, at least I have no evidence to prove that. If the temple were here today, I could not do what the Levites are supposed to do. It would be a sin punishable by death if I tried. If you are not a Levite, you cannot touch the Ark, something Uzzah learned the hard way in 2nd Samuel chapter 6. Within Torah, there are commands for men, women, the land, judges/leaders, business owners, the Levites, and various commands for situations most of us rarely run into, if at all. As we study the instructions of our

Heavenly Father, understanding whether a command has conditions is liberating. It helps you determine if you are walking out Torah properly.

Ultimately, Torah is designed to fully function under a government completely submitted to the voice of the Heavenly Father, with control of the Heavenly Father's identified land. Israel has not had this opportunity since around the late 180s BC, when the Roman Empire began to occupy the land. The current world government, known as Israel, founded in 1948, does not submit to Torah entirely or mostly. The world government known as Israel today is a religious melting pot that protects freedom of religion and protects the LGBTQ community. Their Knesset (Congress) has Jewish, Christian, atheist, and Muslim representation, a structure that stands against fundamental ideals of Torah overall.

Some commands cannot be observed today because we do not have the government for them, we do not live in the land (Most of us), they do not apply to us, or the conditions to keep those commands are just not there. For most of the world today, slavery is a thing of the past. It is highly unlikely that anyone reading this book would need to apply any of the slave instructions. Identifying the commands that are conditional or unconditional is not just liberating; it also empowers us to practically and properly apply Torah in our lives today just like Yeshua did when he walked the earth.

This book is tackling Torah from a "me" perspective. As you read this book, look at how the commands relate to you. The commands that do not apply to you are still important to identify. The more you know His voice, the closer you draw to Him.

Some of the unconditional commands are unconditional because they can be self-regulated. As law-abiding citizens of Israel dispersed throughout the world, there are times when we need to govern ourselves according to Torah. Torah contains requirements, commands, statutes, and laws, all given through the voice of the Heavenly Father. Follow His

Choose Life

voice! There is no Judgment Day for the citizens of Israel because we judge ourselves daily based on the voice of our Heavenly Father. Yeshua demonstrates a Torah-maximalist lifestyle. Yeshua is dedicated to Torah, as Moses and the prophets wrote. Follow Yeshua and strive to be a Torah maximalist.

#1. Genesis 1:28 ~ To Be Fruitful

Positive
Loving People
Unconditional

From the Peshat level, this command is clearly about human reproduction, but if we go into deeper levels, this instruction can also be seen as a charge for us to be productive and successful in life. One of the main themes of Torah is that the Heavenly Father wants His people to succeed in everything good we do. It makes perfect sense since we are made in His image.

#2. Genesis 1:28 ~ To Have Dominion Over the Earth

Positive
Loving People
Unconditional

The Rambam believed that this command was given so that the earth's animals would not overpower humanity, which makes practical sense. On a deeper level, just like the previous teaching, this can encourage us to seek success in life, in other words, to master our individual lives. Precisely what that looks like could be different from person to person.

#3. Genesis 2:24 ~ To Marry

Positive
Loving People
Unconditional

This instruction does not say that you must get married, but if you do, it establishes that marriage is between a man and a woman. This was not a command given by the Heavenly Father; these are Adam's words. This command is on this list because Yeshua enforced it in Matthew 19:1-12. It shows that when a man is in sync with the Heavenly Father and speaks, the Heavenly Father will support him, another theme seen throughout the scriptures. It also supports the only proper way for humanity to procreate.

Another thing that this teaching shows us is the role of the male in a family environment. Since the male is leaving his mother and father to become one with a woman, he must provide a home for his new family. In a marriage, the goal of the man should be to provide, to meet the needs of his family, and to ensure the best options so that every individual in the family can succeed in life. Today, most households need both the husband and wife to work to survive; however, as men, we should always strive to make sure that the wife's income is not required for survival; it can be used as extra income, income for investments, vacation, or simply money for her to do whatever she wants. This fits perfectly with the first two commands of us being fruitful and having dominion over the earth.

Today, it's not unheard of that a wife can be in a more lucrative field than the husband. In such instances, men can still fulfill their role as leaders of the household. In a recent interview, a very popular female performer claimed that she gives all her paychecks to her husband, a successful entrepreneur in his own right, and he manages their finances. That is a great example of a Proverbs 31:10-31 woman. She makes more money than he does, but he leads the family financially and can still support their lifestyle if she chooses to quit performing. This shows that the husband does not really need to make more money then the wife, as long as the family can still live off his income alone; that is the goal to strive for as husbands.

#4. Genesis 4:7 ~ To Master Sin

Positive
Loving Abba
Unconditional

This instruction reveals a major underlying theme of the entire Bible. We must resist sin because failing to do so brings sin to reality upon the earth. To master sin, it must be fought at the root. Yeshua reveals that this battle begins from within (Matthew 15:17-20). Paul sheds more light on mastering sin by instructing us to take every thought captive and make them submissive to the will of Yeshua in 2nd Corinthians 10:3-5.

It is safe to say that when the Heavenly Father gave those words to Cain, he was dwelling in sinful thoughts, and later, we see him ignoring the words of Adonai and acting upon those thoughts of sin against his brother Abel. Another example of sin starting from within is with Eve. In Genesis 3:6, Eve *"saw that the tree was good for food, and that it was a delight to the eyes, and that the tree was to be desired to make one wise"*. Eve didn't just listen to the serpent and take the fruit; she thought about it and dwelt on it first. Eve's thoughts produced the action of taking the fruit, eating it, and giving it to Adam to eat as well. This is how sin works; when we accept it in our minds, it gets digested into our hearts, then it comes out in our words and/or actions.

#5. Genesis 9:4 ~ Not to Consume Blood

Negative
Loving Abba
Unconditional

Repeated 7 times in:

- Leviticus 3:17 (169)
- Leviticus 7:26-27 (197)
- Leviticus 17:10-12 (244)
- Leviticus 19:26 (302)
- Deuteronomy 12:16 (601)
- Deuteronomy 12:23-25 (606)
- Deuteronomy 15:23 (658)

This command is about orally digesting blood, unfortunately, it is often misinterpreted. Some religious groups will use this command as a prohibition for medical blood transfusions, which cannot be supported from the Peshat level and is a false way to approach this teaching. Similarly, some would use this command to condemn people who eat rare steaks; also, a false way to approach this instruction. All the blood is drained from the meat when it hits the market due to universal industry regulations. The red liquid seen in a rare steak is not blood but myoglobin. The only people who should be concerned about this command are hunters who butcher their catch. For such individuals, the instruction of #245 and Genesis 32:32 (not counted in this list) are the only things they should concern themselves with.

#6. Genesis 17:10 ~ Circumcision of Men

Positive
Loving Abba
Conditional (Males Only)

The Heavenly Father made it a point to connect this teaching with Passover through command #29, reinforcing that this is a perpetual command for the children of Abraham and anyone who wants to be considered a part of Israel in His eyes. This is more than a command; it is also a covenant. Unfortunately, mainstream religion has made this command a stumbling block, leading many people to believe that this teaching applies only to the Jewish people. Unfortunately, the Jewish people follow suite. Sadly, even within the Messianic/Hebrew Roots community, some people question whether this instruction is a "salvation issue". That is the wrong way to approach this, or any instruction given from the Heavenly Father.

The idea of circumcision is straightforward. For some men, this is not an issue at all since modern medicine promotes circumcision due to its medical benefits, and it is commonly given as an option during birth. The Heavenly Father does not explain why He chose circumcision to be a sign between Himself, Abraham, and the children of Abraham, which makes this a spiritual command despite its physical nature. There is no shortage of information about this instruction. Confusion surrounding this teaching has led me to take a different approach for this book. Let us seek the proper understanding of this instruction and all the commands given by our Heavenly Father. In Genesis chapter 12, we see the first written communication between the Heavenly Father and Abram:

> *"Leave your country, and your relatives, and your father's house, and go to the land that I will show you. I will make of you a great nation. I will bless you and make your name great. You will be a blessing. I will bless those who bless you, and I will curse him who treats you with contempt. All the families of the earth will be blessed through you."* – Genesis 12:1-3

By the time we reached Genesis Chapter 11, Abram and his wife Sarai were already past the age of physically bearing children. Still, in Genesis chapter 12, the Heavenly Father promises they will have children. These children will be later identified as "Children of the Promise". Fast forward to Genesis chapter 17. Abram's name is changed to Abraham; by this point, he already had a child named Ishmael, not from Sarai, now Sarah (See the previous chapter for details). Adonai made a distinction between Ishmael and the children of the promise. Through this chapter, the Heavenly Father reveals that two types of children come from Abraham:

- Biological Children, who can claim they are children by physical DNA.
- Spiritual Children, who can claim they are his children by living as he did.

> They answered him, "Our father is Abraham." Yeshua said to them, "If you were Abraham's children, you would do the works of Abraham" - John 8:39

The Bible doesn't speak much about Ishmael or Isaac, but we can see that Isaac shared the same faith in the Heavenly Father as Abraham did, and Ishmael did not. The physical children of Abraham can also be children of the promise. It is safe to assume that the Heavenly Father's perfect will is for all who come from the seed of Abraham to be the children of the promise, but that is not always the case. With examples like Ishmael, King Saul, Esau, and the Jewish men Yeshua spoke to in John 8:39, not all the physical children of Abraham follow Abraham. When you act like Abraham, you share in his spiritual DNA.

Do not twist what I am saying! This is not replacement theology. Judah is Israel and holds the scepter until the return of the Messiah (see Genesis 49:10). Judah will always be the Heavenly Father's people first, and Israel, most understood as the Jewish people today, is the tree that the world is grafted into (see Romans 1:16, Jeremiah 11:16, and Romans 11:1-24).

> *For this cause, it is of faith, that it may be according to grace, to the end that the promise may be sure to all the offspring, not to that only which is of the law, but to that also which is of the faith of Abraham, who is the father of us all.* - Romans 4:16

> *I tell the truth in Messiah. I am not lying, my conscience testifying with me in the Set-Apart Spirit, that I have great sorrow and unceasing pain in my heart. For I could wish that I myself were accursed from Messiah for my brothers' sake, my relatives according to the flesh, who are Israelites; whose is the adoption, the glory, the covenants, the giving of the law, the service, and the promises; of whom are the fathers, and from whom is Messiah as concerning the flesh, who is over all, Elohim, blessed forever. Amen. But it is not as though the word of Elohim has come to nothing. For they are not all Israel, that are of Israel. Neither, because they are Abraham's offspring, are they all children. But, "your offspring will be accounted as from Isaac." That is, it is not the children of the flesh who are children of Elohim, but the children of the promise are counted as heirs.* - Romans 9:1-8

The faith of Abraham is revealed in Genesis 26:4-5, when Adonai tells Isaac that Abraham obeyed His voice and kept His requirements, commandments, statutes, and laws. Contrary to popular belief, faith is not a philosophy; it is a verb. This is taught throughout the entire scriptures; see Hebrews chapter 11 as one example. Just like blood can connect people to Abraham, acting like Abraham can also spiritually connect us to him. Circumcision is a physical connection to Abraham, given directly by the All-Mighty. Circumcision allows anyone from the nations to be a part of the family physically and spiritually. There are all kinds of arguments for and against circumcision, but at the end of the day, it is as simple as whether you are a promised child of Abraham or not. If you are, be his child of the promise and do as Abraham did. That is how the promises of Genesis 12:1-3 are continually fulfilled.

Before moving on to the next command, please note: Some men cannot get circumcised mainly for medical reasons, and there could easily be other legitimate reasons that I am not aware of as I write this. Circumcision is not the "golden ticket" to a forever life, and it does not guarantee that you are a part of Israel (see Romans 2:25-29). If you are in a situation where you cannot get circumcised, but you desire to do so, don't worry about it. In such situations, the Heavenly Father will honor your circumcised heart (583). If you cannot get circumcised due to financial reasons, then plan and save up for it. If you breathe your last breath before getting enough money for circumcision, Elohim will still honor the circumcised heart. When it comes to circumcision, "can't do it" and "won't do it" are two serious distinctions.

#7. Genesis 17:12 ~ Circumcision of 8-Day-Old Boys

Positive
Loving Abba
Conditional (Males Only)

Repeated in Leviticus 12:3 (223).

Choose Life

Judaism teaches us that this command is so important that if the 8th day falls on Yom Kippur, the circumcision must still occur. However, if the parents cannot or will not do the circumcision on the 8th day, then it cannot be done on a Shabbat. If the parents completely neglect it or they cannot do it, when the child comes of age, it becomes his responsibility to get circumcised based on what the Heavenly Father says in Genesis 17:14.

If you are new to the Messianic faith and you are a parent of minors, this command can raise some questions about whether to circumcise your children. First off, if you are married, you and your spouse must agree! This should not be a point of strife in a marriage. If you have an infant who is three months old or younger, and you feel a strong conviction to get them circumcised, then it is generally fine to get them circumcised during that time. However, if the baby has developed enough motor control of their arms and hands, there is a risk that they could injure themselves during recovery. If that is the case, teach them about the command and let them decide. The same rule should apply if they are old enough to participate in Bible studies. This is not something that you want to force upon your children or influence them to do. Doing so can cause extreme damage to their relationship with the Heavenly Father. Torah is not meant to be forced upon others in any way, shape, or form. It is a gift freely given to the world for people to choose freely.

NOTE: For Genesis 32:32, Judaism accepts this as a command, but it appears to be more of a tradition, and it is not reinforced anywhere else. I'm not saying it shouldn't be observed, but under the guidelines for this book, it cannot be justified as a command, but it can be honored as a tradition. The sinew, or silver skin, is very tough to eat, and it is usually removed during the butchering process. This is to remember that Jacob overcame with the Heavenly Father and was given the name Israel. Israel means overcoming with the Heavenly Father.

#8. Exodus 12:2 ~ Beginning of New Moons (Observing Rosh Chodesh)

Positive
Loving Abba
Unconditional

This command is repeated in Deuteronomy 16:1 (659).

For the Hebrew calendar, it is important to know that the beginning of months and the beginning of years fall on two separate days. This instruction establishes the beginning of months. We will later see the beginning of years addressed in command #432.

The Jewish calendar is lunar. This understanding is based on Genesis chapter 1, where every day begins in the evening and then the morning (see Genesis 1:5, 8, 13, 19, 23, and 31). When celebrating the Heavenly Father's appointed times or feasts, they begin at sundown and end the following sundown. For example, the weekly Shabbat starts on Friday night and ends on Saturday night. The Hebrew days are numbered.

- Yom Rishon - First day, Sunday
- Yom Sheni - Second day, Monday
- Yom Shlishi - Third day, Tuesday
- Yom Revi'i - Fourth day, Wednesday
- Yom Chamishi - Fifth day, Thursday
- Yom Shishi - Sixth day, Friday

The seventh day is called Yom Shabbat. It means the day of rest or peace. This is a weekly set-apart day because Elohim rested on the 7th day of creation, sanctified it (Genesis 2:2-3), and made it a sign between Himself and those who believe in Him (133).

Israel adapted the names of the months from Babylon during the captivity. Some people reject those names, giving some months multiple names. From new moon to new moon, there are 29 days, 12 hours, 44 minutes, and 3 1/3 seconds. The Jewish calendar months have either 29 days (Months of Iyar, Tammuz, Elul, Tevet, and Adar) or 30 days (Months of Nisan, Sivan, Av, Tishrei, and Shevat). The months of Cheshvan and Kislev can have either 29 or 30 days.

Rosh Chodesh is observed the night after the new moon appears. During the 29-day month, it is observed once. For Judaism, in the months that have 30 days, Rosh Chodesh is observed on both the last day of the outgoing month and the first day of the new month.

Because the lunar calendar is about 11 days shorter than the solar calendar, Israel needed to adjust the calendar days from the beginning; otherwise, events like Passover could occur during the winter. To prevent this, an additional month called Adar Sheni was added. This month is added seven times every 19 years and shows up after Nisan.

During biblical times, the Sanhedrin in Jerusalem determined whether a month had 29 or 30 days. They also kept track of discrepancies between the solar and lunar years. After the destruction of the Temple in 70 AD, the responsibility for declaring the new moon was transferred to the head of the court at Yavneh. According to Jewish history, even though Judaism was generally apprehensive about the Christian faith, the Jewish leadership still considered them a Jewish sect and communicated the days of the new moon to them as well. This communication continued until the 4th century, when the Catholic leaders said they no longer wanted to know about the new moons. Shortly after, Hillel II created a fixed calendar based on astronomical calculations. Hillel's calendar is still followed to this day. You can view the calendar by visiting www.jewishpeople.com and selecting the Jewish calendar link.

#9. Exodus 12:3-5 ~ To Observe the Passover Lamb for 4 Days Starting on the 10th of Nisan

Positive
Loving Abba
Conditional

This command and all commands involving sacrifices are conditional due to instructions such as #598 and #599. As a result, observing the lamb on the 10th of Nisan is a moot point today. For today's believers, we can use these four days to prepare spiritually for the feasts of Passover and Unleavened Bread. If we could keep this command, Leviticus 22:21-25 (370) and Leviticus 22:27 (371) give us the details of what to look for.

The 10th of Nisan is a special date. The first 10th of Nisan fell on a Shabbat. When the Israelites were spotted by the Egyptian residents taking lambs and goats to their homes, the Egyptians asked them what they were doing. This was very dangerous because the Egyptians would have seen the butchering of lambs/goats as a blasphemous act, a concern that Moses brought up to Pharaoh in Exodus 8:26, when Pharaoh suggested that Israel sacrifice in Egypt. Moses warned that such sacrifices would be offensive to the Egyptians. However, by this time, the Egyptians feared the Heavenly Father and did not dare attack Israel. If the Israelites did this at any other time in the past, they would have most likely been destroyed. Because Israel survived the first 10th of Nisan, the Shabbat before Passover is known as the Great Shabbat, or Shabbat HaGadol.

There are various notable historical events tied to the 10th of Nisan. The first-born Egyptians revolt against Pharaoh, Miriam's death, Israel crossing the Jordan, and Ezekiel's vision of a future temple is believed to have been given to him on the 10th of Nisan. Today, in Israel, Yom HaAliyah takes place on the 10th of Nisan. Another reason the 10th of

Nisan is special is its connection to mainstream religion. If you Google the 10th of Nisan, it won't take long before you see that it is identified as the day when Yeshua rode into Jerusalem on a donkey; an event that mainstream religion calls "Palm Sunday." If this is true, it proves that Yeshua was crucified on a Wednesday. This also makes the words of Yeshua literal in Matthew 12:40.

Many people believe that Yeshua died in 33 A.D. on a Friday because the Catholics picked that date from the modern Gregorian calendar. This calendar was first introduced to the world in 1582 by Pope Gregory XIII. The Gregorian calendar is a reformed version of the Julian calendar used before. According to the Gregorian calendar, March 28, 0033 would have been the 10th of Nisan that year, which fell on Monday. This would place Passover on Friday, April 1st, in that year. However, this information exposes a colossal conflict of information that cannot be ignored. If the 10th of Nisan fell on a Sunday, according to the origins of Palm Sunday, Yeshua could have been crucified in either 30 AD or 37 AD, as the 10th of Nisan fell on the correct day for those years.

#10. Exodus 12:6 ~ To Slaughter the Passover Lamb

Positive
Loving Abba
Conditional

This first Passover command is presented in a way that virtually has no limitations, except that it is only for Israel. All the limitations were added after the initial Passover. The initial Passover has elements that made it unique from all the others. Putting blood on the doorpost (Exodus 12:7), eating the lamb whole (Exodus 12:9), and eating it in haste (Exodus 12:11). For that first Passover, there was no time to butcher the lamb, and boiling it would take too long. Israel needed to be ready to depart Egypt immediately after the meal. The act of putting blood on the doorpost was done to protect the households from the death of the firstborn; an act of Elohim that was never repeated. I've heard that some people do the doorpost thing today. It can be harmless if they do not say it must be done. It depends on how they present it.

#11. Exodus 12:8 ~ To Eat the Passover Meal

Positive
Loving Abba
Unconditional

According to the scriptures, the Passover meal only consists of roasted lamb and bitter herbs. If that is all you do, you've met the requirements for this command. Most of what we do today is added traditions. Some people strongly oppose traditions because Yeshua spoke against them frequently; however, he was only opposed to traditions that cancelled or changed what Moses wrote.

There is a difference between eating the Passover meal and observing Passover. Our Jewish brothers have created an order (Sedar) for the meal that helps us do both. The Sedar is filled with traditions that help us remember Passover, how the Heavenly Father freed us from Egypt, and the promises He made.

#12. Exodus 12:9 ~ To Eat it Whole, Do Not Break the Bone

Positive
Loving Abba
Conditional

This command is repeated only once, within the same chapter, in Exodus 12:46. This suggests that it was only for the Exodus generation.

For the Exodus generation, there wasn't time for butchering; Israel had to cook the meal, eat it, and then leave Egypt immediately. Judaism teaches that the whole, unbroken lamb represents a complete and unified Israel. This can also be tied to Yeshua, who died on the cross without any broken bones, unlike the two who died with him.

#13. Exodus 12:14 ~ To Observe Passover Every Year

Positive
Loving Abba
Conditional

Repeated 8 times:

- Exodus 12:24 (20)
- Exodus 12:47 (28)
- Leviticus 23:5 (380)
- Numbers 9:2-3 (473)
- Numbers 9:13 (475)
- Numbers 28:16 (504)
- Deuteronomy 16:1 (660)
- 1st Corinthians 5:7-8 (859)

Due to the limiting factors introduced later, we do not do a full Passover today. Instead, we hold a memorial to Passover. There are two aspects to Passover: The instructions to eat the Passover meal and the teaching to observe Passover. Many people think they are the same, but the fact that they are two separate commands shows us otherwise. In this command, we are instructed to observe Passover every year. For uncircumcised people, observing Passover seems to be fine, but eating the meal is not (29). This is something that should be made extremely clear. Why is Passover so important?

The events of Exodus chapters 7 to 12 should never be forgotten. Through 10 powerful plagues, the Heavenly Father brought the strongest country of that time to its knees and showed the world that all the gods of Egypt were nothing compared to the One True Elohim. Passover is not just about events that have already happened but also about promises to come. Just like Israel was freed from Egypt, Israel all around the world will be freed from all nations, and we will experience another exodus so big that the first one will be overshadowed.

Passover stands apart from the rest of the feasts. Passover is not a full-day feast; it is an event traditionally observed around the late afternoon of the 14th of Nisan. However, the Heavenly Father makes it very clear that it is important to Him. Passover is the only feast with a makeup date (474), highlighting the necessity of preparation. Passover is not an open feast. All the other feasts and appointed times are public events. Passover is designed only for covenanted people and people exploring the idea of getting covenanted. A covenant relationship is the only proper relationship mankind can have with the Heavenly Father (45). Last, Passover is the only feast directly reaffirmed for believers to keep after Yeshua's biography letters.

#14. Exodus 12:15 ~ To Observe the Week of Unleavened Bread

Positive
Loving Abba
Unconditional

Repeated 6 times:

- Exodus 12:17 (16)
- Exodus 13:3 (32)
- Exodus 13:10 (39)
- Exodus 34:18 (137)

- Leviticus 23:6 (381)
- Numbers 28:17 (505)

Many people are unaware of this feast because Judaism typically calls it the week of Passover. The reason is that Passover rolls into the feast of Unleavened Bread; however, they are two separate feasts and should be treated as such. As the name suggests, the week of Unleavened Bread is when we abstain from eating anything with yeast (18). Yeast is not sin, but Elohim uses yeast as a symbol of sin in various places in the Bible. Throughout Torah, specific offerings are not allowed with yeast; even Paul uses yeast to illustrate how sin spreads (1ˢᵗ Corinthians 5:6-8).

This command says, "*Even the first day you shall put away yeast out of your houses...*" Typically, you'd want this task completed before the Passover meal, but sometimes life can get in the way. Since the first day of Unleavened Bread is a Shabbat (the 15ᵗʰ of Nisan), you should have time to meet the requirements of this command on that day. If the leaven is removed by sundown on the first day of Unleavened Bread, you will not be guilty of breaking this command.

#15. Exodus 12:16 ~ The First and Last Day of Unleavened Bread is a Shabbat

Positive
Loving Abba
Unconditional

Repeated 6 times:

- Exodus 13:6 (34)
- Leviticus 23:7 (382)
- Leviticus 23:8 (384)
- Numbers 28:18 (506)
- Numbers 28:25 (508)

- Deuteronomy 16:8 (670)

The first day of Unleavened Bread is the Shabbat that the Pharisees were worried about as Yeshua was on the cross, not the weekly Shabbat, as most people believe. The Passover Sedar begins around the mid to late afternoon of the 14th of Nisan, and by the time it ends, we have entered the feast of Unleavened Bread. Unlike the weekly Saturday Shabbat, Unleavened Bread's first and last days can fall on any day of the week each year (Depending on when you begin to count the Omer, see command #391 for more information); I call them roaming Shabbats. For most roaming Shabbats, cooking is allowed, and some light work is allowed, but like the weekly Shabbats, working for pay is prohibited (More on this later). If a roaming Shabbat falls on a weekly Shabbat, the rule of the weekly Shabbat is to be observed with the following exceptions.

- Yom Kippur trumps the weekly Shabbat.
- If it is Erev Shabbat, that is not much of an issue, but if it falls right after Shabbat ends, then Passover can trump the weekly Shabbat since preparations are needed for the meal.

#16. Exodus 12:17 ~ To Guard the Feast of Unleavened Bread

Positive
Loving Abba
Unconditional

See #14 for more information.

This command is why we cannot simply merge the Feast of Unleavened Bread with Passover. Part of guarding the feast is recognizing that it is a feast of its own.

#17. Exodus 12:18 ~ To Eat Unleavened Bread Every Day for the Feast of Unleavened Bread

Positive
Loving Abba
Unconditional

Repeated 4 times:

- Exodus 13:6 (33)
- Exodus 13:7 (35)
- Deuteronomy 16:3 (663)
- Deuteronomy 16:8 (671)

Unleavened bread, commonly known as Matzah, can be found in grocery stores today. It is also easy to make at home, and you can find recipes online. Back then, it was known as מַצָּה (maṣṣâ H4682), derived from the root word מָצַץ (māṣaṣ H4711), which was a sweet bread/cake-like product. The way this command is worded allows for some creative freedom so that you do not have to eat Matzah plain all week long. There are many tasty ways that people meet the requirements for this teaching. Some people eat Matzah with eggs for breakfast, others cover it with melted chocolate and nuts, and there are various other ways to enjoy it. You can find all kinds of recipes online.

#18. Exodus 12:19 ~ No Leaven in the House During the Week of Unleavened Bread

Negative
Loving Abba
Unconditional

Repeated twice:

- Exodus 13:7 (36)
- Deuteronomy 16:4 (664)

Leaven is a substance used to produce fermentation in dough or liquids. Other names for leaven are yeast, ferment, barm, fungus, and raising agent. Although Baking Soda acts like leavening, it is not the same as yeast.

Bread is commonly made with yeast. Other products made with yeast include beer, certain cereals, certain candies, kombucha, soy sauce, and wine. Please note: This is not a complete list of products made with yeast. From time to time, I still discover new things that are made from yeast, so I strongly encourage everyone to do their due diligence to ensure their house is yeast-free for the Feast of Unleavened Bread. You can look up wines that are approved for Passover according to Judaism, but does it matter? All wine is made with yeast, including the approved wines for Passover. This is all said in the spirit of striving to be Torah maximalists; however, this command can be viewed more specifically.

In this instruction, leaven comes from the Hebrew word שְׂאֹר (śᵊ'ōr H7603). Yeast is all around us in the air. To get the yeast back then, people would leave the dough out for a while, allowing the natural yeast in the air to ferment the dough. That is what śᵊ'ōr is, a lump of fermented dough that can be used when making bread later by adding it to a new lump of dough to raise it. The term "leavened bread" is from the Hebrew word חָמֵץ (ḥāmēṣ H2557), which means leavened bread. When it comes to the Week of Unleavened Bread, we need to remove ḥāmēṣ and śᵊ'ōr from our homes. Judaism has added more to this command, but it is all about ḥāmēṣ and śᵊ'ōr.

Ashkenazic Jewish leaders have added rice and millet to the list. They have also added a list of foods known as "kitniyot." Kitniyot is loosely translated as legumes and includes buckwheat, peas, corn, beans, and lentils. Some authorities have also included peanuts in the list. The logic behind this kitniyot list is that these items are usually stored together. It would make it possible for individuals to break this command unknowingly. It is possible for stored flour to be mixed with yeast. Yeast can contaminate its surrounding foods, and the human eye can easily miss it. However, this is all optional and is not an actual part of the command. If this is a concern, ensure your products are well-isolated.

#19. Exodus 12:20 ~ Do Not Eat Anything with Leaven During the Week of Unleavened Bread

Negative
Loving Abba
Unconditional

Not eating anything with leaven for a whole week is a physical exercise that symbolizes our efforts to resist sin. Since this command is about eating, not drinking, this command allows room for wine. Torah is a series of commands designed to bring us into sync with the Heavenly Father. The Week of Unleavened Bread can reveal your spiritual state based on your struggle with not eating bread. Of course, it can also reveal other problems, such as addiction to carbs and other possible health-related issues.

#20. Exodus 12:24 ~ To Remember Passover Forever

Positive
Loving Abba
Unconditional

See #13 for more information.

#21. Exodus 12:26-27 ~ To Teach Children About Passover

Positive
Loving People
Unconditional

Proverbs 13:22 reads, "*A good man leaves an inheritance to his children's children, but the wealth of the sinner is stored for the righteous.*" On the Peshat level, this refers to something tangible. However, from a spiritual level, what spiritual inheritance is greater than teaching our children about Adonai's feasts, appointed times, and commands?

> *Train up a child in the way he should go, and when he is old he will not depart from it.* - Proverbs 22:6

#22. Exodus 12:43 ~ Uncovenanted People Cannot Eat the Passover Meal

Negative
Loving Abba
Unconditional

Repeated once in Exodus 12:45 (24).

Passover is a family-only affair, and circumcision is the only physical requirement for men to eat the meal by the Heavenly Father. While circumcision is not the golden ticket to a forever life, it is something that the Heavenly Father considers when identifying with the children of Abraham, the children of the promise. According to command #29, it is required to participate in the Passover meal.

Messianic congregations have been known to invite churches to the feast, but Passover is not a public event. If you want to use Passover to evangelize and teach non-covenanted people (see #45 for more information), Torah does not prohibit you from doing a mock Passover Sedar on another night. Just make sure it is not done on the makeup night for Passover either (474).

#23. Exodus 12:44 ~ Servants That Are Covenanted May Eat the Passover Meal

Positive
Loving People
Unconditional

#24. Exodus 12:45 ~ Uncovenanted People and Uncovenanted Servants, cannot eat the Passover Meal

Negative
Loving Abba
Unconditional

See #22 for more information.

#25-26. Exodus 12:46 ~ To Eat the Passover Meal in One House/Not to Take Any of the Flesh Outside

Positive
Loving Abba
Conditional

Repeated once:
- Exodus 34:25 (146)

As we look at these two commands from a Peshat level, we can see that these instructions were for the initial Passover meal. Although we do not do the full Passover today, the meal can be considered set-apart. Some congregations symbolically honor this command by discarding any leftovers from the Seder, while others do not.

#27. Exodus 12:46 ~ Do Not Break the Bone

Negative
Loving Abba
Conditional

See #12 for more information.

#28. Exodus 12:47 ~ All of Israel is to Observe the Passover

Positive
Loving Abba
Unconditional

See #13 for more information.

#29. Exodus 12:48 ~ Only Circumcised Males Can Partake of the Passover Meal

Negative
Loving Abba
Unconditional

This is the only physical requirement for men to partake in the Passover meal. Once you are circumcised, and have agreed to covenant with our Heavenly Father, you become a full citizen of Israel, a child of Abraham, and a member of the family. Since women cannot be physically circumcised, it is safe to believe that the foreskins of their hearts must be circumcised (583). This command is the difference between foreigners dwelling in Israel and an Israelite. This is also how foreign slaves became Israelite slaves, gaining the right to be free in the Year of Jubilee, as well as all the other rights of an Israelite slave. This idea is very different from what we are accustomed to today. For example, if someone comes to America through the proper channels, obtains a visa or green card, and later becomes a citizen, they still hold on to their culture and identity from the country they came from. When you covenant with the Heavenly Father and become a part of Israel, you bring yourself to the table and leave behind worldly customs that conflict with Torah, holidays, and ways of thinking, fully embracing the Torah way of life.

#30. Exodus 12:49 ~ One Torah for All

Positive
Loving Abba
Unconditional

Repeated twice in:

- Numbers 9:14 (477)
- Numbers 15:13-16 (481)

Torah draws all of Israel to the One who freed us from Egypt, and it is the primary uniting factor for the people of Israel. Torah is the foundation of the faith. It is how we are unified in worship of the Heavenly Father. Unfortunately, some Jewish Messianic groups believe those coming in from the nations do not need to follow Torah and teach people something called "Noahide Laws." Elements of Noahide Laws can be found throughout the Bible, but it is not specifically instructed as a way of life for those who believe in the Heavenly Father. Torah is for all who wish to worship the Elohim of Abraham, Isaac, and Jacob. Torah aligns us with Yeshua, without Torah, we cannot imitate him. When we keep Torah, we fulfill the purpose of human beings from Genesis 1:26 because Torah is not just a list of dos and don'ts, it is a written description of who the Heavenly Father is. The more we are committed to Torah as individuals, the more unified we become with Yeshua and the Father. There is a reason why the Heavenly Father had Moses write this 3 times.

#31. Exodus 13:2 ~ To Sanctify the First-Born Males

Positive
Loving Abba
Conditional

Key word: Sanctify (Hebrew: qadash, קָדַשׁ)

This verb means "to consecrate," "to set apart (make holy = qadosh)," or "to dedicate" something or someone for Abba's exclusive use. This is often believed to involve ritual preparation or separation from the common and/or the profane. It focuses on making someone holy rather than freeing, but one can argue that it frees you from the world. It's frequently tied to worship, priesthood, or readiness for Elohim's presence. For Israel, this is accomplished through obedience to a Torah Lifestyle, something we will explore in detail when we get to Exodus 19:4-6.

This command introduces us to the concept of sanctifying all firstborns whether human or animal. It is possible that this command is a reference pointing to Yeshua who is the Heavenly Father's "Only Begotten Son" (John 1:14, 1:18, 3:16, 3:18, & 1st John 4:9). This command is not directly repeated which makes some people believe that it is only for the exodus generation, however, the Heaven Father does see fit to reaffirm the concept that all firstborns belong to Him in Exodus 34:19, Numbers 3:13, & Numbers 8:17. It is possible that there could have been a warped view of firstborns at that time that needed to be corrected. It could also be a message that He is the Elohim who controls the womb; Sarah, Rebecca, and Rachel were barren, and it was Elohim who allowed them to bare children who eventually became the nation of Israel. From a simpler standpoint, it could just be a way to help Israel remember the final plague of Egypt where every house who did not have the blood of the lamb on their door posts suffered the death of their firstborn directly at the hands of Elohim (See Exodus 11:4-5).

In Exodus 19:10 -Adonai said to Moses, "Go to the people, and sanctify them today and tomorrow. Let them wash their clothing..." (preparing Israel for Sinai and receiving the 10 Commandments). In Leviticus 20:7-8, it's a call to personal holiness: "So consecrate (Sanctify) yourselves and be holy, for I am Adonai your Elohim. You are to keep My statutes, and do them. I am Adonai who sanctifies you." These words strongly make the point that it is through obeying the instructions of Elohim that we can be sanctified.

For Animals, sanctification involved being sacrificed or ransomed in the case for donkeys. For human first born males, we must admire the practical wisdom behind this command. Now that we know what the word sanctify means, the firstborn male would be instructed and groomed to live a Torah lifestyle from birth, this could easily increase the chances of his younger siblings following suite. The combination of the father, mother, and firstborn male dedicated to the Torah lifestyle can easily set a solid Torah foundation for the whole family. Of course, this command is far more challenging today than it was back in that world. In today's world, this command has the best chance of succeeding if both the father and mother are unified in worshipping the Heavenly Father. Otherwise, the difficulties of succeeding in this command in today's world increase exponentially.

#32. Exodus 13:3 ~ To Remember the First Day of Unleavened Bread as the Day Israel Left Egypt

Positive
Loving Abba
Unconditional

See #14 for more information.

#33. Exodus 13:6 ~ To Eat Unleavened Bread for 7 Days

Positive
Loving Abba
Unconditional

Repeated 3 times:

- Exodus 13:7 (35)
- Deuteronomy 16:3 (663)
- Deuteronomy 16:8 (669)

Deuteronomy 16:3 explains the reason for this command. Unleavened bread is called the "bread of affliction" because it was often the only thing Israel could eat as slaves in Egypt. Another reason for this command is to remember that Israel left Egypt on the first day of the Feast of Unleavened Bread.

#34. Exodus 13:6 ~ The Seventh Day of Unleavened Bread is a Shabbat

Positive
Loving Abba
Unconditional

See #15 for more information.

#35. Exodus 13:7 ~ To Eat Unleavened Bread for 7 Days

Positive
Loving Abba
Unconditional

See #33 for more information.

#36. Exodus 13:7 ~ Nothing with Leaven is to be Seen on Your Property During Unleavened Bread

Negative
Loving Abba
Unconditional

See #18 for more information.

#37. Exodus 13:8 ~ To Teach Children About the Feast of Unleavened Bread

Positive
Loving People
Unconditional

See #21 for more information.

#38. Exodus 13:9 ~ To Remember That the Heavenly Father Freed Israel from Egypt

Positive
Loving Abba
Unconditional

Repeated 3 times in:

- Exodus 20:2 (46)
- Deuteronomy 5:6 (537)
- Deuteronomy 5:15 (543)

Also mentioned 20 times throughout the Scriptures, including:

- Exodus 13:3 (32)
- Exodus 16:6
- Exodus 16:32
- Leviticus 19:36 (315)
- Leviticus 22:33 (377)
- Leviticus 25:38
- Leviticus 26:13
- Numbers 15:41
- Deuteronomy 4:20
- Deuteronomy 4:37
- Deuteronomy 6:12
- Deuteronomy 7:8
- Deuteronomy 7:19
- Deuteronomy 8:14
- Deuteronomy 13:5 (621)
- Deuteronomy 13:10 (623)
- Deuteronomy 16:1 (659)
- Joshua 24:5
- Judges 2:1
- Judges 6:8

For thousands of years, Judah has wondered why the Heavenly Father introduces Himself in Exodus 20:2 by saying, *"YHWH your Elohim, who brought you out of the land of Egypt, out of the house of bondage."* The Heavenly Father could have introduced Himself as the Elohim of Abraham, Isaac, Jacob, and Joseph. Israel was not around to see the creation of the universe and did not witness His relationship with Abraham, Isaac, and Jacob. However, the exodus generation witnessed the 10 plagues, saw the distinction made between the Egyptians and Israel, and how Pharaoh was forced to let us go. There is another reason why the Heavenly Father attaches Himself to freeing Israel from Egypt more than anything else: It is a unique identifier.

There is no shortage of false gods who claim the creation of the universe and all life within. Today, two of the world's three largest religions claim to be physical descendants of Abraham. However, only the Elohim of Abraham, Isaac, and Jacob is attached to what happened to Egypt, and only He can take credit for taking Israel out of the world's most powerful nation at the time and establishing us to be a nation unto ourselves. No one else can take credit for that.

#39. Exodus 13:10 ~ To Guard the Feast of Unleavened Bread Every Year

Positive
Loving Abba
Unconditional

See #14 for more information.

#40. Exodus 13:11-12 ~ All Firstborn Males Belong to the Heavenly Father

Positive
Loving People
Conditional

See #31 for more information.

#41. Exodus 13:13 ~ To Ransom the First-Born Donkey with a Lamb

Positive
Loving People
Conditional

This command is repeated once, in Exodus 34:20 (138).

Donkeys are considered unclean animals, yet they are the only ones from that category who get firstborn rights. The Bible does not explain why; however, Judah has long told the tale of how the donkeys of Israel gained supernatural strength on the night of the exodus and were able to take on a load of transporting everyone's belongings as Israel left Egypt. It is believed that this is the reason why donkeys have firstborn rights.

It is hard to ignore the symbolic message behind this command. For a donkey, an unclean animal, to be successfully redeemed, the priesthood would need to receive a lamb that they would sacrifice, freeing the donkey back to its owner and marking it as sacred. Sin makes us unclean. Just as the donkey needs a lamb to be redeemed, humanity needs Yeshua to be redeemed from the clutches of death, an act done even while we were still sinners.

#42. Exodus 13:13 ~ To Ransom All First-Born Males

Positive
Loving Abba
Unconditional

See #31 for more information.

#43. Exodus 13:14-16 ~ Teach Children About How the Heavenly Father Freed Israel from Egypt

Positive
Loving People
Unconditional

See #21 for more information. Falls in line with Deuteronomy 6:7.

#44. Exodus 15:26 ~ To Carefully Obey the Voice of the Heavenly Father

Positive
Loving People (see 1 John 5:2)
Unconditional

Repeated 7 times in:

- Exodus 19:5-6 (45)
- Exodus 23:13 (124)
- Deuteronomy 8:1 (573)
- Deuteronomy 8:11 (577)
- Deuteronomy 13:4 (618)
- Deuteronomy 27:10 (806)
- Deuteronomy 30:20 (815)

A few more examples are:

- Deuteronomy 4:30
- Deuteronomy 4:36
- Deuteronomy 15:4-5
- Deuteronomy 28:1-2
- Deuteronomy 28:15
- Jeremiah 38:20
- Hebrews 4:7
- Revelation 3:20

This command is the quintessential command of the entire scriptures. There are only three ways you can go as far as the voice of the Heavenly Father goes:

- You can obey His voice and benefit from a proper relationship with the Heavenly Father

- You can ignore His voice, not having a relationship with Him at all (See Proverbs 28:9 & John 9:31)

- Or, suffer the consequences of ignoring Adonai after you've agreed to obey His voice (See Deuteronomy chapter 28)

When the Heavenly Father told Adam not to eat from the tree of the knowledge of good and evil, it wasn't just a test or matter of choice; it was also for the benefit of all humanity! Every commandment He gives is for our benefit and protection. With that protection comes the power of the Heavenly Father. There is so much power in the voice of the Heavenly Father!

> YHWH's voice is on the waters. The Elohim of glory thunders, even YHWH on many waters. YHWH's voice is powerful. YHWH's voice is full of majesty. YHWH's voice breaks the cedars. Yes, YHWH breaks in pieces the cedars of Lebanon. YHWH's voice

strikes with flashes of lightning. YHWH's voice shakes the wilderness. YHWH shakes the wilderness of Kadesh. YHWH's voice makes the deer calve and strips the forests bare. In his temple everything says, "Glory!" - Psalms 29:3-9

Yeshua lived a sinless life by perfectly submitting to the voice of the Heavenly Father, and He taught us to do the same. Obeying the voice of the Heavenly Father is how you enter the most important covenant in the Bible, seen in Exodus 19:5-6 (45). When we agree to live by His voice, He listens to our prayers, watches over us, blesses us, and protects us. When we go through hard times, we can trust our Heavenly Father, that everything will work out because we trust Him as the Author and Perfecter of our lives. Only through obeying His voice can we have a proper relationship with the Heavenly Father, fulfill our purpose in Genesis 1:26, and realize our full potential.

Obeying the voice of the Heavenly Father not only affects you but also those who come from you. Once a human being covenants with the Heavenly Father, all of Deuteronomy chapter 28 affects them and every human that comes from them. Many times, people refer to something called "generational curses." For the most part, a generational curse is learned bad behavior that moves down from generation to generation. However, sometimes, if things are just not going your way, the Heavenly Father may be trying to get your attention because someone in your genealogy covenanted with Him.

#45. Exodus 19:5-6 ~ The Covenant of Relationship

Positive
Loving Abba
Unconditional

This is the most important covenant, not only for Israel but for all humanity. This covenant is referenced throughout the Bible, the four biographical books of Yeshua, and the letters of the Apostles. The reason why this command is so important is because it is the only identifiable way for individual humans to have a proper relationship with the Heavenly Father. This covenant is simple to enter. It does not involve ceremonies, rituals, public confirmations, or special prayers. All it takes is the choice to live by the voice of the Heavenly Father. After Israel heard the words of Exodus 19:5-6, Israel officially came into this covenant by saying, "*All that YHWH has spoken we will do.* (Exodus 19:8)." This covenant is the foundation of the only true faith in the world. With a humble and contrite heart, anyone can join this covenant of relationship and become a part of Israel. The words and life of Yeshua draws everyone into this covenant (Ephesians 2:11-12).

In the book of Ruth, we are introduced to a woman named Naomi, an Israelite who moved to the land of Moab. Naomi's husband passed away, and her two sons married Moabite women. One of Naomi's daughters-in-law was called Ruth. Ruth was a Moabite, and according to command #742, Moabites do not enter the assembly of Israel. However, when Ruth said, "*Where you go, I will go; and where you stay, I will stay. Your people will be my people, and your Elohim my Elohim...* (Ruth 1:16-17)" At that point, her citizenship changed from Moabite to Israel. She becomes a part of Yeshua's lineage. Ruth is a perfect example of the promise made to Abraham in Genesis 12:1-3 and she also displays the heart that those coming from the nations to join with Israel should have.

Right before offering this covenant to Israel in Exodus 19:5, the Heavenly Father said, "*You have seen what I did to the Egyptians, and how I bore you on eagles' wings, and brought you to myself* (Verse 4)." These words reveal two important facts about this covenant.

Choose Life

First, this covenant is about who He is. For the Exodus generation, Adonai revealed Himself through the plagues and how He freed them from Egypt. About 2000 years ago, the Heavenly Father revealed Himself to the world through Yeshua and His death on the cross while we were still sinners. The Heavenly Father shows us who He is every millisecond of every day. Without Him, there is no air to breathe, earth to walk on, rain, stars, or sunshine. Science is baffled by the laws He has established to sustain the universe. Whether you believe in Him or not, nothing could exist without Him. That is more than enough to listen to His voice.

The second important part about the covenant: It is not about knowledge of the commandments. This covenant is all about the heart of listening to His voice and obeying, just like Abraham did. When Israel committed to this covenant, they had not heard the 10 Commandments yet. This covenant is all about faith based on listening to His voice. As you walk in this faith, you will grow spiritually. It does not start with you knowing all the commands. It can start right now, right where you are, with what you know, and then you learn as you go. Don't worry about getting over the learning curve. The learning curve of this faith may take the rest of your life, at least that seems to be the case for everyone, or almost everyone.

It doesn't matter who you are, where you are, where you are from, or what you have done; once you commit to living according to the voice of the All-Mighty, He accepts you with open arms as a citizen of Israel, and Yeshua sees you as a part of the family (See Luke 8:20-21). When we properly believe in Yeshua, paying close attention to everything he says and how he lives, he draws us into this covenant, this cannot be stated enough. According to what the Heavenly Father tells Moses in Exodus 19:9, this covenant has no expiration date.

#46. Exodus 20:2 ~ To Acknowledge the Heavenly Father Who Freed Israel

Positive
Loving Abba
Unconditional

See #38 for more information.

#47. Exodus 20:3 ~ Do Not Worship Other Gods

Negative
Loving Abba
Unconditional

Repeated in #529.

This teaching is sprinkled throughout Torah. It is presented in different ways, allowing us to explore it from various aspects for a full understanding. When it comes to not worshipping other gods, Paul gives us an idea of how we should approach this command.

> *But I say that the things which the Gentiles sacrifice, they sacrifice to demons, and not to Elohim, and I don't desire that you would have fellowship with demons.* - 1st Corinthians 10:20

All other "gods" are demons, evil spirits, or created by man's imagination. Our Heavenly Father is the only true Elohim. This cannot be compromised in any way, shape, or form. Worship of any other god is worship of demons or nothing at all. There is a popular belief in this world that Christianity, Islam, Judaism, and Hinduism all come from the same god. From a demonic standpoint, that could be true. However, anyone who believes that the Elohim of Abraham, Isaac, and Jacob is a part of that mess does not believe in the One True Elohim of Israel.

#48. Exodus 20:4-5 ~ Not to Make Statues, Idols, or Figures to Worship

Negative
Loving Abba
Unconditional

Repeated 10 times in:

- Exodus 20:23 (61)
- Leviticus 19:4 (273)
- Leviticus 19:4 (274)
- Leviticus 26:1 (453)
- Leviticus 26:1 (454)
- Leviticus 26:1 (455)
- Deuteronomy 5:8-9 (539)
- Deuteronomy 4:16-19 (529)
- Deuteronomy 16:21 (683)
- Deuteronomy 16:22 (684)

In modern English, an idol is a person or thing that is greatly admired, loved, or revered. The word for idol in this verse comes from the Hebrew word פֶּסֶל (peh'-sel). It is a carved object used for worship. Its common synonyms are icon, representation of a god, image, effigy, statue, figure, figurine, fetish, or totem. This teaching found in Exodus 20:4 is meant to prevent Israel from worshipping false gods. Because the Heavenly Father is Spirit, nothing can properly represent Him; in fact, nothing within the scriptures describes what the Heavenly Father looks like. Depending on the Bible you are using, it might say sculptured image, graven image, or simply an idol. Whichever word your Bible uses, this term talks about three-dimensional objects, big or small, that are like statues. The word likeness means a symbolic image that can be drawn, sculpted, or fashioned in any manner. This instruction also means you cannot acquire or even possess an idol.

In today's world, what would fall under this category of idols? Are all statues considered idols? If that is the case, was Solomon's temple defiled because it had statues? Statues, figures, and pictures for decorations, collectibles, or beauty are fine and do not go against this instruction. Pictures and statues are usually made for art, beauty, inspiration, and relaxation, but anything made to provide supernatural service can be considered an idol. For example, Statues or pictures of Yeshua, angels, saints, demons, gargoyles for protection, Indian dream catchers, rabbit's feet, even the cross (with or without Yeshua), and the star of David can all fall into the category of idols if they are made or owned with the idea that they possess a supernatural ability or provide some form of spiritual benefit. Items used for "luck" can be idols because they are believed to provide supernatural benefits while taking glory away from the Heavenly Father when good fortunes fall upon you.

Sometimes, we take things meant for good in the scriptures and twist them into idols; for example, the serpent Moses made in Numbers 21:8-9 eventually became an idol. Even Mezuzahs (561) can be an idol if you believe they do more than remind you of the scriptures when you leave and enter your home. This teaching can take years to master because idolatry is deeply ingrained in the world. Saying things like "good luck" is something we don't even think about. Since faith in the Heavenly Father has nothing to do with luck, what do those words mean?

Israel takes this teaching so seriously that all of Israel has risked total Annihilation multiple times in the past over this command alone. Today, if a Jewish individual goes to see the Statue of Liberty and change falls out of their pockets or they notice that their shoes are untied, that individual will turn away from the statue before bending over, to avoid the impression of worship. Josephus records the event when all of Israel refused to erect a statue of the Roman emperor Caius. Israel was willing to be slaughtered by the Roman Empire rather than allow that statue to be erected in Jerusalem.

NOTE: Exodus 20:6 – To love the Heavenly Father is to keep and guard His commands. The connection between obeying the commands of the Heavenly Father and loving Him is a major theme throughout the entire Bible. Obedience is the Heavenly Father's love language.

#49. Exodus 20:7 ~ Not to Shame the Name of the Heavenly Father

Negative
Loving Abba
Unconditional

Repeated 3 times in:

- Leviticus 18:21 (265)
- Leviticus 24:10-16 (423)
- Deuteronomy 5:11 (540)

In Exodus 20:7, the word used for shame or vain comes from the Hebrew word שָׁוְא (shawv; H7723), which means emptiness, vanity, falsehood, nothingness, the empty speech, lying, and worthlessness. Deuteronomy 5:11 uses the same Hebrew word שָׁוְא (shawv; H7723) as in Exodus 20:7.

The word "profane" used in Leviticus 18:21 comes from the Hebrew word חָלַל (khaw-lal; H2490), which means, properly, to bore — that is, to wound or to dissolve. Figuratively, it means to profane (a person, place, or thing), to break one's word, to begin (as if by an "opening wedge"), to play (the flute), to defile, to treat as common, to pollute, to prostitute, to stain, or to wound. It refers to any act that violates or defiles something set-apart or sacred, reducing it to something common or unworthy.

From Leviticus 24:10-16, the word blaspheme comes from the Hebrew word נָקַב (naw-kab'; H5344) which means literally (to perforate, with violence) or figuratively (to specify, designate, libel): —appoint, blaspheme, bore, curse, express, with holes, name, pierce, strike through.

The verses of Exodus 20:7, Leviticus 18:21, Leviticus 24:10-16, & Deuteronomy 5:11 all use 3 different words that go in the same direction. When you shame the name of the Heavenly Father, you present a false or negative view of who He is. When you profane the name of the Heavenly Father, you are not esteeming Him as set-apart; you are making His name common. When you blaspheme the name of the Heavenly Father, you are causing harm to the name, cursing the name, and placing holes in the character of our Heavenly Father.

To profane the name of the Heavenly Father is to make His name common, to use His name in frivolous subjects, or to say something false in His name. The tetragrammaton (YHWH) is not commonly used in this book to avoid profaning His name. Over the years, Judah has employed Adonai or Hashem to avoid profaning the name of the Heavenly Father. The most common way to shame the name of the Heavenly Father is when you claim to believe in Him, but your actions contradict His voice.

In today's world, one of the most common ways people shame, profane, and blaspheme His name is to claim you believe in Him **and** believe in the idea that Torah is done away with, that Messiah has put an end to Torah and is teaching new commands, or that Paul teaches against Torah; 3 false things that many believe in the world today. The wording of Deuteronomy 13:1-4 leaves no room to accept the idea that our Heavenly Father would ever profane Torah.

#50. Exodus 20:8 ~ To Keep the Weekly Shabbat

Positive
Loving Abba
Unconditional

Repeated 3 times in:

- Exodus 31:16 (136)
- Leviticus 23:3 (378)
- Deuteronomy 5:12 (541)

To guard all Shabbats is repeated 4 times in:

- Exodus 31:13 (133)
- Leviticus 19:3 (272)
- Leviticus 19:30 (309)
- Leviticus 26:2 (456)

In Exodus 31:13, the Heavenly Father says, "*Speak also to the children of Israel, saying, 'Most certainly you shall keep my Sabbaths: for it is a sign between me and you throughout your generations; that you may know that I am Yahweh who sanctifies you.*" The weekly Shabbat of Elohim is not only a sign between Him and those who believe in Him, but according to Exodus 31:16, it is also a covenant. Because the weekly Shabbat is a covenant, it will never be altered, replaced, or done away with.

The weekly Shabbat is a practical way to keep the Heavenly Father at the center of our lives. Through the Shabbats, we revolve around the Heavenly Father. Every week, we must prepare, and throughout the year, we set our plans, vacations, business, and family life around the Shabbats, feasts, and appointed times of the Heavenly Father. When we focus on His Shabbats, He remains at the forefront of our minds. Without His Shabbats, it becomes easy for us to forget Him and make Him revolve around us. At that point, we are not following Him at all. When we properly observe Shabbat, we take a break from the world to focus on Adonai, a time to recalibrate spiritually with Him.

#51. Exodus 20:9-10 ~ To Work 6 Days of the Week

Positive
Loving People
Unconditional

Repeated 6 times:

- Exodus 23:12 (122)
- Exodus 31:15 (135)
- Exodus 34:21 (142)
- Exodus 35:2 (149)
- Leviticus 23:3 (378)
- Deuteronomy 5:13-14 (542)

Every command in Torah is designed to lead us to behave like the Heavenly Father, like the command to work six days and rest on the seventh, just as He did in the first chapter of the book of Genesis, continuing into Genesis 2:3. There are a few things we can learn from this teaching.

In Genesis chapter 1, everything was done in order and with purpose. Each day was designed to support something created later. The sun, stars, and moon would collapse if they were made on the second day. The earth needed to be revealed first for grass and vegetation. All the things created during the first five days are essential to sustain human life created on the sixth day. Each day should have a purpose that sets up something to come. That is the true meaning of a purpose-driven life.

Unfortunately, many of us are in survival mode, stuck in a vicious cycle of working to pay bills from month to month, hoping that we might have something left over to have some fun, but with no bright future to come. We settle on false security because we have a roof over our head, a car, electricity, gas, internet, a computer, or whatever gadgets we are into. If we unexpectedly lose our jobs, it is usually devastating to our way of life. This teaching can help us break free from that rut.

Most people work five days a week and rest for two days. For those of us who take this command seriously, working on a sixth day is an opportunity to pursue our dreams, tackle business projects, improve ourselves, acquire new skills, consider a second job, explore alternative ways to earn extra income, and ultimately strive for a more productive life and/or reach a point of financial strength. For 40 hours a week (or more), we devote time to paying our bills and making someone else's dreams come true. That 6th day can provide an opportunity for us to go the extra mile for ourselves and our families. Working six days a week is repeated more than not working on the Shabbat. That is a message in and of itself, bringing us back to the first two commands in this book.

#52. Jeremiah 17:21-22 ~ To Do No Work on Shabbat

Negative
Loving Abba
Unconditional

Repeated twice in:

- Exodus 31:14 (134)
- Deuteronomy 5:13-14 (542)

In Jeremiah 17:21-22, the word "Burden" comes from the Hebrew word מַשָּׂא (mas-saw'; H4853), and it means load, bearing, tribute, burden, lifting. In other words, physical work. Some people might look at this and believe that no work should be done on Shabbat; however, let us look at the other verses connected to this command.

For Exodus 31:14, the word "work" comes from the Hebrew word מְלָאכָה (mel-aw-kaw'; H4399), which generally means employment (never servile) or work (abstractly or concretely). It also refers to the property (as the result of labor), including terms like business, cattle, industrious, occupation, officer, thing (made), use, (manner of) work (-man, -manship). It is the same word used for Deuteronomy 5:13-14. Unfortunately, many people have interpreted this command in a religious aspect that has caused criticism throughout history, even to this day.

While Yeshua and the disciples were walking through a field on a Shabbat, the disciples began to pluck ears of grain to eat. Some Pharisees saw this and began to scold them for breaking "the law" (Not an actual commandment but a man-made one within Judaism). Yeshua replied, *"Did you never read what David did, when he had need, and was hungry—he, and those who were with him? How he entered into God's house at the time of Abiathar the high priest, and ate the showbread, which is not lawful to eat except for the priests, and gave also to those who were with him? The Sabbath was made for man, not man for the Sabbath. Therefore, the Son of Man is lord even of the Sabbath* (Mark 2:25-28)." Unfortunately, this command is often abused as an excuse to do nothing on Shabbat.

Shabbat is set-apart to focus on the Heavenly Father and avoid things that usually take up our time during the week, things that distract us from the Heavenly Father. Through various commands, we see what that looks like in detail.

When Yeshua healed on the Shabbat and was questioned about it, Yeshua said, "*My Father is still working, so I am working, too.*" (Matthew 5:17). This shows us that even on the Shabbat, there are things that the Heavenly Father finds acceptable for us to do. Every Shabbat, people work to ensure congregations have the best service possible. In Matthew 5:1-17, Yeshua saw someone in need on a Shabbat feast and helped the individual. From the establishment of Israel until the temple was destroyed in 70 A.D. (With the exception of the Babylon captivity of course), the Levites worked every Shabbat to serve the Heavenly Father and the people. Sacrifices were expected on the Shabbats, feast days, and appointed times.

In this world, situations can still happen during Shabbat. It is possible that people can run into problems where they need help during Shabbat. In another example of Yeshua healing on a Shabbat, when the Pharisee leaders challenged Him on it, He replied with, "*Which of you, if your son or an ox fell into a well, wouldn't immediately pull him out on a Sabbath day* (Luke 14:5)?" Shabbat is not an excuse to ignore what needs to be done, that does not represent the Heavenly Father at all. However, for some people, there are legitimate questions.

The Heavenly Father values life: If you work in a field that saves, protects, or preserves life, such services cannot stop on Shabbat. Firefighters, police officers, security guards, emergency responders, doctors, hospital staff, caregivers, biomedical technicians, and more, cannot stop working on Shabbat because people's lives would be at risk. Israel's IDF cannot rest on Shabbat. The IDF need to stay alert every day because history has proven that Israel's enemies would take advantage of any opportunity (Google "Yom Kippur War"), even more recently, look up what happened to Israel on 10/7/2024; that was on a shabbat during the feast of Sukkot. Similarly, if you see someone needing help on Shabbat, or something that cannot wait until the sun goes down, be like Yeshua and help.

#53. Nehemiah 13:15-18 ~ Do Not Conduct Business on Shabbat

Negative
Loving Abba
Unconditional

During the first century, this command was taken so seriously that giving tithes and offerings was conducted on Sundays because that was considered taking care of business. In the book of Acts, the believers followed suit and met on Sundays to conduct business, not to praise and worship as many believe. For us today, this is a clear prohibition for us to avoid things that would bring profit to our lives on Shabbat, which is why some people who work as nurses and so on struggle with this, but as stated in the previous commandment, preserving and saving life on Shabbat is good. If you are in that position and feel guilty about it, you can always tithe that day's pay, but that is completely up to you.

#54. Amos 8:4-7 ~ Do Not Desire Shabbat to End so You Can Do Business

Negative
Loving Abba
Unconditional

This command is deceptively harder than you think because it tugs at our selfish desires. It's not just the desire for Shabbat to end so you can conduct business; we can also add the desire to do the things you enjoy during the week, which can easily fit into this command. If you desire

Shabbat to end for whatever reason, that is where your treasure lies, not in the kingdom (see Matthew 6:21).

NOTE: Exodus 20:11 – We keep Shabbat to remember that the Heavenly Father created the heavens and earth in six days and rested on the seventh. Also see Exodus 31:15-17.

#55. Exodus 20:12 ~ Respect Your Father and Mother

Positive
Loving People
Unconditional

Repeated in Deuteronomy 5:16 (544).

This is one of the few commands with a promise that "*your days may be long in the land which YHWH your Elohim gives you.*" Respecting your parents is the foundation of having a healthy relationship with the Heavenly Father. Since He determines the time and place for us to exist in this life (Acts 17:26-27), He was the one who selected our parents, the first authorities we have in our lives. Respecting our parents respects the Heavenly Father's authority He first gives us. In respecting our parents, we obey them unless they tell us to do something that goes against Torah. We take care of them when they cannot take care of themselves, we do not curse them (Exodus 21:17 #80, Leviticus 20:9 #322), and we do not strike them (Exodus 21:17). Cursing and striking our parents are punishable by death. Such things do not happen by mistake.

Of course, this command is much easier for some people and extremely hard for others because, unfortunately, in this fallen world, not all parents are good. However, even in the roughest situations, there are ways to honor your parents, even if the relationship has been severed. If you are someone who has a bad relationship with your parents, the first step to honor them is to forgive them for your peace of mind, allowing you to move on and heal. This would allow you to emotionally let go of the hurt and grow as an individual. This doesn't mean forgetting and acting like it never happened. In most situations, for proper reconciliation to take place, all who did wrong need to acknowledge what they did, apologize, and repent from the hurtful act. Sometimes that never happens; regardless, that should not stop you from forgiving them so you can move on and not stay emotionally trapped in whatever wrong was done to you.

The other step is not to speak badly of your parents. Most people don't need to know what happened, so avoid murdering your parents' reputation as much as possible. If you are in counseling or therapy, talk about it and get help. If you are married, it is ok to share with your spouse, but do not dump or vent in a way that would dishonor your parents.

The last step in honoring parents who have done you wrong is to keep the door open for reconciliation. This does not mean that you must actively seek to reconcile, but it does mean that you do not lock the door on the opportunity should it arise. Of course, this commentary is not a "one-size-fits-all" solution. If you are in a situation where your relationship with your parents is bad for whatever reason, please seek the proper help you need so that you can heal and move on to the best of your ability, and hope that one day the door opens for the relationship to be restored.

#56. Exodus 20:13 ~ Do Not Murder

Negative
Loving People
Unconditional

Repeated in:

- Deuteronomy 5:17 (545)
- Matthew 5:21-26

The punishment for murder is repeated in:

- Exodus 21:12 (75)
- Exodus 21:14 (77)
- Leviticus 19:16 (292)
- Leviticus 24:17 (425)
- Leviticus 24:21 (429)

Unfortunately, some Bibles translate the Hebrew word רָצַח (raw-tsakh'; H7523) as kill but murdering and killing are two different things. Killing is something that sometimes cannot be avoided in this fallen world; otherwise, Israel could not go to war, Israel's judges could not sentence people to death, and sometimes, these are necessary evils. Murder is usually personal, emotionally charged, and filled with rage, hatred, and malice towards another human being to the point where you do not care if they live or die, or you feel that you cannot have satisfaction unless they no longer exist in the world.

According to the Heavenly Father, there are two kinds of murder; a conscious choice and plot to end another human being's life. In these situations, the guilty party must be executed. The other instance is murder by accident; something completely unintentional. In such situations, the murderer can flee to a refuge city (76). Such individuals would be protected from people who would try to take revenge for their fallen loved one and await a proper trial to determine his/her fate. The fact that the Heavenly Father even thought of refuge cities is a testament to how much He understands the struggles of this world.

In Matthew 5:21-26, Yeshua shows us the internal aspect of keeping this command by advocating that we should avoid being angry with people because that puts us in danger of judgment. Jails and prisons are filled with people who act upon their emotions instead of having logical self-control. Yeshua encourages us to see the value of people and not see anyone as worthless (Raca, from Matthew 5:22, comes from the Greek word ῥακά; G4469, and it means worthless). When we get angry at someone, it is easy to value their lives as worthless. Yeshua also advocates for us to seek peace with our adversaries. According to James 1:20, nothing good comes from man's anger, and there are plenty of examples in life and the scriptures to show that. It was anger that prevented Moses from entering the land.

In this life, for many of us, if not all of us, it is impossible never to get angry, so do not think that anger is a sin; it is simply a gateway to sin when left unchecked. Even in anger, we can exhibit self-control. Paul said, "*Be angry, and don't sin. Don't let the sun go down on your wrath, and don't give place to the devil* (Ephesians 4:26)." Paul used words from Psalms 4:4 to show us that it's ok to get angry, but we should never stay there because when we dwell in anger, that is when sin can easily come to life. With command #4, Cain was stewing in negative emotions, and shortly after, we read the account of humanity's first murder.

#57. Exodus 20:14 ~ Not to Commit Adultery

Negative
Loving people
Unconditional

This command is repeated in Deuteronomy 5:18. The consequences for breaking this command are found in:

- Leviticus 20:10 (323)
- Deuteronomy 5:18 (546)
- Deuteronomy 22:22 (752)
- Deuteronomy 22:23-24 (753)

Choose Life

In today's world, adultery is when people who are committed in relationships engage in inappropriate relations with others outside their relationships. Within the Torah, adultery is defined as a man who has sexual relations with a married woman (Deuteronomy 22:22) or a man sleeping with an engaged woman (Deuteronomy 22:23-24). If the man is married and the woman is single, it is not a sin against the Heavenly Father, but it can still be a sin against the wife of that married man and others. During biblical times, the wife didn't have much say in such matters, especially since polygamy was a commonly accepted practice back then. This is why only men had a course of action within Torah if they suspected their wives had an affair, see Numbers 5:11-31. However, it is important to note that when it comes to polygamy and the righteous men in the Bible, it was the wife who initiated, not the husband.

So far, we've only talked about a physical affair between a man and a married woman. Yeshua reveals the spiritual layer of this command when he says, "*You have heard that it was said, 'You shall not commit adultery, but I tell you that everyone who gazes at a woman to lust after her has committed adultery with her already in his heart* (Matthew 5:27-28)." This can easily describe what some call "emotional adultery" and it can be just as painful as discovering your significant other has slept with someone else. This lines up with Job's final appeal to Adonai when he asks, "*I made a covenant with my eyes, how then should I look lustfully at a young woman? (Job 31:1)*"

According to Deuteronomy 22:22-24 and Leviticus 20:10, both the man and the woman must be executed when caught in adultery. However, this verdict is not as easy as most people believe. Deuteronomy 17:6 (687) dictates that the death penalty can only happen under two or more witnesses, and they are the ones who throw the first stones (See Deuteronomy 17:7, #688). Most of the time, when people are caught in the act of adultery, it is usually by one eyewitness.

If the witnesses turn out to be false, they risk the punishment meant for those accused, which is a good deterrent to prevent people from providing false accusations. Also, consider this; if someone has been in a relationship with another and really loves them, finds out that the person has cheated, how many people would truly want to see that person dead? Of course there are people out there like that, but not everyone is like that. With all that said, let us look at the account of John 8:1-11.

Some people like to use John 8:1-11 to teach that Yeshua has "done away" with Torah because he showed "grace and mercy" to this woman who was "caught in adultery" instead of having her stoned as Torah dictates; however, verse 6 says they were testing him to find something to accuse him of. This reveals that there was a distortion of Torah within the whole situation. For example, Yeshua was not a judge nor a part of the Sanhedrin leadership for the Jewish people at that time. If that woman was truly caught in adultery, there was no reason for them to bring her to Yeshua. She needed to go to the official leaders of Israel to face a proper trial. Another distortion with that whole scenario was the absence of the man! If only the woman were stoned and not the man, Torah would have been broken.

When Yeshua says, *"He who is without sin among you, let him throw the first stone at her."* (Verse 7), He placed them all in checkmate, and they were convicted by their conscience (Verse 9). The scriptures do not say exactly what was eating away at their conscience. From their reaction, it is possible that the woman may not have committed adultery at all, possibly was a victim of rumors. It is also possible that she did commit adultery, but there were never two or more eyewitnesses to testify against her, who would risk their lives for a lie? Ultimately, it was never about the woman. This was all about trapping Yeshua into publicly sinning, which would have discredited his authority. The fact that they were trying to trick him shows evil motivation; nothing about their actions was for the righteousness of the Heavenly Father. When we carefully examine this account and pin it against the actual commands for this situation one thing is clear: In that entire scene, Yeshua was not discarding Torah; he was the only one honoring the instructions for that situation.

#58. Exodus 20:15 ~ Do Not Steal

Negative
Loving People
Unconditional

Repeated twice in:

- Leviticus 19:11 (279)
- Deuteronomy 5:19 (547)

This teaching can easily be tied to different commands. Commands such as #447, #739, #800, #181, #60, and #279-#281 all talk about us not profiting in deceitful ways or gaining something at the expense of someone else's loss. All these things, and more, can result in stealing.

#59. Exodus 20:16 ~ Do Not Lie About Others

Negative
Loving People
Unconditional

Repeated in:

- Exodus 32:1 (113)
- Leviticus 19:16 (291)
- Deuteronomy 5:20 (548)

Within Judaism, there is a belief that when you bear false witness against someone, you are guilty of breaking command #56 because spreading false information about someone is murdering their character and creating a fictitious version of them that does not exist. When these false accusations spread, people will behave towards that person based on such false information, and like yeast, it spreads, causing problems that could have been avoided. Unfortunately, this type of situation is common in this fallen world, and many people do it without thinking or believing it is harmless. Always avoid spreading negative information about people. Even if it is true, don't do it unless it is a situation where it is the right thing to do, such as a court case.

One of the biggest misconceptions about this command is that some Bibles present it as "You should not lie." Every instruction that addresses not lying teaches us not to lie negatively about people, not to lie to get people in trouble in court, or not to lie for dishonest gain. In this world, sometimes lying can be a good thing. Sometimes we withhold information for the greater good or lie to encourage someone. During the holocaust, Germans who sheltered Jews and lied about it did a good thing. Abraham lied, saying that Sarah was his sister. That lie was not meant to shame anyone; his only goal was survival. The Heavenly Father didn't punish Abraham for it, and He even stopped the Pharaoh from sinning because of it. So don't feel guilty if your grandmother proudly comes to you with the ugliest dress you've ever seen, asking if she looks good.

#60. Exodus 20:17 ~ Do Not Desire What Belongs to Other People

Negative
Loving People
Unconditional

Choose Life

This command is repeated in Deuteronomy 5:21 (549)

There is nothing wrong with going to someone's house, seeing something, and saying, "I want one like that," then you go out and buy that item for yourself. This command is about wanting what belongs explicitly to someone else. This desire can easily drive people to robbery or worse. If the Heavenly Father blesses you, it will be in a way where nobody gets the shorthand, and always through blessing your efforts. When you desire what belongs to someone else, how can you be grateful for what the Heavenly Father has given you? Coveting what belongs to someone else stirs up selfishness and greed within and is the root that sprouts sin.

> *Be free from the love of money, content with such things as you have, for he has said, 'I will in no way leave you, neither will I in any way forsake you.* - Hebrews 13:5

Torah is not just about physically doing or not doing things; it is about internal change, wanting to do or not do something from within, that is the true definition of being born again. This is how Torah truly becomes a part of you. With command #830, Yeshua speaks about lusting after other women, a desire to want a woman who belongs to someone else. It doesn't matter if you are not doing anything physically, but if you fantasize about it and allow your mind to run wild with scenarios about it, you are breaking this command.

#61. Exodus 20:23 ~ Not to Make Idols Out of Silver or Gold

Negative
Loving Abba
Unconditional

See #48 for more information.

#62. Exodus 20:24 ~ To Make a Slaughter Place for Sacrifices

Positive
Loving Abba
Conditional

Biblically, this command and the following two could have only been applied 3 times. The first time was when the Tabernacle was created, the second was when King Solomon built the Temple, and the 3rd time was when the Babylon exile ended, and the temple was rebuilt. According to the scriptures, there will be at least one other time when this command and the following 2 can be applied.

#63. Exodus 20:25 ~ To Make the Slaughter Place with Natural Stones

Positive
Loving Abba
Conditional

This simple expression of humility shows that the Heavenly Father is open to anyone who wishes to worship Him. You don't have to be rich, full of resources, or have special abilities to build an altar of worship to the Heavenly Father. This concept aligns perfectly with Yeshua's words when He said, "Come to me, all you who labor and are heavily burdened, and I will give you rest. Take my yoke upon you and learn from me, for I am gentle and humble in heart; and you will find rest for your souls. For my yoke is easy, and my burden is light. (Matthew 11:28-30)." The fact that the stones are not to be touched by iron can also point us to the idea that we serve the Elohim of all nature and King over heaven and earth.

This was where all the sacrifices took place, at the Tabernacle courtyard. The altar played a major role for Israel because it was where divine atonement was made. Later, the altar would be moved to the Temple court, the only place where the Heavenly Father accepts sacrifices to this day. Because this teaching deals with the altar, it is specifically for Levites only, as they were the ones who administered the sacrifices. Some people argue that building an altar should not be conditional because the patriarchs did it in the book of Genesis. While this is true, such individuals fail to realize that from this teaching forward, we have no record of anyone else building altars outside the Tabernacle and, later, the Temple.

#64. Exodus 20:26 ~ Not to Make Steps Leading to the Slaughtering Place

Negative
Loving Abba
Conditional

Within Judaism, this teaching represents the Heavenly Father's desire for us to be modest and mindful of ourselves wherever we are. To ensure this teaching was properly observed, the Levites' approach to the altar was on an inclined plane, taking small steps to the altar to avoid accidentally revealing themselves to the Heavenly Father, contradicting the message of modesty throughout Torah.

During the age of monarchies, kings would have their thrones elevated to display their superiority over everyone else in the throne room. Although the Heavenly Father is high above all, He does not want us to ascend to Him. We cannot ascend to Him in this life, so why illustrate the practice with His altar? This is one of the reasons why Yeshua came down to us and is the bridge that fills the gap between Israel and the Heavenly Father; and as Israel, it is our job to invite the world to join us so that they can become a part of Israel and have that connection to the Father. Throughout the Bible, the Heavenly Father always comes to us, not because we are worthy, but because He is merciful and loves those who seek and love Him. We truly serve an awesome Elohim!

#65. Exodus 21:2 ~ Male Hebrew Slaves Can Go Free After 7 Years

Positive
Loving People
Conditional

This command is repeated with Leviticus 25:10 (434).

For Israel, there were two types of slaves: The foreign slave and the native Israelite slave. Foreign slaves were usually obtained as spoils of war only when the Heavenly Father permitted it and within certain guidelines that He establishes. When it came to Israelite slaves, there were a few official reasons why a native Israelite would become a slave; either they could not repay a debt they owed, as a part of restitution due to theft, or through some kind of other legal judgment. Unofficially, a family member could be sold for money to improve their status as well as the status of the one being sold. Some Israelites would sell themselves into slavery to escape financial ruin. Yes, you read that last part correctly; Israel treated slavery differently than all other nations, as you will see with other commandments on the subject.

One thing to understand is that slavery for Israel was nothing like the horrific atrocities we read about in American history. This type of slavery was more like indentured servitude. The biggest difference between a foreign slave and a domestic slave is that a domestic slave had the option to leave slavery in the Year of Jubilee. Command #29 gives foreign slaves a way to become Israelites and gain the same rights as the domestic slaves.

#66. Exodus 21:3 ~ Male Hebrew Slaves Who Become Slaves While Single Leave Single; Those Married Before Being Slaves Leave with Their Spouse/Family.

Positive
Loving People
Conditional

#67. Exodus 21:4 ~ Single Male Hebrew Slaves Who Are Given a Wife to Marry by The Master; The Slave Can Leave Without His Family; They Belong to The Master.

Positive
Loving People
Conditional

#68. Exodus 21:5-6 ~ Option for Male Slaves Who Want to Stay with Family

Positive
Loving People
Conditional

It is possible that masters would give their slaves wives as an incentive for the slaves to stay.

#69. Exodus 21:7 ~ Female Hebrew Slaves Do Not Go Out Like Male Slaves After 7 Years

Negative
Loving People
Conditional

Females usually became slaves as a way for a family to escape poverty and/or to ensure that the young woman would be taken care of by a wealthy master. Usually, the expectation was marriage, if not to the master himself, then to one of his sons, or maybe even an honored servant. The family selling the woman did so with a belief that she would be cared for the rest of her life. This is made clear in the next command, which instructs the master to redeem the woman if he is not pleased with her because he dealt with her deceitfully. The master oversaw taking care of her, but for whatever reason, he reneged on what he was supposed to do, which allowed the maiden to go free.

#70. Exodus 21:8 ~ To Ransom Displeasing Female Hebrew Slaves

Positive
Loving People
Conditional

#71. Exodus 21:8 ~ Not to Sell Female Hebrew Slaves to Foreigners

Negative
Loving People
Conditional

#72. Exodus 21:9 ~ If the Master Gives a Female Hebrew Slave to His Son for Marriage (1st wife), She is No Longer a Slave.

Positive
Loving People
Conditional

#73. Exodus 21:10 ~ If the Son of the Master Marries Another, the First Wife (Former Slave) is Still to be Honored as the First Wife

Negative
Loving People
Conditional

#74. Exodus 21:11 ~ If the Son Neglects 1st Wife (Former Slave), She is Free to Leave Him Without Obligations (Possibly for All 1st Wives' Situations)

Positive
Loving People
Conditional

#75. Exodus 21:12 ~ He Who Murders on Purpose Must be Executed

Positive
Loving People
Conditional

See #56 for more information.

#76. Exodus 21:13 ~ He Who Murders by Mistake May Flee (To a City of Refuge)

Positive
Loving people
Conditional

A city of refuge is designed to protect people who murder someone by mistake. These cities can only be constructed by Israel when Israel controls the land (Numbers 35:10) and is fully committed to the commands of the Heavenly Father. There were supposed to be six cities of refuge throughout the land (Numbers 35:13), and they were not just for the Israelites. Citizens of other countries who murdered someone by mistake could take advantage of a city of refuge (Numbers 35:15). Israel was expected to quickly build three refuge cities once they took over the land (718).

Those who flee to a refuge city would face a trial to determine if they murdered someone on purpose or by mistake. After the trial, if the murderer is found innocent, they can stay in the city of refuge until the death of the presiding high priest (Numbers 35:25), then they can return to their home (Numbers 35:28).

If the murderer is found guilty of breaking command #56, then they would be handed over to the Blood Avenger, possibly the prosecutor in the trial, to be executed; only the Avenger had the right to kill the murderer (Numbers 35:19). This was not a "Wild West" situation where anyone could be an Avenger and kill the murderer. A Blood Avenger was usually a family member of the one who was murdered and was legally appointed by the courts to expose the truth and execute the murderer if need be. It is the closest thing to having a real-life Judge Dredd.

During the trial, specific things were looked for. If the murderer had an instrument made of iron or wood, or if they had a stone in their hands when the murder took place, then they would be guilty of breaking command #56 (Numbers 35:16-18). If it is proven in court that he/she planned the murder, they would be guilty of breaking command #56. If the murderer leaves the city of refuge, is caught by the Blood Avenger, and killed, the Blood Avenger is considered innocent of taking that life (Numbers 35:26-28).

According to Deuteronomy 4:41-43, a person who murders by mistake is someone who did not plan to murder someone or never displayed hatred in the past for the one who was murdered. This should motivate us to listen to what Yeshua says in Matthew 5:21-26; it is most likely the reason why Yeshua said those words. It is possible that if the family of the fallen were convinced that the murder was an accident, then a Blood Avenger may never be assigned, and everyone can move on. In Deuteronomy 19:8-10, the Heavenly Father made it clear that as Israel's borders expanded, more cities of refuge were expected to be made.

#77. Exodus 21:14 ~ Those Who Plot Murder Must Be Executed

Positive
Loving People
Conditional

See #56 for more information.

#78. Exodus 21:15 ~ Those Who Strike Their Parents Must be Executed

Positive
Loving people
Conditional

See #55 for more information.

#79. Exodus 21:16 ~ Those Who Kidnap Must Be Executed

Positive
Loving people
Conditional

Repeated in Deuteronomy 24:7 (779).

#80. Exodus 21:17 ~ Those Who Curse Their Parents Must be Executed

Positive
Loving people
Conditional

See #55 for more information.

#81. Exodus 21:18-19 ~ Those Who Injure Another in a Fight Must Cover Wages Lost and Medical Expenses

Positive
Loving people
Unconditional

This command is unconditional because it is one of those commands that we should be able to regulate ourselves, no matter where we are. When we carefully examine the words of this command, it doesn't matter who started the fight or how it got started. If you hospitalize someone during a fight, you are responsible for taking care of them. This command can mend broken relationships and set the stage for reconciliation between you and the person you were fighting with. This is another instruction that brings us to the words of Yeshua in Matthew 5:21-26. If this is done quickly and correctly, it is possible that you can avoid legal action against you. Ideally, this command is for the community of Israel, but since we are in a state of dispersion, there is no reason why this cannot be applied anywhere in the world if possible.

Indirectly, this command encourages us to be financially strong. If you cannot pay someone's medical bills, do not start fights or take up martial arts or some form of self-defense. If you get into a fight, and you are trained, it increases the chance that no one ends up in the hospital. Surprisingly enough, fighting is not against Torah! It is safe to say that fighting is not something that the Heavenly Father wants us to be a part of, but as stated before, He understands the struggles of this world.

#82. Exodus 21:20 ~ Those Who Murder a Slave Must be Punished

Positive
Loving People
Conditional

According to Judaism, the punishment can be death.

#83. Exodus 21:21 ~ No Restitution for Slaves Injured (Minor injuries) by Slave Masters

Positive
Loving People
Conditional

We must remember the time when Torah was given. During this time, slaves belonged to their masters, and if that person saw it necessary to physically punish a slave, it was within their right to do so. According to instruction #86, if the injury was permanent, the slave had every right to leave, which served as a way for Israelite slave masters not to abuse their punishments.

#84. Exodus 21:22 ~ If a Man Strikes a Pregnant Woman and there is no Injury, the Husband Can Seek Justice Through a Judge.

Positive
Loving People
Conditional

See #85 for more information.

#85. Exodus 21:22-25 ~ Eye for Eye, Tooth for Tooth

Negative
Loving People
Unconditional

Repeated as a part of:

- Deuteronomy 19:16-21 (723)
- Matthew 5:38 (836)

This teaching is speaking to the husband for the previous command (84). Most people read the part about "eye for an eye" and interpret it to mean that if someone takes out your eye, you can take out their eye. However, the Heavenly Father is the source of love, wisdom, and righteousness. He does not encourage His people to seek revenge (Deuteronomy 32:35, Leviticus 19:18, & Romans 12:19); these words are used for something else. The truth is that this teaching does not promote human mutilation for revenge or tit-for-tat. It is about valuing humans and/or their body parts in legal judgments.

In ancient times, civilizations determined that each part of the human body had value. For Israel, this command was about recognizing the value of human body parts that were damaged and ensuring that the plaintiff could not seek more than the damage done. During the Mesopotamian era, if someone stole a loaf of bread, they could lose everything they owned, including their life! With this command, the Heavenly Father sets reasonable limits, unlike the practices of surrounding nations that took things to extremes over bread. Now, let's examine what Yeshua says about this command.

> *You have heard that it was said, "An eye for an eye, and a tooth for a tooth." But I tell you, don't resist him who is evil; but whoever strikes you on your right cheek, turn to him the other also. If anyone sues you to take away your coat, let him have your cloak also. Whoever compels you to go one mile, go with him two. Give to him who asks you, and don't turn away him who desires to borrow from you.* - Matthew 5:38-42

It is unfortunate that when most people read this verse, they think Yeshua is advocating for the people of Israel to be the punching bags of the world. However, that is not what He is talking about here! Within Israel, striking someone for wrongdoing can be a judgment made in court (see Deuteronomy 25:2-3, #795). The words of Yeshua in Matthew 5:38-42 are directed at those who were found guilty in a trial and *"eye for an eye, tooth for tooth"* was wrongfully abused. Based on Yeshua's words, people took advantage of command #795 and used it in an unrighteous way. Instead of fighting against the abuse, Yeshua teaches us to still go above and beyond for restitution. This teaching aligns with other instructions of our Heavenly Father, such as command #93.

Of course, we should always strive for peace with everyone. However, in times when fighting cannot be avoided, defend yourself! As stated in command #81, fighting is not against Torah. The only exception to this rule is if you catch someone breaking into your house (94).

This command is unconditional because it is something we can self-regulate. Many people have heard the story of the woman who sued McDonald's because her coffee was too hot and received millions. America's court system is filled with such stories. The Heavenly Father does not want us to take advantage of bad situations. If you must take someone to court, go after only what is owed to you, and do not allow money-hungry lawyers to convince you otherwise. Anything beyond that is a violation of this command.

#86. Exodus 21:26-27 ~ Slaves Are Free to Leave Their Master if Their Master Causes Them Permanent Physical Injuries

Positive
Loving People
Conditional

There are no distinctions between Hebrew and non-Hebrew slaves in the wording of this command. This also sets a distinction from how Israel was treated in Egypt as slaves.

#87. Exodus 21:28 ~ If an Ox Kills Someone, it Must be Stoned; No One is to Benefit from it. The Owner is Innocent.

Positive
Loving People
Unconditional

In this situation, no benefit is to come from the remains of the ox; you can't eat it or use any of the remains for anything beneficial. The entire animal is buried, and that is it. This supports the idea that the Heavenly Father does not want His people to benefit from bad situations.

#88. Exodus 21:29 ~ If an Ox Has Been Known to Injure People Before, and it Kills Someone

Positive
Loving People
Conditional

In the previous command, no one is at fault if the animal has never attacked someone before. In that situation, the animal is put to death, and that is the end of the subject. In this situation, the animal has injured people before, making this a more serious situation. Now it becomes the fault of the owner because it shows negligence and disregard for other's well-being.

#89. Exodus 21:30-31 ~ In case of a Sin Covering (If the Owner is Redeemed) Then He Shall Pay a Ransom Determined by a Judge.

Positive
Loving People
Conditional

If the owner of the ox is ransomed (sin covering, redeemed), most likely a firstborn son, then the judge would determine how much he should pay for restitution. This instruction also reveals the importance and protection of the redeeming system.

#90. Exodus 21:32 ~ If an Ox Injures a Slave, They Give the Master 30 Shekels, and the Ox is Stoned to Death.

Positive
Loving People
Unconditional

In this situation, it appears that the ox's remains could be utilized productively. We don't know exactly what the 30 shekels are for. It may cover the cost of destroying the animal.

#91. Exodus 21:33-34 ~ If an Animal Dies Due to an Uncovered Pit

Positive
Loving People
Unconditional

Pits were used during ancient civilizations for various reasons before aqueducts and sewage systems were invented. People don't usually make pits anymore. The lesson behind this message is that if you do something that causes someone's animal to die, you are responsible for making restitution. This is something we can self-regulate, which is why this command is unconditional.

#92. Exodus 21:35-36 ~ If a Person's Animal Kills an Animal That Belongs to Another.

Positive
Loving People
Unconditional

#93. Exodus 22:1 ~ When Someone Steals an Ox or Sheep to Slaughter or Sell

Positive
Loving People
Conditional

As people of Israel, we do not steal. If you have stolen before covenanting with the All-Mighty and want to make restitution, you can self-regulate according to Torah. Part of preparing for Yom Kippur each year is reflecting on any wrongs we've done to others and making things right (240).

#94. Exodus 22:2 ~ If a Thief is Caught in the Act of Breaking in and is Killed

Positive
Loving People
Unconditional

With command #76, we learned about people who murder by mistake. In #81, if we get into a fight with someone and injure them to the point where they miss work and/or are hospitalized, we are responsible for paying for the medical bills and lost wages. This command shows us the only exception to those rules. You don't have to kill someone caught in your house, but if you do, you would not be guilty of murder in the eyes of the Heavenly Father because you are defending and protecting what is yours. However, keep in mind that local government laws may see things differently. Know your rights in case you find yourself in this situation.

#95. Exodus 22:3 ~ Do Not Hold a Thief Hostage to Kill Later

Negative
Loving People
Unconditional

#96. Exodus 22:4 ~ If a Stolen Ox, Sheep, or Donkey is Found Alive in the Hand of a Thief

Positive
Loving People
Conditional (Lack of proper government)

If you were a thief before covenanting, you can self-govern this command as a way for restitution.

#97. Exodus 22:5 ~ If Livestock is Feeding on Another Man's Property Without Permission

Positive
Loving People
Unconditional (Self-Govern)

Sometimes when we are studying Torah, we must go beyond the words. The modern translation for this instruction and others like it is: If your dog destroys your neighbor's yard, you must make restitution and pay for the damage. Your neighbor should not feel the need to take you to court if you take ownership and act quickly. If you believe yourself to be covenanted with the Elohim of Israel and truly are Torah observant, in situations where your pet attacks someone, teachings such as #87 - #90 should be taken seriously. Once again, as law-abiding citizens of Israel, sometimes we need to self-regulate according to Torah.

#98. Exodus 22:6 ~ The One Who Starts a Fire Must Pay for Damages

Positive
Loving People
Unconditional (Self-Govern)

#99. Exodus 22:7-8 ~ If You Hold onto a Neighbor's Possession and it Gets Stolen

Positive
Loving People
Conditional (Lack of proper government)

Of course, the parties involved here would be expected to go to a Levite or a judge to handle this dispute. This command can be unconditional, but it would require all parties to be a part of the same Torah-observant community with anointed and appointed leaders willing to adhere to the guidelines of this command.

#100. Exodus 22:9 ~ For Unresolved Disputed Civil Matters

Positive
Loving People
Conditional (Lack of proper government)

#101. Exodus 22:10-15 ~ If Something Happens to What is Borrowed

Positive
Loving People
Unconditional

#102. Exodus 22:16-17 ~ If a Man Sleeps with a Virgin Out of Wedlock

Positive
Loving People
Conditional

This is another instruction (Like #99) that can be unconditional if all parties are committed to Torah with anointed and appointed leaders. Of course, if either of the individuals involved is not covenanted, then this cannot be applied at all. Although fornication is frowned upon, this command provides a way to make it right. Since whoring is against Torah (308) and polygamy was acceptable for men, this instruction protects the women. This command also solidifies the idea that sexual activities are for marriage, a concept that many in today's world ignore.

#103. Exodus 22:18 ~ To Execute Those Who Practice Witchcraft

Positive
Loving People
Conditional (Lack of proper government)

Witchcraft is the use of alleged supernatural powers or magic. Traditionally, "witchcraft" means the use of magic or any mystical powers to inflict harm or misfortune on others, and this remains the most widespread meaning. Voodoo also falls under the category of witchcraft. The most important thing that this command tells us is that the Heavenly Father would never communicate with His people through witchcraft. Unfortunately, it is not uncommon for people who practice witchcraft to tell you otherwise.

#104. Exodus 22:19 ~ To Execute Those Who Have Sexual Relations with Animals

Positive
Loving Abba
Conditional

#105. Exodus 22:20 ~ To Execute Those Who Sacrifice to Other Gods

Positive
Loving Abba
Conditional

NOTE: To be put "under the ban" means no redemption for that individual; see Deuteronomy 7:2.

#106. Exodus 22:21 ~ Not to Oppress Those Uncovenanted Within Israel

Negative
Loving People
Unconditional

Repeated in:

- Exodus 23:9 (120)
- Leviticus 19:33 (313)

We see an example of this in Acts 15:1-21. The events of Acts 15:1-21 is directly tied to everything Paul says in Galatians chapter 3. When the Pharisee believers in the faith were telling the Gentiles that they must get circumcised to complete their salvation, that was a form of oppression because it was forcing people to get circumcised without really understanding why. James corrects the situation by giving those coming from the nations 4 prohibitions that were common pagan practices at the time. It is also possible that those 4 prohibitions were starting points of the Noahide laws which would allow the Jewish community to accept them into the synagogues, allowing the new converts access to learn from Moses for themselves. It would allow them to naturally come to their own convictions about circumcision and give room for the Set-Apart Spirit to lead them. Remember, in the first century, unless you were wealthy or held a powerful government position, the Jewish synagogues on Shabbat were the only way the average person could be exposed to the written oracles of Elohim.

#107. Exodus 22:22 ~ Do No Wrong to Widows and Orphans

Negative
Loving People
Unconditional

James refers to this command as part of the "perfect religion" according to the Heavenly Father in James 1:27. Since this is an outward act, it fits the description of what religion means.

#108. Exodus 22:25 ~ When Lending to the Poor Within the Body, Do Not Add Interest

Negative
Loving People
Unconditional

Repeated in Deuteronomy 23:19 (766).

This command is one of the running themes of Torah that encourages financial strength for the citizens of Israel. Command #836 teaches us to lend when asked. This shows that we should always be financially strong enough to lend when the time comes. Unfortunately, this command comes with a caution sticker in today's world.

When someone asks to lend money for business or investment purposes, you'd want to ensure you are not putting money into a doomed business venture. However, when someone requests a loan for personal reasons, we must approach the situation with wisdom, discernment, and discretion, not because you need your money back, but to ensure it is best for that individual and the situation.

Whenever someone within the kingdom asks to borrow money to pay a bill, a debt, an emergency, or for food, it should raise alarms. Sometimes it can simply be a case of unforeseen circumstances beyond their control. In such situations, lending them money can be all they need to get back on track. Other times, it can be a sign of bigger financial problems. If they are bad with money, lending them more money can only be a temporary band-aid at best, or it might place them in worse financial troubles.

Far too often, people make poor financial choices and seek a quick fix without sacrifices. Such people only apply a band-aid to their situation without taking ownership of their poor financial judgments, and without making the proper changes for permanent solutions. A situation like this brings up the old saying, "Give a man a fish, you feed him for a day. Teach a man how to fish, and you feed him for a lifetime." Sadly, we live in a world where many people are bad with their finances. Giving such individuals money can cause more harm than good. Sometimes, the best course of action is to lay your life down and help someone get their finances together.

#109. Exodus 22:26-27 ~ If You Borrow Your Neighbor's Garment, Return It Before Sundown

Positive
Loving people
Unconditional

This instruction emphasizes mercy and compassion in dealing with the poor or vulnerable, a characteristic we see from our Heavenly Father throughout the Bible. In this situation, someone lends money or goods and takes a cloak or garment as a good-faith collateral to ensure repayment or the return of the borrowed item(s). Even with the best intentions, sometimes, plans do not go as we expect. The borrower may struggle to pay back or return as promised. The idea behind this command is simple: Even if you're legally owed something, you can't leave the debtor without their basic needs, in this case, warmth at night. Returning the garment by sunset ensures they aren't left shivering or humiliated.

This command highlights the love and compassion of our Heavenly Father and destroys the idea that Torah is without mercy and love. This command is not really about the garment. With this command, the Heavenly Father shows that He prioritizes mercy over strict justice. In today's world, you can view this command as a call to avoid screwing over people who are already struggling. Do not strip people of their dignity or survival to enforce a debt. This command is less about garments and more about basic human decency towards one another. If you lend money or an item and need it back, maybe you should not lend it in the first place.

#110. Exodus 22:28 ~ Do Not Disrespect Leaders

Negative
Loving Abba
Unconditional

This command applies directly to leaders within Israel's congregations. If your leaders are doing or saying something you disagree with, speak with them. Speak with them directly and privately. Do not speak about your leaders unless it is positive, do not vent to others about them. If you cannot agree, you have two options:

1. If you believe that the leadership is anointed and appointed, pray about it, place that grievance on the shelf, and in due time, you may get the revelation you need to move forward.
2. If you do not believe your leadership is anointed and appointed by the Heavenly Father, find one and join that congregation.

Whether you are right or wrong, you must never show disrespect to leadership. Some people would argue, "Yeshua stood up to the leaders of his time!" My response: If you truly believe that the Heavenly Father has sent you to fight against established leaders, you better make sure you are right! It's not impossible, but it is also highly unlikely.

The practicality of this command should also extend beyond the body of believers. Do not speak disrespectfully of political leaders. You can express disagreement with their policies, beliefs, or voting records on Capitol Hill, but do not disrespect them. Of course, this command can also be applied in the workplace, where disrespecting your leader is a guaranteed way to lose your job. Once again, it doesn't matter if you are right or wrong; never disrespect leadership.

#111. Exodus 22:29-30 ~ To Sanctify the Firstborn Animals on the Eighth Day.

Positive
Loving People
Conditional

#112. Exodus 22:31 ~ Do Not Eat Animals Torn in the Fields

Negative
Loving Abba
Unconditional

Repeated 4 times in:

- Leviticus 7:24 (196)
- Leviticus 17:15-16 (246)
- Leviticus 22:8 (361)
- Deuteronomy 14:21 (637)

Torah is the All-Mighty's definition of how humanity should behave as human beings. In this command, we are instructed not to eat animals torn in the field, and this distinguishes us from people who do not live by Torah, making us set-apart for the Heavenly Father. Instead, we are told to feed the dogs with such animals.

In Leviticus 7:24, we see that the remains of animals can be used for various things. For example, fur can be used for clothing or shelter, teeth and bones can be crafted into various weapons and tools, and so on. The meat could even be sold for consumption to foreigners (Deuteronomy 14:21). In Leviticus 22:8, we see that eating such meat defiles us. However, if someone does eat of an animal torn, Adonai shows us how to be clean in Leviticus 17:15. In today's world, as Torah maximalists, we should consider including roadkill for this command.

#113. Exodus 23:1 ~ Do Not Provide False Testimony

Negative
Loving People
Unconditional

See #59 for more information.

#114. Exodus 23:2 ~ Do Not Follow a Crowd into Evil

Negative
Loving People
Unconditional

This command calls for independent moral judgment, for us to stand firm for righteousness rather than submit to popular opinion to avoid conflict, gain favor, or fit in. Yeshua is a great example of successfully keeping this command. A recent example of people failing this command is the George Floyd murder case, where jurors admitted to political pressures. Evidence that could have supported reasonable doubt was ignored so that Derek Chauvin could be found guilty of murder. On a more personal note, this command could be that big event happening on a Shabbat, like a birthday, wedding, graduation, and the like. Everyone will be going, and you will be a bad person if you don't go. This command applies to any situation where people pressure you to go against the voice of the Heavenly Father.

#115. Exodus 23:3 ~ Do Not Favor the Poor in Legal Judgments

Negative
Loving People
Conditional

This command is broken far too commonly within the world's court systems. It is not unheard of for someone to sue a corporation with a losing case but end up with some reward because many judges believe it won't hurt anyone. Even if a corporation can afford it, it is still not justice. The fact that this is a command within Torah is a testament to the idea that humanity has not changed in this regard.

#116. Exodus 23:4-5 ~ Do Not Neglect Your Enemy's Animal in Distress; Return it to Its Owner.

Positive
Loving People
Unconditional

The wisdom in this instruction cannot be stressed enough! Of course, this command is most likely talking about enemies within the body of believers, but its practical application is well suited in the current state of dispersion that Israel is in. In this world, being kind to your enemy will not always work, but in most cases, being kind to your enemies can remove hostilities and make the situation much better.

On the Peshat level, this instruction is talking about your enemy's animal in distress, back then, this would have been a huge gesture of kindness. Today, this command would be if your enemy's dog got loose while they were at work and you take it in and protect it until the owner comes home. This can be a situation where you find your enemy's wallet and return it to them fully intact, or you see an uncontrolled fire in their backyard, and you rush to warn them and/or put it out yourself. It can also be a situation where you spot someone breaking into their home and you call 911. Do you see how such actions would remove tensions and open the door to a healthy relationship? Worst case scenario is that they are ungrateful and still treat you with contempt, but the Heavenly Father would still reward your righteous heart.

#117. Exodus 23:6 ~ Do Not Neglect the Right Rulings of the Poor

Negative
Loving People
Conditional

Command #115 instructs us not to favor the poor. This command teaches the importance of justice in the courts. Status should not sway a righteous judgement. Regardless of the person, true justice respects the facts unincumbered.

#118. Exodus 23:7 ~ Stay Away from False Matters

Negative
Loving People
Unconditional

See #59 for more information.

#119. Exodus 23:8 ~ Do Not Take Bribes

Negative
Loving People
Unconditional

#120. Exodus 23:9 ~ Do Not Oppress Those Uncovenanted Within the Body

Negative
Loving People
Unconditional

Repeated in:

- Exodus 22:21 (Command 106)
- Leviticus 19:33 (Command 313)

See #106 for more information.

#121. Exodus 23:10-11 ~ The 7th Year Rest of the Land

Positive
Loving The Father
Conditional

#122. Exodus 23:12 ~ To Work 6 Days and Rest on Shabbat

Positive
Loving People
Unconditional

See #51 for more information.

#123. Exodus 23:13 ~ Do Not Mention the Names of False Gods

Negative
Loving Abba
Unconditional

#124. Exodus 23:13 ~ Be Careful to Do as the Heavenly Father Says

Positive
Loving Abba
Unconditional

See #44 for more information.

#125. Exodus 23:14-17 ~ To Appear 3 Times a Year Before the Heavenly Father

Positive
Loving Abba
Unconditional (Conditional)

Repeated 3 times in:

- Exodus 34:23 (144)
- Deuteronomy 16:16 (676)
- Deuteronomy 16:16-17 (677)

Each year, we meet before the Heavenly Father as a body at Passover, Shavuot, and Sukkot. Command #678 dictates that we are supposed to meet the Heavenly Father at His decided location: Jerusalem. After the failed Bar Kokhba revolt around 132 AD, Israel was banned from the land, and to add insult to injury, Emperor Hadrian changed the name of the land from Jerusalem to Syria Palaestina around 135 AD. Jerusalem itself was rebuilt as a Roman colony named Aelia Capitolina. For many years, the Heavenly Father's believers could not keep this command as fully intended.

Yet, even today, Israel gathers, around the world, to observe the three feasts; after all, when two or more gather in His name, He will be there (Malachi 3:16 & Matthew 18:20), which is why we can keep this command still and why this command is both conditional and unconditional. You may wonder, what about the world government known as Israel, established in 1948? It is not the same as the Biblical Israel. It is not devoted to Torah; it doesn't count because it is just another world government. If you can afford to go to the land 3 times a year for the feasts, why not? Until the restoration of the Kingdom within the land, such pilgrimages remain optional.

When we gather for the three feasts, we are expected not to appear empty-handed (679). Within Torah, there are 3 tithes. The most popular tithe is the 10% tithe seen in command #493. There is also a 2nd tithe dedicated for personal use during the feasts throughout the year covered in #642. The 2nd tithe is what allows us not to appear before the Heavenly Father empty-handed during the feasts; it should be used up fully at Sukkot, and restart again for the next year's three feasts. The 3rd tithe is expected to be given every 3 years during Sukkot, as seen in command #646.

#126. Exodus 23:18 ~ Not to Sacrifice Animals with Leavened Bread

Negative
Loving Abba
Conditional

This is about eating sacrificed animals. When doing so, we do not eat such meals with leavened bread. This is a symbolic message showing that the meal is sin-free.

#127. Exodus 23:18 ~ No Leftovers for the Feasts

Negative
Loving Abba
Conditional

This command is repeated in Exodus 34:25 (146).

The meals of the feasts should be viewed as set apart. They are not ordinary meals; therefore, no leftovers should remain for the following day, nor should any be given for others to take home. This command is conditional because we don't sacrifice for the feasts today. However, when the future temple or altar is erected, commands such as this will trigger some heated conversations around the world.

#128. Exodus 23:19~ Bring the First Fruits to the House of the Heavenly Father

Positive
Loving People
Conditional

Repeated in #147.

This command ensured Levites had the resources to serve Israel and the Heavenly Father 24/7. It also provided a source of benevolence for those in need. Although this command is conditional, we can practice it by providing offerings beyond our regular tithe each spring to a congregation with anointed and appointed leadership. If you receive an income tax return or a bonus check during the year, that can be a source for this offering.

#129. Exodus 23:19 ~ Not to Cook a Goat in its Mother's Milk

Negative
Loving Abba
Unconditional

Repeated in:

- Exodus 34:26 (148)

- Deuteronomy 14:21 (637, 638 & 639)

Judaism has long believed and taught that this command prohibits mixing meat and dairy while eating. However, the words of Genesis 18:1-8 seem to contradict that belief as our Elohim sat down with Abraham and ate bread, milk, and a calf. Some would argue that time passed between eating each of those items during that meal; that could be possible, but it is more likely that all those items were prepared and brought together. People have always liked drinking something while they eat. Nonetheless, the scriptures do not give us hints one way or the other.

There are a couple of reasons why this command raises eyebrows. First, there are no world historical references to cooking young goats in their mother's milk. The Rambam and some archaeologists speculate that it was a fertility rite done by people in that region at that time. If that is the case, then we should stay away from this practice due to its pagan origins. However, there is no outside solid historical evidence to support that.

With command #85, we talked about valuing human body parts. World history shows us that this was a thing during the Mesopotamian era, as well as Jewish historical records. While studying Torah, there are some topics that we can look at in world history to fill in gaps, but cooking a young goat in its mother's milk is nowhere to be found! There are no direct references to it outside of the 3 verses that mention this practice in the Bible.

If this were an actual practice, then cruelty is clear. Cooking a kid in the same milk used for nourishment disrespects the life of goat and the mother. Taking this command at the Peshat level makes perfect sense and is a very safe approach. However, another reason this command seems odd is that it appears in the middle of thoughts that do not connect with it, making it appear to be a very random statement each time it is used.

> *The first of the first fruits of your ground you shall bring into the house of YHWH your Elohim. **You shall not boil a young goat in its mother's milk**. Behold, I send an angel before you, to keep you by the way, and to bring you into the place which I have prepared. -* Exodus 23:19-20

> *You shall not offer the blood of my sacrifice with leavened bread. The sacrifice of the feast of the Passover shall not be left to the morning. You shall bring the first of the first fruits of your ground to the house of YHWH your Elohim. **You shall not boil a young goat in its mother's milk**. YHWH said to Moses, "Write you these words: for in accordance with these words I have made a covenant with you and with Israel." He was there with Yahweh forty days and forty nights; he neither ate bread, nor drank water. He wrote on the tablets the words of the covenant, the ten commandments. -* Exodus 34:25-28

> *You shall not eat of anything that dies of itself. You may give it to the foreigner living among you who is within your gates, that he may eat it; or you may sell it to a foreigner; for you are a holy people to YHWH your Elohim. **You shall not boil a young goat in its mother's milk**. You shall surely tithe all the*

increase of your seed, that which comes out of the field year by year. - Deuteronomy 14:21-22

The placement of commas, periods, and even paragraph structures in the Bible is 100% subjective and varies depending on the version of the Bible you are reading. The grammatical structures we are familiar with today didn't start until the medieval period. Modern Bible translators/authors have complete autonomy and creative freedom to present how the written thoughts are structured in the Bible translations we have today. Bible translations are normally based on the translator's understanding of what they believe the original author was trying to say. This can create a huge problem in the translations we read today because where periods and commas go can radically change a written thought. This command, not to cook a goat in its mother's milk, is separated by a period, suggesting that it is an independent thought, but it is possible that it could be the ending part of the sentence that comes before it.

In Exodus 23:19 and 34:26, Adonai talks about bringing the first fruits of the ground into His house, and then immediately refers to not cooking a young goat in its mother's milk. The first fruits of the ground that go to His house must be set-apart, mixing the first fruits of the ground with other fruits would defile the offering. The key to understanding this command is in its 3rd use in Deuteronomy 14:21. Israel is commanded not to eat animals that die of themselves; by default, this means that such meat needs to be separated from the meat that Israel can eat so it can be sold to foreigners or used for other things. The Heavenly Father explains that Israel is not to eat such meat because Israel is set-apart from the rest of the nations, but it is ok for everyone else to eat it.

I submit that the phrase, "Not to cook a goat in its mother's milk," is an idiom lost to time, and it means to keep the set-apart things separate from what is common or defiled. This fits the theme of all 3 verses in which it is used. In all 3 examples, the Heavenly Father talks about what is set-apart or what is defiled and completes His thought with "Not to cook a goat in its mother's milk." This means keeping the set-apart and/or things defiled separate from everything else.

#130. Exodus 23:21 ~ Do Not Rebel Against the Heavenly Father's Anointed Appointed People

Negative
Loving Abba
Unconditional

Repeated in Deuteronomy 18:15 & 19 (716).

The anointed and appointed people of the Heavenly Father should be treated with respect because they are representatives of the Heavenly Father. In Ephesians 4:11, Paul describes 5 types of anointed people designed to bring the body of Yeshua to spiritual maturity. Today, when we speak about anointed and appointed people from above, we are talking about apostles, prophets, evangelists, shepherds, and teachers within the body of believers. People whom the Heavenly Father has given special drive and skills to help the people of Israel grow in their spiritual walk. These anointed people can have anywhere from one to all five of the skills Paul mentions.

Disrespecting an anointed appointed from the Heavenly Father is equal to disrespecting the Heavenly Father. We see this with Korah's rebellion in Numbers 16. Adonai supported Moses, and Korah died along with everyone who followed him. We also see it with Aaron and Miriam in Numbers 12 when they disrespected Moses for whom he married. People who are anointed and appointed by the Heavenly Father should be honored because they represent the Father, speak His words, and do His will.

As human beings, there are various kinds of characteristics, and some characteristic traits can clash with others. This is no different for our Heavenly Father's anointed and appointed people. As human beings, we all have things that we can personally improve upon. This is no different for our Heavenly Father's anointed and appointed people. We don't have to be best friends with anointed and appointed people (It would be a bonus if we could), but we do need to respect them.

#131. Exodus 23:24 ~ Do Not Submit to the Gods of Other Nations

Negative
Loving Abba
Unconditional

Repeated in:

- Deuteronomy 6:14 (565)
- Deuteronomy 11:16 (592)
- Deuteronomy 12:30 (611)

When we look at the entire verse, we can see that these words are to the exodus generation but are also relevant for believers today. Holidays such as Christmas, Easter, Valentine's Day, and Halloween came from paganism. Some people would argue that there is no harm in participating in these holidays today. However, if those actions originally came from false gods and demons, participating in them is a form of submission to those spirits. We submit to the Heavenly Father when we follow His commands, so why wouldn't the same logic apply to false gods?

Through the instructions of Adonai, we have been given a culture, a way of thinking, that shows us how to live so we are set apart from everyone else. We risk breaking this command when we start doing things that come from world religions or beliefs. We are commanded to be careful not to break this command (592), meaning we do not seek other gods, learn their ways (565 & 611), or do the things they require of their followers.

#132. Exodus 23:25 ~ To Serve the Heavenly Father

Positive
Loving Abba
Unconditional

Repeated 4 times in:

- Deuteronomy 6:13 (563)
- Deuteronomy 10:12 (581)
- Deuteronomy 10:20 (586)
- Deuteronomy 13:4 (619)

According to Judaism, the three daily sacrifices offered in the Temple were called "*Avodah*", which means service. When the Temple was destroyed, the avodah was replaced with "*Avodah she-b'lev*," which means service of the heart. This is why people in Judaism began praying three times a day to replace the sacrifices that cannot be offered at this time. Those sacrifices performed in the temple were an act of service to Adonai. There is no doubt that praying is a part of serving Adonai, but is praying the only way we can serve Him? Let us look at Abraham.

> But you, Israel, my servant, Jacob whom I have chosen, the offspring of Abraham my friend, you whom I have taken hold of from the ends of the earth, and called from its corners, and said to you, 'You are

my servant, I have chosen you and have not cast you
away. - Isaiah 41:8-9

Abraham, the father of our faith (See Galatians 3:6-9), believed in the Almighty and showed the Heavenly Father that he was truly His friend (James 2:23). A key component of friendships is that friends trust each other, look out for one another, and support each other's goals. In Genesis chapter 18, Adonai told Abraham He was about to destroy Sodom and Gomorrah. Any negative effects from the destruction would have been minimal, if any at all, to Abraham. How many of us would have interceded the way Abraham did? Was he interceding because he knew Lot and his family were there? Or was there something more to why Abraham was interceding for Sodom and Gomorrah? If you pay close attention to the words of Abraham, his concern was for the righteous who could be living in that location. This parallels the parable of the tares and wheat in Matthew 13:24-30 and 36-43, where the wheat is protected. Abraham was concerned because he knew Adonai loves the righteous and would not want them destroyed.

In Exodus 32, Israel built a golden calf to worship Elohim. The Heavenly Father told Moses that He would go down to destroy Israel and start over with him. How many of us would have stood there in silence? How many of us would have agreed and watched as Israel got destroyed?

Moses had already felt the frustrations of leading Israel and was given a "get out of jail free" card. Moses could have used that opportunity to take the easy way out, but instead, Moses thought about what was best for Adonai. Moses demonstrated that he was not just someone who did what Adonai told him, but he was fully committed to the goals of the Heavenly Father. He protested for the sake of Adonai's reputation.

Moses understood that if the Heavenly Father destroyed Israel at that time, Egypt would have told the world that Elohim freed Israel only to lure them into the wilderness for evil. A reputation that would have been devastating to the goals of Elohim drawing people unto Him, an act that would harm how the nations view Him to this day. Of course, this was a test for Moses, and he passed it with flying colors. Abraham and Moses both demonstrated a desire to help the Heavenly Father with His vision and goals. They served the Heavenly Father by knowing who He is, considering what He wants, and what is best for His goals.

Who is the Heavenly Father? What does He want? What are His visions and goals? His vision is for humanity to behave like Him (Genesis 1:26), His goal is for the whole world to be blessed through Abraham (Genesis 12:1-3), to believe in Messiah (John 3:16), to listen to Moses (Exodus 19:9) and Messiah (Mark 9:7) so He can dwell with us forever (Revelation 21). Paul puts it best when he wrote, "*I exhort therefore, first of all, that petitions, prayers, intercessions, and givings of thanks, be made for all men: for kings and all who are in high places; that we may lead a tranquil and quiet life in all godliness and reverence. For this is good and acceptable in the sight of Elohim our Savior; who desires all people to be saved and come to full knowledge of the truth*" (1st Timothy 2:1-4).

To properly serve the Heavenly Father, we must commit to His vision for humanity, which requires spiritual maturity. We need a level of faith that goes beyond "our salvation" and has everything to do with how we can help Adonai to carry out His vision and goals to the best of our ability, like a true friend. When we truly serve the Heavenly Father, we are not motivated by selfish gains for this world!

Joseph demonstrated this kind of service when he refused to sleep with Potiphar's wife. David served Adonai when he stepped up to fight Goliath while the soldiers of Israel were afraid. The prophets served Adonai when they spoke His words at the risk of their own lives. Paul served Adonai by trying to evangelize the leaders of Rome instead of fighting for his freedom. None of these people did what they did for the sake of their "salvation"; they believe in the Heavenly Father, in His words, His promises, His vision, the direction He wants humanity to go, and His goals. Our ultimate example of serving the Heavenly Father is in Yeshua Messiah, who only did and spoke as the Father instructed Him. He did it as an act of love and obedience towards the Heavenly Father, and as an example for people to follow.

When someone genuinely serves another, they do so out of the kindness of their heart and without any expectations of reward or praise. We fulfill this command when our actions are not based on salvation but on loving the Heavenly Father for who He is. This command forces us to go beyond ourselves and dig deeper, to go beyond the letters and understand the spiritual goals behind them. When we can achieve this, we can begin to serve the Heavenly Father selflessly, as friends, and be fully committed to His vision and goals, just like Abraham and Moses show us. This is why Yeshua said, "*If anyone desires to come after me, let him deny himself, and take up his cross, and follow me. For whoever desires to save his life will lose it, and whoever will lose his life for my sake will find it*" (Matthew 16:24-25).

NOTE: Exodus 23:32 is clearly for the exodus generation; however, we should always be careful when dealing with non-covenanted people. See 2nd Corinthians 6:14.

#133. Exodus 31:13 ~ To Guard the Shabbats of the Heavenly Father

Positive
Loving Abba
Unconditional

See #50 for more information.

#134. Exodus 31:14 ~ To Not Work on Shabbat

Negative
Loving Abba
Unconditional

See #52 for more information.

#135. Exodus 31:15 ~ Work 6 Days and Rest on Shabbat

Positive
Loving People
Unconditional

See #51 for more information.

#136. Exodus 31:16 ~ Guard the 7th Day Shabbat

Positive
Loving Abba
Unconditional

See #50 for more information. Explained in the next verse.

#137. Exodus 34:18 ~ To Guard the Feast of Unleavened Bread

Positive
Loving Abba
Unconditional

See #14 for more information.

#138. Exodus 34:20 ~ To Ransom the Firstborn Donkey with a Lamb

Positive
Loving People
Conditional

See #41 for more information.

#139. Exodus 34:20 ~ To Break the Neck of a Firstborn Donkey Not Being Redeemed

Positive
Loving Abba
Conditional

Since donkeys are unclean animals, the Levites needed to come up with a different way to terminate the life of an unredeemed donkey so that people would not mistake the act for a sacrifice. This can also symbolize how people who reject Yeshua will not be redeemed.

#140. Exodus 34:20 ~ To Ransom All Firstborn Sons

Positive
Loving Abba
Unconditional

See #31 for more information.

#141. Exodus 34:20 ~ Ransomed Firstborn Sons Will Not Appear Before the Heavenly Father Empty-Handed

Positive
Loving People
Unconditional

This command is connected to the 2nd tithe command of #642. Although it is directed for redeemed first borns, this is generally accepted for all of Israel.

#142. Exodus 34:21 ~ Work 6 Days and Rest on Shabbat

Positive
Loving Abba
Unconditional

See #51 for more information.

#143. Exodus 34:22 ~ To Observe Sukkot

Positive
Loving Abba
Unconditional

Repeated 3 times in:

- Leviticus 23:34 (411)
- Numbers 29:12 (514)
- Deuteronomy 16:13-14 (674)

Connecting commands are:

- Leviticus 23:35 (412)
- Leviticus 23:36 (414)
- Leviticus 23:39 (417)
- Leviticus 23:41 (419)
- Leviticus 23:42 (420)
- Deuteronomy 16:15 (675)

Sukkot ends what is commonly known as the "High Holy Days," which begin with the Feast of Trumpets and include Yom Kippur. Sukkot is an eight-day celebration where the first day is a Shabbat (412), and the eighth day is a Shabbat (414). That final day of Sukkot is also known as Shemini Atzeret, the day that the yearly Torah cycle comes to an end. Torah scrolls are reset back to Genesis 1:1, and we start a new Torah cycle on the following weekly Shabbat.

Another aspect of this command is dwelling in booths (420). The word "Booths" in Leviticus 23:42 comes from the Hebrew word סֻכָּה (sook-kaw'; H5521), which means a hut or lair: —booth, cottage, covert, pavilion, tabernacle, tent. All these words result in temporary dwelling places. Many Messianic/Hebrew Roots people gather on Sukkot and dwell in tents to honor this command; however, hotels can also fit the description for this feast. We know that Yeshua was born around one of the three major gathering feasts, most likely Sukkot, because none of the hotels had rooms for Joseph and Mary.

Some people teach that dwelling in booths is a reminder that Israel lived in the wilderness for 40 years, but that is debatable. The spring feast Days of Passover, Unleavened Bread, First Fruits, and Shavuot all represent things that have already happened, things that Yeshua fulfilled or represented. The High Holy Days represent things that we are still waiting for.

The Feast of Trumpets is about the return of Yeshua. Yom Kippur is the Day of Judgement. Sukkot represents the Millennial Reign of Yeshua; this is why Sukkot should be observed with rejoicing (676). The

Millennial Reign will be awesome, but as its name suggests, it will not last forever. The Millennial Reign will last until everything is fulfilled, all sin is destroyed, and that is when the Heavenly Father comes down from heaven with the New Jerusalem (Revelation chapter 21), which will be our home forever.

#144. Exodus 34:23 ~ To Gather 3 Times a Year Before the Heavenly Father

Positive
Loving Abba
Unconditional

See #125 for more information.

#145. Exodus 34:25 ~ The Passover Lamb is Not to be Eaten with Leavened Bread

Negative
Loving Abba
Unconditional

This command is repeated in Deuteronomy 16:3 (662).

Because Passover rolls into the Feast of Unleavened Bread, it makes sense not to have leavened bread with the meal. Judaism has also considered not consuming yeast products after noon on the 14th of Nisan to give your body time to digest yeast for the feast. Some people go as far as only eating yeast products for breakfast on the 14th of Nisan and then cutting them off to prepare for Passover.

#146. Exodus 34:25 ~ No Leftovers for Passover Meal

Negative
Loving Abba
Conditional

See command #127 for more information. This command is conditional because it only applies when doing the actual Passover. We are performing a memorial for the Passover today.

#147. Exodus 34:26 ~ To Bring the First Fruits to the House of the Heavenly Father

Positive
Loving People
Unconditional

Repeated with #128.

#148. Exodus 34:26 ~ Not to Boil a Young Goat in its Mother's Milk

Negative
Loving Abba
Unconditional

See #129 for more information.

#149. Exodus 35:2 ~ Work 6 Days and Rest on the Shabbat

Positive
Loving People
Unconditional

See #51 & #52 for more information.

#150. Exodus 35:3 ~ To Not Kindle Fire on Shabbat

Negative
Loving Abba
Unconditional

In today's world, this teaching is commonly understood as not cooking on Shabbat. When Israel first heard these words, they meant a lot more. Back then, fire stayed lit in the house all day long. Fire was used for many things needed in day-to-day life. A kindled fire meant that work was being done. Even starting a fire with the knowledge and tools they had required some physical work, a far contrast to us just turning a knob today.

#151. Leviticus 1:1-9 ~ Ascending Offering of the Herd (Ox, Bulls, Cows)

Positive
Loving People
Conditional

#152. Leviticus 1:10-13 ~ Ascending Offering from the Flock (Sheep or Goat)

Positive
Loving People
Conditional

#153. Leviticus 1:14-17 ~ Ascending Offering of Birds

Positive
Loving Abba
Conditional

#154. Leviticus 2:1-3 & Leviticus 2:8-10 ~ Grain Offering

Positive
Loving People
Conditional

#155. Leviticus 2:4 & Leviticus 2:8-10 ~ Baked Grain Offering

Positive
Loving People
Conditional

#156. Leviticus 2:5-6 & Leviticus 2:8-10 ~ Griddled Grain Offering

Positive
Loving People
Conditional

#157. Leviticus 2:7-10 ~ Stewing-Pot Grain Offering

Positive
Loving People
Conditional

#158. Leviticus 2:11 ~ Not to Burn Leaven with the Grain Offering

Negative
Loving Abba
Conditional

#159. Leviticus 2:11 ~ Not to Burn Honey with the Grain Offering

Negative
Loving Abba
Conditional

#160. Leviticus 2:11-12 ~ To Bring Honey and Leaven to First Fruits

Positive
Loving Abba
Conditional

#161. Leviticus 2:13 ~ To Season the Grain Offerings with Salt (Salt Covenant)

Positive
Loving Abba
Conditional

A salt covenant is something we know very little about today, but during the Mesopotamian era, it was a common practice. People realized very early on that salt is an element that never changes. If Noah had preserved a pile of salt that miraculously survived, it could still be used to season food today. Salt represents something that never changes. During ancient times, when people were getting into business together or when kingdoms joined forces, they would bring salt as a part of sealing the deal.

The salt covenant is repeated in Numbers 18:19. It is also mentioned as tied to the throne of David in 2nd Chronicles 13:5, which also connects to Yeshua, who will be King of Israel forever on that same throne. In Matthew 5:13, when Yeshua called the crowd the "*salt of the earth*," he was referencing the salt covenant between the Heavenly Father and Israel. It is reasonable that most within that Jewish crowd would have understood the reference.

#162. Leviticus 2:14 ~ Grain Offerings for First Fruits

Positive
Loving Abba
Conditional

#163. Leviticus 2:15 ~ To Add Oil and Frankincense to the First Fruits Grain Offering

Positive
Loving Abba
Conditional

#164. Leviticus 2:16 ~ Burning the Remembrance Portion

Positive
Loving Abba
Conditional

#165. Leviticus 3:1-5 ~ Peace Offering from the Herd

Positive
Loving People
Conditional

This command is tied to:

- Deuteronomy 12:17-18 (602)
- Deuteronomy 12:26 (607)
- Deuteronomy 23:21 (768)

Contrary to popular belief, not all sacrifices were about sin. A peace offering was given from a heart filled with thanksgiving, gratitude, and love for the Heavenly Father. It was usually done when someone was delivered from peril, a bad situation, or to complete a vow in which the person acknowledges that the Heavenly Father answered their prayers. A peace offering was a way to praise the All-Mighty publicly. This was usually a festive offering shared with the Levites who administered the sacrifice. These were big events with family, servants, and friends of the one hosting the offering. Believers of Yeshua likely offered peace offerings until the temple was destroyed.

#166. Leviticus 3:6 ~ Male or Female from the Flock is Permissible for Peace Offering

Positive
Loving Abba
Conditional

#167. Leviticus 3:7-11 ~ Peace Offering of a Lamb

Positive
Loving People
Conditional

#168. Leviticus 3:12-16 ~ Peace Offering of Goat

Positive
Loving People
Conditional

#169. Leviticus 3:17 ~ Not to Eat the Blood or Fat of the Sacrifices

Negative
Loving Abba
Unconditional

See #5 for more information.

NOTE: The instructions for sin offerings in Leviticus chapter 4 are only for unintentional sins (see verse 2). There are no provisions for sinning intentionally in the Bible because rebellion against the All-Mighty is a conscious choice.

#170. Leviticus 4:1-12 ~ Sin Offerings for Anointed Priests

Positive
Loving People
Conditional

#171. Leviticus 4:13-21 ~ Sin Offerings for Israel

Positive
Loving People
Conditional

#172. Leviticus 4:22-26 ~ Sin Offerings for Rulers

Positive
Loving people
Conditional

#173. Leviticus 4:27-31 ~ Sin Offerings for Individuals of Israel with a Goat

Positive
Loving People
Conditional

#174. Leviticus 4:32-35 ~ Sin Offerings for Individuals of Israel with a Lamb

Positive
Loving People
Conditional

#175. Leviticus 5:1 ~ To Truthfully Testify to an Oath Made

Positive
Loving People
Unconditional

#176. Leviticus 5:2 ~ Touching Anything Unclean Makes You Unclean and Guilty

Negative
Loving Abba
Unconditional

This is the first commandment dealing with the idea of clean vs unclean. Numbers 5:1-4 show us that being clean/unclean has to do with being in the presence of the Heavenly Father (Also see Numbers 19:13 and Numbers 19:20). These commands are unconditional because what makes us unclean is still around, and what normally needs to be done to correct uncleanness is to have good hygiene.

Once the Tabernacle was completed, the presence of our Elohim entered the Holiest of Holies, and He dwelt within the midst of Israel; see Numbers 9:15-23. The same thing happened when Solomon's Temple was created (1 Kings 8:10-11). Israel had not had this opportunity since before captivity in Babylon. Israel has not had the chance to be in that spiritual state since the late 180s BC when Rome began to occupy the land. For the current world government known as Israel to get to that point again, it would take a massive upheaval of that government, a nationwide devotion to Torah, a commitment to remove all elements that stand against Torah, and most likely a civil war in which the surrounding enemies of Israel would take full advantage. Sounds very similar to what will happen when Yeshua returns, according to scripture (Zechariah 14:1-5, Thessalonians 1:7-10 & Revelation 19:11-21 are just a few examples).

To be unclean is different than being in sin. With proper awareness, discipline, and willingness to submit to Torah, sin can be avoided, but sometimes it is impossible to be clean in our day-to-day lives. Torah gives us various ways people can become unclean in this life. If a four-legged insect lands on you, that makes you unclean (206). If you touch the dead, touching dead animals, sexual intercourse, monthly women's cycles, and more. Becoming unclean is a part of this life. There are necessary jobs for society to function properly that make some people unclean almost every day.

Leviticus 5:2 says that unclean people are guilty. Once someone realizes that they are unclean, depending on how they become unclean, there is a time limit for what they must do to be clean again. This is made clear in command #177. Usually, making yourself clean involves washing yourself and sometimes even the clothes you wore when you became unclean. Sometimes, being unclean may call for people to be outside the camp for a time, such as during war.

In ancient times, being unclean was a huge deal, but over time, humanity's hygiene practices improved. If the kingdom were fully restored today, and the presence of the Heavenly Father once again dwelt within the midst of His people, being clean/unclean would be much less of a concern because it is much easier to wash daily today.

#177. Leviticus 5:3 ~ Touching Uncleanness of Man Makes You Guilty

Negative
Loving Abba
Unconditional

#178. Leviticus 5:4 ~ Rashly Making Vows Makes You Guilty

Negative
Loving People
Unconditional

#179. Leviticus 5:5-13 ~ To Atone for Not Exposing Sin, Touching Something Unclean, Touching Uncleanness of Man, or Swearing Rashly.

Positive
Loving People
Conditional

#180. Leviticus 5:14-19 ~ Guilt Offerings

Positive
Loving People
Conditional

The guilt offerings are sins against the set-apart matters of the Heavenly Father.

#181. Leviticus 6:1-5 ~ Do Not Deceive for Personal Gains

Positive
Loving People
Unconditional

#182. Leviticus 6:6-7 ~ Trespass Offerings for Deceitful Gains

Positive
Loving People
Conditional

#183. Leviticus 6:8-13 ~ The Ascending Offering of the Priesthood

Positive
Loving Abba
Conditional

#184. Leviticus 6:14-18 ~ Grain Offering for the Priesthood

Positive
Loving People
Conditional

#185. Leviticus 6:19-23 ~ Offering of Anointing for the Start of the High Priest and Priesthood

Positive
Loving People
Conditional

#186. Leviticus 6:24-30 ~ Sin Offerings from the Priesthood

Positive
Loving People
Conditional

#187. Leviticus 7:1-6 ~ Guilt Offerings from the Priesthood

Positive
Loving People
Conditional

#188. Leviticus 7:7 ~ Sin Offering is the Same as a Guilt Offering for the Priesthood

Positive
Loving Abba
Conditional

#189. Leviticus 7:7 ~ The Priest Who Makes Atonement for Sin or Guilt is His Offering

Positive
Loving Abba
Conditional

#190. Leviticus 7:8 ~ The Priest Who Brings Someone's Ascending Offering, it Belongs to That Priest

Positive
Loving People
Conditional

This suggests that the priests were active in the community, not waiting for people to come to them.

#191. Leviticus 7:9 ~ Grain, Meal, Pan, and Griddle Offerings Belong to The Priest Who Brings Them in and Offers Them

Positive
Loving People
Conditional

Not necessarily tied to animal sacrifices, this is conditional because it is for the Levites.

#192. Leviticus 7:10 ~ Grain Offering Mixed with Oil or Dried Belongs to the Priesthood

Positive
Loving People
Conditional

Not necessarily tied to animal sacrifices, this is conditional because it is for the Levites.

#193. Leviticus 7:11-20 ~ Peace Offerings from the Priesthood

Positive
Loving people
Conditional

#194. Leviticus 7:21 ~ Priests Cannot be Unclean and Eat of the Peace Offering

Negative
Loving Abba
Conditional

See #176 about unclean.

#195. Leviticus 7:23 & 25 ~ Not to Eat the Fat of Bulls, Sheep, or Goat That Are Sacrificed

Negative
Loving Abba
Conditional

Some people teach that it is a sin to eat the fat of animals because of this command, but it is about sacrifices (verse 25), which cannot be done at this time.

#196. Leviticus 7:24 ~ Not to Consume the Fat of a Dead Animal Torn

Negative
Loving Abba
Unconditional

See #112 for more information.

#197. Leviticus 7:26-27 ~ Not to Consume Blood

Negative
Loving Abba
Unconditional

See #5 for more information.

#198. Leviticus 7:29-36 ~ Bringing the slaughtering of the peace offering

Positive
Loving People
Conditional

#199. Leviticus 10:9-11 ~ Priesthood is Not to Drink Strong Drink Before Going into the Tent of Appointment

Negative
Loving People
Unconditional

It is important to note that this command does not say that the priest is not allowed to get drunk; they are not allowed to be drunk in the tent of appointment while serving Israel and the Heavenly Father. With that said, as a spiritual leader, you can drink alcohol, you can even get drunk at times, but you shouldn't be known as someone who gets drunk frequently (See 1st Timothy 3:1-7 and Titus 1:7).

#200. Leviticus 11:2-3 ~ Animals That Are Good for Food

Positive
Loving Abba
Unconditional

Repeated in Deuteronomy 14:4-6.

With this command, we have begun the instructions for what we can and cannot eat regarding meat. These instructions are found throughout Leviticus chapter 11. They also cover animals, fish, birds, and insects that can make us unclean. There is an abridged version of this list in Deuteronomy 14:1-21. Everything we need to know about what Adonai approves for food concerning animals, fish, birds, and insects is here. Grains, fruits, and vegetables are not mentioned here because the Heavenly Father does not change and has already made them food back in Genesis 1:29.

Other than the tree of the knowledge of good and evil, if there were any grains, fruits, or vegetables that we should not eat, the Heavenly Father would have made that clear. Throughout mankind's existence, through trials and errors, we have identified what is poison to us, what is useful, and what can be used as medicine. Adonai might not have forbidden poisonous plants because they can still help humanity in various ways. Except for sacrifices where the animals must be perfect, what Adonai has established as food has no restrictions. Any rules added to what we can eat are man-made.

In Mark 7:1-23, the Pharisees accused the disciples of eating what was "defiled." In verses 3-4, we get the explanation of what those Pharisees were talking about, a key part of the context many people overlook. There are no indications within Genesis 1:29, Leviticus chapter 11, or Deuteronomy 14:1-21 that hint at the idea that someone must wash their hands before eating anything. Those Pharisees were referring to a Jewish law that is still observed today, a man-made tradition that the Pharisees even acknowledged as such in Mark 7:5 when they called it the "tradition of the elders", not a command of Moses or something given by the Heavenly Father.

From a logical standpoint, the tradition of washing your hands before touching food is not bad in and of itself. If it weren't for this specific tradition, the Jewish people would have suffered high numbers of tragic deaths from the Black Plague, like everyone else in Europe, from 1347 to 1353. The problem with this tradition is that it alters what Adonai identifies as food by introducing the idea that touching food with unwashed hands makes it unclean. That cannot be supported within Torah.

When people use Mark 7:1-23 to justify ignoring Leviticus 11 and Deuteronomy 14:1-21, they fail to see that the item declared defiled was wheat touched with hands not ritually cleansed. For all the people that were there, Yeshua's words in verses 6-23 did not bring them to the conclusion that they could eat shrimp, pork, or gator tails (Things that are out of context for the narrative); they understood that touching food with unwashed hands does not make food unclean or defiled.

#201. Leviticus 11:4-7, 26-27 ~ Animals of the Earth You Do Not Eat

Negative
Loving Abba
Unconditional

This command is repeated in Deuteronomy 14:7-8.

#202. Leviticus 11:8 ~ Do Not Touch the Carcasses of Animals You Do Not Eat

Negative
Loving Abba
Unconditional

This instruction does not say you are unclean if you touch them while they are alive; otherwise, people would not be allowed to have pets or tend to pigs which are useful to have in farming and other areas of life. Since this command doesn't go into detail, it is safe to say that you can use gloves or a shovel to move the remains if needed. Not touching the carcasses also means not touching them as food products either. If you work in the food industry, this command is something to take seriously.

#203. Leviticus 11:9 ~ Creatures of the Water That Can Be Eaten

Positive
Loving Abba
Unconditional

This instruction is repeated in Deuteronomy 14:9.

For this command we must consider the fact that not all tuna is kosher. When it comes to tuna that we know for sure are kosher we can depend on skipjack, yellowfin, bluefin, albacore, and bigeye to be safe for this command. Some tuna and their sub-species have been debatable such as King mackerel, Spanish mackerel and the Scombridae Family. For this subject, it is better to error on the side of caution and stay away from what could be questionable. When shopping, always look for kosher certifications (e.g., OU, OK, Star-K) on the label to ensure no non-kosher additives or processing issues. In case you are wondering, Mahi-Mahi is also considered kosher for this command.

#204. Leviticus 11:10-12 ~ Creatures of the Water That Are Not for Food Are an Abomination

Negative
Loving Abba
Unconditional

Due to the nature of our society today, it is important to identify the fish that many people commonly eat but are not kosher according to this command.

- Catfish – No scales.
- Shark – No scales.
- Swordfish – No scales in their edible form (They have scales when they are young).
- Sturgeon – Not real scales because they are bony and not easily detachable.
- Eel – No scales.
- Monkfish – No scales.
- Pufferfish – No scales. Although this one is rare, people still eat it.
- Lamprey – No scales.

NOTE: The word Kosher in this book is used more as a Hebrew cultural term. It is not a biblical word.

#205. Leviticus 11:13-19 ~ Birds That Should Not Be Eaten Are Abominations

Negative
Loving Abba
Unconditional

The list of unclean birds is repeated in Deuteronomy 14:11-18.

#206. Leviticus 11:20 & 23 ~ Flying Insects That Creep on All Fours Are Abominations

Negative
Loving Abba
Unconditional

Many crawling insects, such as flies and beetles, are connected to decay, filth, or death because they often gather around waste, including the dead. With Torah observance, contact with dead bodies or unclean things makes us unclean (Leviticus 11:24-25); these insects could be seen as inherently defiling.

#207. Leviticus 11:21-22 ~ Insects That Can Be Eaten

Positive
Loving Abba
Unconditional

#208. Leviticus 11:24-25 ~ Touching Insects Not for Food Makes You Unclean

Negative
Loving Abba
Unconditional

#209. Leviticus 11:26-28 ~ Touching the Carcasses of Animals Not to Eat Makes You Unclean

Negative
Loving Abba
Unconditional

First seen in #202.

#210. Leviticus 11:29-30 ~ Creeping Creatures That Are Not for Food

Negative
Loving Abba
Unconditional

#211. Leviticus 11:31 ~ Touching Creeping Creatures Not for Food Makes You Unclean

Negative
Loving Abba
Unconditional

#212. Leviticus 11:32-38 ~ Instructions of Unclean Creeping Creatures Dying on Objects

Positive
Loving Abba
Unconditional

#213. Leviticus 11:39-40 ~ Touching the Carcass of a Clean Animal Makes You Unclean Until Evening

Negative
Loving Abba
Unconditional

#214. Leviticus 11:41-42 ~ Swarming Creatures Are Not to be Eaten

Negative
Loving Abba
Unconditional

There is something to take note of here regarding swarming creatures. In Leviticus 11:41-45, we have five distinct instructions. This instruction tells us that they are not to be eaten. Commands #215, #216, #217, and #219 warn us not to be abominable, unclean, or defiled by swarming creatures. Then, the Heavenly Father tells us to be set apart with command #218 and completes His thoughts by repeating it with command #220. While the Heavenly Father does not explain why this is so important, modern science teaches us that swarming insects carry diseases. This is just another confirmation that the teachings of Adonai benefit humanity.

#215. Leviticus 11:41-42 ~ Swarming Creatures Are Abominations

Negative
Loving Abba
Unconditional

See #214 for more information.

#216. Leviticus 11:43 ~ Not to Make Oneself Abominable with Swarming Creatures

Negative
Loving Abba
Unconditional

See #214 for more information.

#217. Leviticus 11:43 ~ Not to Make Oneself Unclean with Swarming Creatures

Negative
Loving Abba
Unconditional

See #214 for more information.

#218. Leviticus 11:44 ~ To Be Set-Apart for the Heavenly Father

Positive
Loving Abba
Unconditional

Repeated 5 times in:

- Leviticus 11:45 (220)
- Leviticus 19:2 (270)
- Leviticus 20:7 (320)
- Leviticus 20:26 (337)
- Deuteronomy 7:6 (571)

Contrary to popular belief, this command is not a stand-alone thought. It is usually tied to a series of teachings and used as a statement that if we do the instructions related to it, then Adonai will see us as set-apart for Him. Instructions #218 and #220 are connected to the dietary instructions and avoiding swarming insects. Teaching #270 in Leviticus 19:2 begins a series of commands about one-another relationship. When we next see this command in Leviticus 20:7 (320), it comes on the heels of Adonai speaking against things done for Molech. With command #337, to be set apart is tied to keeping His commands, not following the ways of the nations, and distinguishing between clean and unclean animals. Finally, we last see this teaching in Deuteronomy 7:6, where Moses reminds us that we are set apart people unto Adonai because He loves us and because of the promises made to Abraham.

#219. Leviticus 11:44 ~ Do Not Defile Oneself with Swarming Creatures

Negative
Loving Abba
Unconditional

See command #214 for more information.

#220. Leviticus 11:45 ~ To Be Set Apart for the Heavenly Father

Positive
Loving Abba
Unconditional

See command #218 for more information.

#221. Leviticus 11:46-47 ~ To Distinguish Between What You Can and Cannot Eat

Positive
Loving Abba
Unconditional

Repeated in Leviticus 20:25 (336).

#222. Leviticus 12:1-2, 4, 6-8 ~ Purification After Male Childbirth

Positive
Loving Abba
Conditional

#223. Leviticus 12:3 ~ Circumcision of 8-Day-Old Boys

Positive
Loving Abba
Unconditional

See Command #7 for more information.

#224. Leviticus 12:5-8 ~ Purification After Female Childbirth

Positive
Loving Abba
Conditional

#225. Leviticus 13:1-28 ~ The Priesthood Identifying Unclean Leprosy

Positive
Loving Abba
Conditional

In ancient times, leprosy meant something different than what we understand today. In Hebrew, there are 2 words for Leprosy. For this teaching, the word leprosy comes from the Hebrew word צָרַעַת (ṣāraʿaṯ; H6883), which is described as a skin disease, something like chicken pox or measles (Chapters 13-14). It can also be mildew or mold in clothing (Leviticus 13:47-52) or a building (Leviticus 14:34-53). Why would people go to the Levites for a medical condition? Why not go to a carpenter if there is mold in the house? The reason is that it could be tied to something spiritual.

In Numbers chapter 12, Miriam was punished with leprosy after speaking negatively against Moses. In Hebrew, the term is called "*Lashon hara,*" which means the evil tongue. Based on Numbers chapter 12, it is possible that the difference between clean leprosy and unclean leprosy could be whether it is purely medical, natural, or the result of a spiritual matter.

Throughout Leviticus chapters 13 and 14, the Levites look for conditions to see if someone or someone's place is clean or unclean. When looking at these symptoms, it is possible that someone can get unclean by eating, touching, or doing/not doing something that biblically makes you unclean. The symptoms described various infections, possibly allergic reactions, or rashes, such as being allergic to eating shellfish. The infections can even be caused by contact with swarming bugs or bad hygiene, which can cause similar types of rashes described in these verses.

#226. Leviticus 13:29-37 ~ The Priesthood Identifying Infections

Positive
Loving Abba
Conditional

See #225 for more information.

#227. Leviticus 13:38-39 ~ The Priesthood Examining Bright Spots on the Skin

Positive
Loving Abba
Conditional

See #225 for more information.

#228. Leviticus 13:40-44 ~ Baldness Concerning Leprosy

Positive
Loving Abba
Conditional

See #225 for more information.

#229. Leviticus 13:45-59 ~ A Leper and Their Garments

Positive
Loving Abba
Conditional

See #225 for more information.

#230. Leviticus 14:1-32 ~ Cleansing Someone from Leprosy

Positive
Loving Abba
Conditional

See #225 for more information.

#231. Leviticus 14:33-57 ~ Cleansing a House of Leprosy

Positive
Loving Abba
Conditional

#232. Leviticus 15:1-12 ~ Unclean Due to Bodily Discharge

Negative
Loving Abba
Unconditional

The word for "issue" in this instruction comes from the Hebrew word זוֹב (H2101 - zôḇ/zov), a flow, issue, discharge, flux. Semen, discharge (venereal disease) (of men); issue, flux (of women). You can learn more about bodily discharges at: https://www.dovemed.com/health-topics/focused-health-topics/discharge-types-causes-normal-vs-abnormal-and-when-seek-medical-advice.

#233. Leviticus 15:13-15 ~ Cleansing from Bodily Discharge (Non-Sexual)

Positive
Loving Abba
Conditional

#234. Leviticus 15:16-18 ~ When There is Sexual Discharge

Positive
Loving Abba
Unconditional

#235. Leviticus 15:19-23 ~ Women Unclean from Bodily Discharge

Negative
Loving Abba
Unconditional

#236. Leviticus 15:24 ~ Men Who Have Sexual Relations with a Woman Who Is Unclean from Discharge

Negative
Loving Abba
Unconditional

#237. Leviticus 15:25-27 ~ Women with Extended Abnormal Discharge

Negative
Loving Abba
Unconditional

An account of this is seen in:

- Matthew 9:20-22
- Mark 5:25-34
- Luke 8:43-48

#238. Leviticus 15:28-30 ~ After a Woman's Discharge is Complete

Positive
Loving Abba
Conditional

#239. Leviticus 16:2 ~ The High Priest Is Not Allowed to Enter the Set Apart Place Except for Yom Kippur

Negative
Loving Abba
Conditional

#240. Leviticus 16:3-34 ~ Instructions for Yom Kippur

Positive
Loving Abba
Conditional

Commands connected to Yom Kippur are:

- Leviticus 23:27 ~ To observe Yom Kippur (401) & Numbers 29:7 ~ To observe Yom Kippur (512)
- Leviticus 23:27 ~ To fast on Yom Kippur (402) & Leviticus 23:32 ~ To fast on Yom Kippur (405)
- Leviticus 23:28 ~ Yom Kippur is a Shabbat (403)
- Leviticus 23:31 ~ To do no work at all on Yom Kippur (404)
- Isaiah 58:13-14 ~ Do not do your pleasures on Yom Kippur (406)
- Isaiah 58:13-14 ~ To call Yom Kippur a delight (407)
- Isaiah 58:13-14 ~ To esteem Yom Kippur (408)
- Isaiah 58:13-14 ~ To not do your way on Yom Kippur (409)
- Isaiah 58:13-14 ~ To not speak your own words on Yom Kippur (410)
- Numbers 29:8-11 ~ Instructions for Yom Kippur offerings (513)

Adonai spoke to Moses, saying, "However on the tenth day of this seventh month is the day of atonement: it shall be a holy convocation to you, and you shall afflict yourselves; and you shall offer an offering made by fire to Adonai. You shall do no kind of work in that same day; for it is a day of atonement, to make atonement for you before Adonai your Elohim. For whoever it is who shall not deny himself in that same day; shall be cut off from his people. Whoever it is who does any kind of work in that same day, that person I will destroy from among his people. You shall do no kind of work: it is a statute forever throughout your generations in all your dwellings. It shall be a Sabbath of solemn rest for you, and you shall deny yourselves. In the ninth day of the month at evening, from evening to evening, you shall keep your Sabbath." - Leviticus 23:26-32

Yom Kippur, also known as Yom HaKippurim, Day of Atonement, or Day of the Coverings, is an important day for Israel. The days from the Feast of Trumpets (399) to Yom Kippur are called the "10 Days of Awe" because during this time, we reflect inwardly. We look back at the year, confess our wrongdoings, and seek forgiveness and/or reconciliation if we have wronged anyone. We also take this time to do a spiritual self-assessment of where we are spiritually by identifying the teachings of Torah that we've struggled with. This is how you properly measure spiritual growth from year to year.

When people sin throughout the year, we are expected to confess and do whatever is appropriate within Torah for that infraction. Yom Kippur is when Israel corporately gets a clean slate from sin. The people of Israel depended on the High Priest to be on point; otherwise, the rituals we see in Leviticus 16:3-34 may not be accepted by Adonai. In Israel's history, High Priests have entered the Holy of Holies and never came back out, their bodies rotting for a whole year until the next High Priest goes in and gets the body out. At one point, Priests would have ropes tied around them so that their bodies would be dragged out if they died. This caused concerns every year, which is why the writer of Hebrews talks about Yeshua being our High Priest in the Melchizedek order (Hebrews chapters 7-8) and how Yeshua, as our High Priest, is better than the Levitical Priesthood because he never sinned.

#241. Leviticus 17:2-6 ~ The Heavenly Father Accepts Sacrifices in One Place

Negative
Loving Abba
Unconditional

Repeated 8 times in:

* Deuteronomy 12:5-7 (596)
* Deuteronomy 12:11 (598)
* Deuteronomy 12:13-14 (599)
* Deuteronomy 12:21 (604)
* Deuteronomy 14:23 (641)
* Deuteronomy 15:20 (654)
* Deuteronomy 16:2 (661)
* Deuteronomy 16:5-6 (666)

This is one of the main reasons why sacrifices cannot be made today. Although there are some debates concerning where exactly this place is, many believe it is where the Muslims' golden dome resides on the Temple Mount.

While in the wilderness, Israel was only allowed to sacrifice at the door of the tent of appointment (243). When Solomon's temple was built, sacrifices were made in the temple court (See Ezekiel 40:41). The Heavenly Father has never identified another place where He accepts sacrifices. Outside of the three major feasts, if people within the boundaries of Israel lived far from where Adonai chose for sacrifices, they could have been done in other locations still within the land (604).

These were not for ritual sacrifices; everyone was still expected to appear where our Heavenly Father places His name 3 times a year.

#242. Leviticus 17:7 ~ Not to Sacrifice to Any False Gods

Negative
Loving Abba
Unconditional

A sin so serious that it demands execution according to command #105.

#243. Leviticus 17:8-9 ~ Sacrifices Are Only Allowed at the Door of the Tent of Appointment

Negative
Loving Abba
Conditional

See #241 for more information.

#244. Leviticus 17:10-12 ~ No One is Allowed to Consume Blood, Not Israel nor the People with Israel

Negative
Loving Abba
Unconditional

See #5 for more information.

#245. Leviticus 17:13-14 ~ When Hunting, You Must Drain and Bury the Blood

Positive
Loving Abba
Unconditional

See #5 for more information.

#246. Leviticus 17:15-16 ~ If You Eat Animals Torn by a Beast or That Died Naturally

Positive
Loving Abba
Unconditional

See #112 for more information.

#247. Leviticus 18:4 ~ To Guard and Follow Torah

Positive
Loving People
Unconditional

The most repeated command in all of Torah, seen twenty-seven times in:

- Leviticus 18:26 (268)
- Leviticus 18:30 (269)
- Leviticus 19:19 (297)
- Leviticus 19:37 (316)
- Leviticus 20:8 (321)
- Leviticus 20:22 (335)
- Leviticus 22:31 (375)
- Deuteronomy 4:6 (522)
- Deuteronomy 4:23 (530)
- Deuteronomy 4:40 (533)
- Deuteronomy 5:1 (536)
- Deuteronomy 5:29 (551)
- Deuteronomy 6:2 (555)
- Deuteronomy 6:17 (567)
- Deuteronomy 7:11 (572)

- Deuteronomy 8:6 (574)
- Deuteronomy 10:13 (582)
- Deuteronomy 11:8 (590)
- Deuteronomy 12:28 (609 & 610)
- Deuteronomy 12:32 (612)
- Deuteronomy 13:4 (617)
- Deuteronomy 27:1 (804)
- Deuteronomy 29:9 (806)
- Deuteronomy 30:16 (810)
- Deuteronomy 30:16 (811)
- John 14:15 (857)

The Hebrew word שָׁמַר (shaw-mar'; H8104) means to keep, guard, protect, retain, treasure up, observe, celebrate, and preserve. The fact that this is the most repeated command in all of Torah is a strong sign that the Heavenly Father will not sway from the instructions He has given to Israel through Moses. In Exodus 19:9, Adonai said that He wants Israel to believe what Moses says forever. In Deuteronomy 13:1-4, the Heavenly Father says He will test Israel by allowing people to try and persuade us to walk away from Torah. When the Heavenly Father speaks of a coming covenant in Ezekiel 11:19-20, 36:26-27, and Jeremiah 31:33, He describes it as the Set-Apart Spirit dwelling in us and causing us to want to keep what Moses wrote. There is no room to think that new commands will replace what Moses wrote.

In Matthew 5:18, Yeshua says, "For most certainly, I tell you, until heaven and earth pass away, not even one smallest letter or one tiny pen stroke shall in any way pass away from Torah, until all things are accomplished." There are still prophecies that we are waiting for to be fulfilled. Paul reinforces the idea that Torah still defines sin when he writes, "What shall we say then? Is the law sin? May it never be! However, I wouldn't have known sin, except through the law. For I wouldn't have known coveting, unless the law had said, "You shall not covet. (Romans 7:7)" In 1st John 5:3, the author writes, "For this is loving Elohim, that we keep his commandments. His commandments are not grievous." Revelation 12:17 & 14:12 show us that we cannot resist the beast without faith in Yeshua and obedience to Torah. We need Torah to resist the beast!

> *Now faith is the substance of things hoped for, the evidence of realities not seen.* – Hebrews 11:1(TLV)

When we live by Torah, we demonstrate that we believe in the Heavenly Father's order in this universe. Torah is the faith of the Heavenly Father given by the Heavenly Father. When we guard Torah, we hope the Heavenly Father is who He says He is and will keep His promises. We believe He hears our prayers, blesses us, protects us, and guides us in all truth when we guard Torah. This does not mean we will not face troubles and hardships in life, but it does mean that we have complete faith in Him and trust that in the end, it will all be worth it. When we guard Torah, we advertise to the world that the Elohim who freed Israel from Egypt is real! By guarding Torah, we become that "Light of the world" and "City on a hill" that Yeshua refers to in Matthew 5:14.

One more reason, and this cannot be said enough: Yeshua kept Torah perfectly not because he had to, but because it is who he is. If Yeshua said anything that contradicted one command of Torah, we would know he is false. If Yeshua did anything against one of the commands, we would know he is false. As we guard Torah, we become more like Yeshua, not just outwardly, but inwardly as well. Yeshua guarded Torah to the utmost, and if we claim to believe in him, we should follow suit.

This command is all about loving people because when we wholeheartedly keep Torah, the people around us do not have to worry about us stealing, deceiving them for personal gains, spreading negative rumors about them, doing anything that would cause them harm, or cheating them in any way! When we properly keep Torah, if our neighbor drops their wallet in the street with $1000 in it and we find it, we will return it to them fully intact! If a $100 bill flies into our yard from our neighbor's yard, we will take it back to them. If we are mechanics, lawyers, doctors, business owners, no one should worry about us taking advantage of people for the sake of making as much money as we can. Torah abiding citizens of Israel do not slander others or take advantage of others. We look out for the best interest of those around us because Torah teaches us to do so.

#248. Leviticus 18:5 ~ To Live by Torah

Positive
Loving People
Unconditional

Repeated twice in:

- Leviticus 19:37 (317)
- James 2:10 (872)

This is an essential command. To live by Torah is a commitment that changes human beings from people of the world into people set-apart for Adonai. To live by Torah means that your life revolves around what the Heavenly Father has established through His voice. Whatever the Heavenly Father identifies as bad is bad; whatever He says is good is good. When Adonai says something is abominable, that is what it is, and whatever judgments He has made, that is the final word on that subject.

Because the Heavenly Father does not change, His words will never change. Through this command, there is a practical way to measure your spiritual growth, to see how in sync you are with Yeshua and the

Choose Life

Heavenly Father. As you examine each instruction, look within yourself to see if you wholeheartedly align with it or if there is some resistance. Maybe it is something you disagree with, don't understand, or a weakness the flesh does not want to give up. Remember, Torah is not just a list of dos and don'ts; Torah is the tool used to transform us into the likeness of Yeshua and the Heavenly Father from within. Any resistance towards the commands is an opportunity to overcome the flesh.

This command can also free you from religious bondage. Torah is not a religion; it is a covenant. Torah focuses on internal changes, while religion is more externally focused. Religion has been the cause of mental suffering and emotional torment for thousands of years due to unrealistic expectations of what they believe faith should look like. When we live by Torah, we submit only to Adonai's definition of sin. This alone can break bondages. From behind pulpits, people have said all kinds of things that are "sin" but are not according to the Heavenly Father. Here is a surprising list (Not a complete list) of things that are not sinful within Torah, but many think they are.

- Drinking Alcohol
- Doing Drugs (Unless it is illegal where you are)
- Smoking Cigarettes or Cigars
- Fighting/Self-defense or otherwise
- Getting seconds at the dinner table
- An unattached man having sex with an unattached woman (755)
- Getting divorced (conditional)
- Going to nightclubs
- Masturbation
- Killing someone caught in the act of breaking into your home or in self-defense

Torah for Modern Messiah Believers

In my 25+ years of seeking the face of our Heavenly Father, I have heard preachers repeatedly call these things (and more) sin, and I have seen many people suffer from guilt, feelings of inferiority, and become discouraged in their faith because of it. Don't get me wrong, everything mentioned in the above list, if uncontrolled, can cause problems in people's lives. If you suffer from drug addiction, alcoholism, or can't control your anger or sexual urges, these are known to have negative impacts on people's lives, and you should seek help. Such things do not go with the overall goals of Torah and usually lead to actual sin. While you are fighting to overcome such things, recognize the wisdom, love, and compassion within Torah. As stated before, the Heavenly Father understands the struggles of this world, and how He has chosen to present His voice demonstrates that.

To live by Torah means that we follow all of it; we do not pick and choose which commands to follow or agree with. This is the very nature of the covenant found in Exodus 19:5. It does not mean that you must do every command within Torah, but it does mean that you should always recognize what flows with or against Torah all around you. To live by Torah means that you can identify what is pleasing and not pleasing to the Heavenly Father at any time. To know how the Heavenly Father would want certain situations handled, either by yourself or if someone is seeking advice. If someone claims that the kingdom of Israel was fully restored today, Torah exposes what it should look like and where it should be.

Torah is not a matter of convenience; you cannot pick and choose when to apply Torah. Torah is not something you can turn on and off at will. You cannot agree with some commands while discarding others. With that said, some commands are not for you, some are for situations you may never find yourself in, and there are commands where the conditions are not there to apply. Overall, Torah is a mentality, a lifestyle that becomes a part of who you are. Torah is an all-or-nothing deal. This is what James was saying in James 2:1-13.

#249. Leviticus 18:6 ~ Do Not Have Sexual Relations with Family Members

Negative
Loving People
Unconditional

Commands #250-261 cover the details of this command.

#250. Leviticus 18:7 ~ Do Not Have Sexual Relations with Father or Mother

Negative
Loving People
Unconditional

This command applies to biological, adoptive, or in-law parents. Also, see 1st Corinthians 5:1-2. We can also reference Romans 1:26-27. This passage focuses on unnatural relations as an example of "dishonorable passions." It is a part of a larger argument about humanity's rejection of the Heavenly Father's design for proper relationships, which could implicitly include incestuous acts as deviations from the natural order.

Throughout this chapter, Moses often uses the term "the nakedness of..." which connects it to sexual immorality. The same term is used in Genesis Chapter 9, which sheds light on what happened between Ham, Noah, Noah's wife, and Canaan. It was more than Ham walking in on his drunk dad naked in bed. It even suggests that Canaan could have been the result of Ham sleeping with Noah's wife, which is why Noah cursed Canaan, his grandson, instead of cursing Ham, who committed the sinful act.

This also reveals a pattern: children born outside of the natural order tend to become enemies of Israel. The Canaanites became enemies of Israel. Lot's descendants, the Moabites and Ammonites (See Genesis 19:31-38), became enemies of Israel.

#251. Leviticus 18:8 ~ Do Not Have Sexual Relations with Your Father's Wife

Negative
Loving People
Unconditional

This instruction is repeated in Deuteronomy 22:30 (757).

This refers to the woman your father marries. It covers both biological and non-biological mothers.

#252. Leviticus 18:9 ~ Do Not Have Sexual Relations with Your Sister Born of Your Father or Mother

Negative
Loving People
Unconditional

This command refers to a sister.

#253. Leviticus 18:10 ~ Do Not Have Sexual Relations with a Daughter Born from Your Son or Daughter

Negative
Loving People
Unconditional

This command refers to grandchildren.

#254. Leviticus 18:11 ~ Do Not Have Sexual Relations with the Daughter of Your Father's Wife

Negative
Loving People
Unconditional

Sister-in-law.

#255. Leviticus 18:12 ~ Do Not Have Sexual Relations with Your Father's Sister

Negative
Loving People
Unconditional

Repeated in #332.

This instruction refers to an aunt from your father's side.

#256. Leviticus 18:13 ~ Do Not Have Sexual Relations with Your Mother's Sister

Negative
Loving People
Unconditional

Repeated in #332.

This instruction refers to an aunt from your mother's side.

#257. Leviticus 18:14 ~ Do Not Have Sexual Relations with Your Father's Brother or His Wife

Negative
Loving People
Unconditional

This instruction refers to an uncle from your father's side and his wife.

#258. Leviticus 18:15 ~ Do Not Have Sexual Relations with Your Daughter-in-Law

Negative
Loving People
Unconditional

This refers to a woman married to your son.

#259. Leviticus 18:16 ~ Do Not Have Sexual Relations with Your Brother's Wife

Negative
Loving People
Unconditional

Repeated in #334.

This command refers to a sister-in-law.

#260. Leviticus 18:17 ~ Do Not Have Sexual Relations with a Woman and Her Daughter, Her Son's Daughter or Daughter's Daughter

Negative
Loving People
Unconditional

This command refers to the woman, her daughter, and her grandchildren.

#261. Leviticus 18:18 ~ Do Not Marry Your Wife's Sister While Your Wife is Still Alive

Negative
Loving People
Unconditional

#262. Leviticus 18:19 ~ Do Not Have Sexual Relations with a Woman During Her Monthly Uncleanness

Negative
Loving Abba
Unconditional

#263. Leviticus 18:20 ~ Do Not Have Sexual Intercourse with Your Neighbor's Wife

Negative
Loving People
Unconditional

Do not even desire it according to Matthew 5:27-28 (830).

#264. Leviticus 18:21 ~ To Not Give Your Children to Molek (or Molech)

Negative
Loving People
Unconditional

Repeated twice in:

- Leviticus 20:1-5 (318)
- Deuteronomy 18:10-11 (711)

According to www.bibleanalysis.org, Molech is often identified as a Canaanite deity associated with child sacrifice. The name "Molech" is thought to be derived from the Hebrew word for "king," emphasizing the prominent role of this deity in the pantheon of Canaanite gods. Ancient texts and archaeological findings suggest that Molech was worshipped through the ritualistic burning of children as sacrifices, a practice that was rejected and condemned in Torah. Some people like to connect this to the abortions that happen today, although they lead to the same results, they are not the same thing.

#265. Leviticus 18:21 ~ Not to Profane the Name YHWH

Negative
Loving Abba
Unconditional

See #49 for more information.

#266. Leviticus 18:22 ~ Men Are Not to Have Sexual Relations with Other Men

Negative
Loving Abba
Unconditional

A sin so severe that it is punishable by death, according to Leviticus 20:13 (326). This can be an example of someone being "under the ban." Despite the severity of this command, let us not use it to discriminate against people who are homosexual. Homosexuality is simply a by-product of this world full of sin. It doesn't matter if people feel like they are born that way, choose to be that way, if they were groomed in that way, or if a traumatic situation caused them to be that way; homosexuality is in this world, and it is something we must tackle because Yeshua died so that everyone can have a chance to escape death!

The action of men having sexual interactions with other men is a sin like any other, and it can be a struggle for some people, just like we all have things that we struggle with. Nonetheless, if such individuals are seeking the face of the Heavenly Father, we have no right to give them no hope. If they are willing to agree to a lifestyle of celibacy to start their walk, that is a huge step in the right direction. That is a true denying of the flesh situation. Maybe they will always be sexually attracted to men, maybe something can happen down the line where they can enjoy a romantic relationship with the opposite sex. Of course, the spirit of this command would be that men are not sexually attracted to other men; so for some men, this can be a hard process, but not impossible.

This is a difficult subject that does not have a clean and simple answer. Regardless, we should always remember that the Heavenly Father does not despise a broken and contrite heart (Psalms 51:17). With the Heavenly Father, all things are possible (Matthew 19:26, Mark 10:27, and Luke 18:27).

#267. Leviticus 18:23 ~ Men and Women Do Not Have Sexual Intercourse with Animals

Negative
Loving Abba
Unconditional

#268. Leviticus 18:26 ~ To Guard Torah, All Israel, and Those with Israel

Positive
Loving People
Unconditional

See #247 for more information.

#269. Leviticus 18:30 ~ To Guard Torah

Positive
Loving People
Unconditional

See #247 for more information.

#270. Leviticus 19:2 ~ To Be Set Apart

Positive
Loving Abba
Unconditional

See #218 for more information.

#271. Leviticus 19:3 ~ To Fear Your Mother and Father

Positive
Loving People
Unconditional

There is a lot more to this command than most people think. Without thinking much about it, we tend to approach the Heavenly Father in the same way we would approach our parents. Since they are the first authorities given to us by Elohim, this is one of the most important relationships we can have that is indirectly connected to the Heavenly

Father. If we cannot fear or respect our parents, whom we can see, hear, and touch, is it even possible to fear and respect YHWH, whom we do not see, hear, or touch?

#272. Leviticus 19:3 ~ To Guard the Shabbats

Positive
Loving Abba
Unconditional

See #50 for more information.

#273. Leviticus 19:4 ~ Do Not Turn to Idols

Negative
Loving Abba
Unconditional

See #48 for more information.

#274. Leviticus 19:4 ~ Do Not Make Figures to Worship

Negative
Loving Abba
Unconditional

See #48 for more information.

#275. Leviticus 19:5 ~ Sacrifices of Peace Offering are For Your Acceptance

Positive
Loving People
Conditional

Sometimes translated as fellowship offering or offering of well-being. The Peace offering sacrifice is a voluntary one, distinct from offerings for sin or guilt. It was typically an expression of gratitude, communion with Adonai, or celebration, and part of the animal was shared among the offeror, the priests, and sometimes the community. It is not impossible to believe that Yeshua's followers made this sacrifice until the destruction of the temple in 70 AD.

#276. Leviticus 19:5-8 ~ To Eat the Sacrifice of a Peace Offering Within 3 Days

Positive
Loving Abba
Conditional

#277. Leviticus 19:5-8 ~ Burn the Remainder of the Sacrifice of the Peace Offering on the 3rd Day

Positive
Loving Abba
Conditional

#278. Leviticus 19:9-10 ~ Do Not Reap the Corners or Gleaning of Your Harvest for the Poor

Negative
Loving People
Conditional

Repeated in:

- Leviticus 23:22 (398)
- Deuteronomy 24:19 (790)

This is a conditional command because it talks to farmers in the land, but spiritually, there is something that we all can learn from this instruction. This command demonstrates a heart for the poor and the homeless. In today's world, most people ignore the poor and homeless, thinking that there are organizations out there helping them. In this command, Adonai does not want us to pass the buck and turn a blind eye to the people who are in need. His heart for the poor is seen throughout the entire Bible. This command, along with all the commands that focus on the poor in this book, is an opportunity to gauge how in sync we are with the Heavenly Father. Upon reviewing this command, it became clear that all of us can fulfill this, even though most of us are not farmers.

When you get paid, put a few dollars in your wallet/purse to give to beggars. Some people don't want to give to beggars because they could be scammers, or they will use it for drugs/alcohol, or they refuse to give because they see beggars as lazy. That is not our place to judge. Many are out there because they are desperate, feel like they have no other options, and do not know what else to do. If you feel uncomfortable giving money to beggars, look for a trustworthy organization to donate to regularly. Can we truly be in sync with the Heavenly Father if we forget the poor, the widow, and orphans? The Heavenly Father never forgets them, and neither should His people.

#279-281. Leviticus 19:11 ~ Do Not Lie to Gain Deceitfully and Steal

Negative
Loving People
Unconditional

This is a 3-in-1 commandment. The first part of "do not steal" is first seen in command #58. The 2nd part is "do not lie", and the 3rd part, "do not deceive", completes the whole thought. The full verse of this command says, "You shall not steal, you shall not lie, and you shall not deceive one another." Many scriptures present this as three different and separate thoughts by presenting it like:

> *"You shall not steal. You shall not lie. You shall not deceive one another."*

Replace the periods with commas, and it becomes one complete thought that teaches us not to lie or deceive for false gains. That is in uniform with all the instructions about lying. Remember, punctuation is 100% subjective for modern scriptures. The only way we can accurately punctuate the scriptures is if someone fluent in ancient Hebrew can go back in time and hear how Moses said it. By replacing the periods with commas, it flows better and makes more sense with the surrounding commands.

#282. Leviticus 19:12 ~ Do Not Swear Falsely in the Name of YHWH

Negative
Loving Abba
Unconditional

#283. Leviticus 19:13 ~ Do Not Oppress Your Neighbor

Negative
Loving people
Unconditional

#284. Leviticus 19:13 ~ Do Not Rob Your Neighbor

Negative
Loving People
Unconditional

#285. Leviticus 19:13 ~ Do Not Delay in Paying Wages

Negative
Loving People
Unconditional

#286. Leviticus 19:14 ~ Do Not Hate or Cause Hardship to the Handicapped

Negative
Loving People
Unconditional

#287. Leviticus 19:14 ~ To Fear the Heavenly Father

Positive
Loving Abba
Unconditional

Repeated 8 times in:

- Deuteronomy 4:10 (527)
- Deuteronomy 5:29 (550)
- Deuteronomy 6:2 (554)
- Deuteronomy 6:13 (562)
- Deuteronomy 8:6 (576)
- Deuteronomy 10:12 (578)
- Deuteronomy 10:20 (585)

- Deuteronomy 13:4 (616)

The word fear here comes from the Hebrew word יָרֵא (yaw-ray': H3372) a primitive root; to fear; morally to revere; causatively to frighten:— affright, be (make) afraid, dread(-ful), (put in) fear(-ful, -fully, -ing), (be had in) reverence(-end), see, terrible (act, -ness, thing). By looking at the full use of the word, we can pinpoint its proper use for this teaching.

The fear that Adonai is talking about is the same as when a child does something wrong and fears that they have let their parents down. Once you submit to the covenant of relationship in Exodus 19:5, Adonai becomes your Elohim, your Heavenly Father. He plans to see you prosper and to protect you. Every command of Torah is for our benefit, and when we do not take Torah seriously, just like any good father would, He punishes us and allows us to suffer the consequences of our actions.

> *The fear of Adonai is the beginning of wisdom. The knowledge of the Holy One is understanding.* – Proverbs 9:10

The Heavenly Father is not asking us to be frightened of Him; the type of fear He is looking for from us is a healthy fear, like the fear of fire. We all use fire daily for cooking, camping, heating our homes, lighting candles, and more. Some people work with fire every day as a part of their profession. Because we use fire so much, many of us have developed a healthy fear of fire, a respectful fear. Because of this respectful fear, we are careful when it comes to handling fire; in the same way, we should not treat Torah carelessly. That is how we fearfully respect the Heavenly Father.

NOTE: The next 3 commands (288-290) are for leaders of Israel; however, if you find yourself in leadership in the world, it will not hurt you to follow these commands, which is why they are unconditional. These are universal principles that every human being wishes for leadership to be.

#288. Leviticus 19:15 ~ For Leaders to be Righteous in Right-Rulings

Positive
Loving People
Unconditional

#289. Leviticus 19:15 ~ Leaders Should Not Be Partial to the Poor nor Favor the Great

Negative
Loving People
Unconditional

#290. Leviticus 19:15 ~ For Leaders to Rightly Rule the People

Positive
Loving People
Unconditional

#291. Leviticus 19:16 ~ Do Not Slander

Negative
Loving People
Unconditional

See #59 for more information.

#292. Leviticus 19:16 ~ Do Not Stand Against the Blood of Your Neighbor

Negative
Loving People
Unconditional

The word blood comes from the Hebrew word דָּם (dawm: Strong's H1818). It is used as murder in this command; also see command #56 for more information.

#293-294. Leviticus 19:17 ~ Do Not Be Bitter Towards Others/To Correct Others When They Sin

Positive
Loving People
Unconditional

These two commands are intertwined: "You shall not hate your brother in your heart, you shall surely rebuke your neighbor and not bear sin because of him." If you see someone who is covenanted sinning and you do not tell them, you are hating them, and you bear sin because you do not tell them. Within the body of believers, we all serve as white cells, protecting the body and fighting against the cancer known as sin. If we see someone sinning out in the world that is not covenanted, it is none of our business (Unless it requires calling 911, of course). Within the body of believers, we cannot let sin slide. Throughout Torah, Adonai punishes Israel corporately. Corporate punishment is done to keep us motivated to look out for one another and keep sin out of the body.

Today, many people are shy to call out sin when they see it within the body of believers. Most people are not mature enough to take corrections without preparation and would normally claim that the accuser is breaking #845 found in Matthew 7:1-5. This is usually a perversion of the command for the sake of pride.

Matthew 18:15-18 talks about confronting someone when they sin against you. The same steps can be used if you see someone sinning within the body. If you cannot confront the person directly, at the very least, you can go to leadership. Whatever you do, never ignore sin when a covenanted member of the body, or someone working towards getting covenanted, is sinning.

#295. Leviticus 19:18 ~ To Not Seek Vengeance

Negative
Loving People
Unconditional

#296. Leviticus 19:18 ~ To Love Your Neighbor as Yourself

Positive
Loving People
Unconditional

#297. Leviticus 19:19 ~ To Guard Torah

Positive
Loving Abba
Unconditional

See #247 for more information.

#298. Leviticus 19:19 ~ To Not Let Livestock Mate with Other Kinds

Negative
Loving Abba
Unconditional

#299. Leviticus 19:19 ~ Not to Sow Fields with Mixed Seeds

Negative
Loving Abba
Conditional

This instruction is repeated in Deuteronomy 22:9 (746).

Logically, it seems that Adonai would not want His creation of fruits and vegetables altered, and the same can be said of the previous command about animals. Historically, sowing different seeds in the same field was allowed with certain guidelines, such as separating the various kinds with a fence or planting them far enough from each other so that they can extract nutrients from the soil without interfering with each other (NC215 from the 613 Mitzvot).

#300. Leviticus 19:19 ~ Do Not Wear a Garment with Two Different Types of Threads

Negative
Loving Abba
Unconditional

It is repeated in Deuteronomy 22:11 (751).

Most people look at this command, scratching their heads and wondering, "What's the point?" On the surface, poor people couldn't afford the materials to make proper clothing and would stitch together all kinds of materials to make their clothes. Once again, one of the major underlying themes of Torah is prosperity for the people of Israel. The people of Israel wearing such outfits go in the opposite direction of what the Heavenly Father wants for Israel. Of course, there are far deeper meanings behind this command.

Thanks again to modern science, it has been proven that this command is another example of how every instruction within Torah is for our benefit. If you Google the term "Effects of clothing materials on the body", you will find the following, along with tons of other information:

- Health implications: Some chemicals used in clothing production, such as fabric coatings, processing chemicals, and toxic dyes, can have health effects.
- Physical and psychological symptoms: Fabric frequencies may disrupt the body's natural balance, leading to physical and psychological symptoms.
- Comfort during exercise: Sports clothing enhances sweat evaporation and provides comfort during exercise in the heat.
- Influence on cardiovascular and respiratory parameters: Wearing clothes made of different fabrics may affect cardiovascular and respiratory parameters during physical effort.

Health implications due to chemicals in our clothes are things that humanity learned through trial and error; the same thing can be said for discomfort with certain clothing materials while exercising. Physical and psychological symptoms regarding fabrics and their influence on cardiovascular and respiratory parameters were not something humans could even imagine when Torah was given. Today, most clothes are made of 100% cotton, and the clothing industry usually identifies the fabric in the clothes they produce, which makes this command easy to keep, only costing us a few seconds to review the fabrics in the clothes we buy.

Last, look at the wording of this teaching carefully, "Don't wear a garment (Singular) made of two kinds of material." The way this command is worded, if you wear a silk shirt with a pair of jeans made with 100% cotton, you may not be breaking this command because those are two separate garments. This command is about one garment made with multiple types of materials. It is easy to find garments made of 1 material today, making this instruction relatively easy to keep.

#301. Leviticus 19:20-22 ~ When a Man Sleeps with a Servant Engaged or Ransomed

Positive
Loving People
Conditional

#302. Leviticus 19:26 ~ Do Not Consume Blood

Negative
Loving Abba
Unconditional

See #5 for more information.

#303. Leviticus 19:26 ~ Do Not Practice Fortune-Telling or Magic

Negative
Loving Abba
Unconditional

Similar commands are in:

Choose Life

- Leviticus 19:31 (311)
- Leviticus 20:6 (319)
- Leviticus 20:27 (338)
- Deuteronomy 18:10-11 (712-715)

Witchcraft, fortune-telling, magic, spiritism, interpretations of omens, and sorcery are all forbidden in Israel. Practicing witchcraft, fortune telling, spiritism, and practicing magic (Not the entertainment, sleight of hand, "magic" we are accustomed to today) are all punishable by death (103). The Heavenly Father does not even want us to turn to such things. Throughout the Bible, Adonai speaks via people He anoints, and those people talk to everyone else. Adonai's anointed people will not use magic, witchcraft, or sorcery, will not interpret omens, or tell fortunes. Throughout history, many people who practice such things have claimed to speak on Adonai's behalf and have all lied. The only exception to this rule would be Balaam, whom the Heavenly Father forced to bless Israel instead of cursing Israel (Numbers 22-24). As followers of the Heavenly Father, we are responsible for identifying and following Adonai's anointed, appointed people. These commands are not just telling us what to avoid; they also convey that Adonai will never communicate with us in those ways.

NOTE: The next four commands are things that history identifies as being done in ancient Egypt and can be verified online. With the commands about beards, it is safe to say that Adonai did not want the Levites to imitate how the Egyptian priests presented themselves. Cutting yourself and getting tattoos were part of ancient funeral rituals. You can also search "ancient pagan rituals for tattooing and cutting at funerals" online.

#304. Leviticus 19:27 ~ Do Not Round the Corners of Your Beard

Negative
Loving Abba
Unconditional

This command is connected to #341.

#305. Leviticus 19:27 ~ Do Not Destroy the Corners of Your Beard

Negative
Loving Abba
Unconditional

This command is connected to #341.

#306. Leviticus 19:28 ~ Not to Cut Yourself for the Dead

Negative
Loving Abba
Unconditional

This instruction is repeated in #627.

#307. Leviticus 19:28 ~ Not to Put on Tattoos for the Dead

Negative
Loving Abba
Unconditional

Many people view this as a stand along command, but historically, putting on tattoos for the dead was a thing. Even today, we see people putting on tattoos to remember a dead relative or people who passed away who was very close to them. Based on the command that come before it, it is most likely that this is about the dead. Once again, punctuation in our Bibles today is 100% subjective and it is possible that commands #306 and #307 is one complete thought and could possibly be translated better as, "You shall not make any cuttings in your flesh, nor tattoo any marks on you, for the dead. I am Adonai."

#308. Leviticus 19:29 ~ Do Not Turn Daughters into Whores

Negative
Loving Abba
Unconditional

In ancient Mesopotamia, texts like the Code of Hammurabi (1750 BCE) hinted at prostitution being recognized as a low-status occupation. Some scholars suggest that families living in extreme poverty may have turned to prostitution to improve their financial situation, although it's not explicitly documented as a widespread practice. In ancient Greece, particularly in cities like Athens, poor families sometimes sold daughters into slavery or concubinage, knowing it could end up in sexual exploitation. The hetaerae—high-class courtesans—were a different story, often educated and independent, but lower-tier prostitutes were more likely to come from desperate circumstances. The nations surrounding Israel saw this as a logical way to make money. This command sets Israel apart from the rest of the nations. This command also solidifies the idea that when a young woman was sold to a wealthy family, it was with the expectation that she would be taken care of and not treated as a prostitute or go into some sort of sex slavery.

#309. Leviticus 19:30 ~ To Keep the Shabbats

Positive
Loving Abba
Unconditional

See #50 for more information.

#310. Leviticus 19:30 ~ To Respect the Set Apart Place

Positive
Loving Abba
Conditional

#311. Leviticus 19:31 ~ Do Not Turn to Mediums, Spiritists, and Magic

Negative
Loving Abba
Unconditional

See #303 for more information.

#312. Leviticus 19:32 ~ To Respect the Elders

Positive
Lovin People
Unconditional

#313. Leviticus 19:33 ~ Do Not Oppress the Uncovenanted Among Israel

Negative
Loving People
Unconditional

Repeated in:

- Exodus 22:21 (106)
- Exodus 23:9 (120)

#314. Leviticus 19:34 ~ To Love the Uncovenanted Among Israel as Israelites

Positive
Loving People
Unconditional

#315. Leviticus 19:35-36 ~ To Be Honorable in Business

Positive
Loving people
Unconditional

#316. Leviticus 19:37 ~ To Guard Torah

Positive
Loving People
Unconditional

See #247 for more information.

#317. Leviticus 19:37 ~ To Live by Torah

Positive
Loving People
Unconditional

See #248 for more information.

#318. Leviticus 20:1-5 ~ To Not Give Children to Molek

Negative
Loving People
Unconditional

See #264 for more information.

#319. Leviticus 20:6 ~ Do Not Turn to Fortune Tellers and Spiritists

Negative
Loving Abba
Unconditional

See #303 for more information.

#320. Leviticus 20:7 ~ To Be Set Apart

Positive
Loving Abba
Unconditional

See #218 for more information.

#321. Leviticus 20:8 ~ To Guard Torah and Live by It

Positive
Loving Abba
Unconditional

See #247 for more information.

#322. Leviticus 20:9 ~ Do Not Curse Your Parents

Negative
Loving People
Unconditional

Back in ancient times, cursing parents wasn't just a personal insult; it was seen as a threat to the family structure, which threatens the covenant community. The harsh penalty reflects the high stakes of maintaining obedience and cohesion in a theocratic society. This is one of many capital offenses listed in Leviticus because you cannot curse your parents by mistake. To do something like that means that you have thought about it and have accepted that thought in your heart.

#323. Leviticus 20:10 ~ To Execute Adulterers, Both the Man and Woman

Positive
Loving People
Conditional

See #57 for more information.

#324. Leviticus 20:11 ~ To Execute Both the Man and the Mother-in-Law Who Has Sexual Relations

Positive
Loving People
Conditional

#325. Leviticus 20:12 ~ To Execute Both the Man and the Daughter-in-Law Who Have Sexual Relations

Positive
Loving People
Conditional

#326. Leviticus 20:13 ~ Both Men Who Have Sexual Relations with Each Other Are to Be Executed

Positive
Loving People
Conditional

#327. Leviticus 20:14 ~ To Execute a Man Who Marries a Woman and Her Mother

Positive
Loving People
Conditional

All three shall be burned.

#328. Leviticus 20:15 ~ To Execute a Man and an Animal Who Has Sexual Relations

Positive
Loving Abba
Conditional

#329. Leviticus 20:16 ~ To Execute a Woman and an Animal Who Has Sexual Relations

Positive
Loving Abba
Conditional

#330. Leviticus 20:17 ~ To Cut Off Siblings Who Have Sexual Relations

Positive
Loving People
Conditional

The Hebrew word כָּרַת (kaw-rath', Strongs H3772) is translated to mean a few things, but based on the context, this is most likely talking about beheading the siblings. Since the Heavenly Father does not change, this command strongly implies that Cain and Seth married women who were not born of Eve.

#331. Leviticus 20:18 ~ Cut Off Couples Who Have Sexual Relations During a Woman's Monthly Uncleanse

Positive
Loving People
Conditional

This instruction is not 100% clear, but it is likely referring to execution.

#332. Leviticus 20:19 ~ Do Not Sleep with Your Aunt

Negative
Loving People
Unconditional

Either from your mother's side or your father's side. Also seen in commands #255 & #256.

#333. Leviticus 20:20 ~ A Man Should Not Have Sexual Relations with His Uncle's Wife

Negative
Loving People
Unconditional

First seen with #257.

"They die childless"- It's not clear if this means to execute them or if Adonai will not allow such a union to bear children within Israel. This command can be conditional if "die childless" means execution.

#334. Leviticus 20:21 ~ Man Should Not Have Sexual Relations with His Brother's Wife

Negative
Loving People
Unconditional

First seen in #259.

"They are childless", not sure if this means to execute them or if the Heavenly Father will not allow such a union to bear children within Israel. This command can be conditional if "die childless" means execution.

#335. Leviticus 20:22 ~ To Guard and Live by Torah

Positive
Loving The Father
Unconditional

See #247 for more information.

NOTE: Leviticus 20:23-24 is for the Exodus Generation. For us today, it could mean not to do as the nations do.

#336. Leviticus 20:25 ~ To Distinguish Between Clean and Unclean Animals

Positive
Loving Abba
Unconditional

This instruction was first seen in Leviticus 11:46-47 (221).

#337. Leviticus 20:26 ~ To Be Set Apart

Positive
Loving Abba
Unconditional

See #218 for more information.

#338. Leviticus 20:27 ~ To Stone Those Who Practice Fortune Telling, Magic, and Spiritism

Positive
Loving People
Conditional

See #303 for more information.

#339. Leviticus 21:1-3 ~ Rule of Defilement from the Dead for the Priesthood

Negative
Loving Abba
Unconditional

#340. Leviticus 21:4-5 ~ The Priesthood is Not Allowed to Make Any Bald Places on Their Heads

Negative
Loving Abba
Unconditional

The command seems to refer to the appearance of the Egyptian priests. We have plenty of examples of what the Egyptian priests looked like. The Levites are not allowed to imitate their appearance. Since Egypt had great influence on the world at that time, it is possible that other nations followed them. This command shows us that the Heavenly Father does not want Israel to follow anybody but Him.

#341. Leviticus 21:4-5 ~ The Priests Are Not Allowed to Shave the Corners of Their Beards

Negative
Loving Abba
Conditional

Like commands #304 & #305. This command is conditional because it is for the Levites who are in active service.

#342. Leviticus 21:4-5 ~ Priests Are Not Allowed to Make Cuts in Their Flesh

Negative
Loving Abba
Unconditional

Another reference to pagan rituals.

#343. Leviticus 21:6 ~ The Priesthood is Set Apart to the Heavenly Father

Positive
Loving Abba
Unconditional

#344. Leviticus 21:7 ~ Who the Priesthood Should Not Marry

Negative
Loving Abba
Unconditional

#345. Leviticus 21:8 ~ The Priesthood Is Set Apart for Israel

Positive
Loving Abba
Unconditional

#346. Leviticus 21:9 ~ To Execute the Daughter of a Priest Who Whores

Positive
Loving People
Conditional

To be burned with fire.

#347. Leviticus 21:10 ~ The Priesthood is Not to Dishonor the Headbands and Garments

Positive
Loving Abba
Conditional

This command could also be about the priesthood's proper grooming. Things such as keeping the head covered or the hair well-groomed.

#348. Leviticus 21:11 ~ The Priesthood is Not Allowed to Go Near the Dead

Negative
Loving Abba
Conditional

#349. Leviticus 21:11 ~ The Priesthood is Not to Defile Themselves for Father or Mother

Negative
Loving Abba
Unconditional

This cannot refer to the death of their parents due to Leviticus 21:2; it could refer to something else, possibly the next command.

#350. Leviticus 21:12 ~ Priesthood is Not to Leave the Set-Apart Place

Negative
Loving people
Conditional

Due to some of the priesthood's responsibilities, this command likely means active Levites should not live outside the set-apart place.

#351. Leviticus 21:12 ~ The Priesthood is Not Allowed to Profane the Set-Apart Place

Negative
Loving Abba
Conditional

This command is tied to Leviticus 22:15-16 (368). Unfortunately, we see an account of this in Matthew 21:12-13, Mark 11:15-17, and Luke 19:45-46.

#352. Leviticus 21:13 ~ Those in the Priesthood Should Marry a Virgin

Positive
Loving Abba
Conditional

#353. Leviticus 21:14 ~ Those in the Priesthood Do Not Marry Widows, Those Defiled, or Whores

Negative
Loving Abba
Conditional

#354. Leviticus 21:15 ~ Those in the Levite Priesthood Marry Within the Levite Tribe Only

Positive
Loving Abba
Conditional

#355. Leviticus 21:17-20 & 23 ~ No Levite with a Defect is to Draw Near to Bring the Bread of the Heavenly Father

Negative
Loving Abba
Conditional

#356. Leviticus 21:21 & 23 ~ No Levite with a Defect is to Draw Near to Bring an Offering Made by Fire to the Heavenly Father

Negative
Loving Abba
Conditional

#357. Leviticus 21:22 ~ Levites with Defects Can Eat the Bread of the Heavenly Father

Negative
Loving Abba
Conditional

#358. Leviticus 22:2 ~ The Priesthood Should Separate Themselves from the Offerings of the People of Israel

Negative
Loving Abba
Conditional

The Heavenly Father commands the priests to approach these offerings with reverence and care. The phrase "separate themselves from" suggests they must maintain a state of ritual purity and avoid misusing or mishandling what has been dedicated to Adonai. This is very much like a fiduciary responsibility; the offerings must be handled with the utmost righteousness. The goal is to prevent the priests from defiling the Heavenly Father's Set-Apart Name. The Heavenly Father's name represents His character, presence, and authority. Any carelessness or irreverence in handling sacred things could be reflected poorly on Him. Since the Levite Priesthood is not active now, we have no idea what that exactly looks like, since they were free to do what they believed was best.

#359. Leviticus 22:3 ~ A Priest Should Not Come Close to the Set-Apart Offerings if He is Unclean

Negative
Loving Abba
Unconditional

#360. Leviticus 22:4-7 ~ An Unclean Levite Is Not to Eat the Set-Apart Offerings

Negative
Loving Abba
Unconditional

#361. Leviticus 22:8 ~ A Levite Does Not Eat What Dies of Natural Causes or Is Torn by Beasts

Negative
Loving Abba
Unconditional

See #112 for more information.

#362. Leviticus 22:9 ~ A Levite Must Guard Torah

Positive
Loving People
Unconditional

#363. Leviticus 22:10 ~ Those Uncovenanted Are Not Allowed to Have the Set-Apart Offering

Negative
Loving Abba
Conditional

#364. Leviticus 22:11 ~ A Levite Priest and His Family Can Eat What He Bought with Silver

Positive
Loving people
Unconditional

#365. Leviticus 22:12 ~ If a Levite's Daughter Marries an Uncovenanted Man, That Daughter Can't Eat of the Set-Apart Offering

Negative
Loving Abba
Conditional

#366. Leviticus 22:13 ~ A Priest's Daughter Who Has Left and Returned

Positive
Loving People
Conditional

#367. Leviticus 22:14 ~ When a Man Eats the Set-Apart Offering by Mistake

Positive
Loving Abba
Conditional

#368. Leviticus 22:15-16 ~ The Levite Priesthood is Not to Profane the Set-Apart Offerings

Negative
Loving Abba
Conditional

This command is repeated in Leviticus 21:12 (351).

#369. Leviticus 22:17-20 ~ Do Not Bring Offerings with Blemishes

Negative
Loving Abba
Conditional

#370. Leviticus 22:21-25 ~ Identifying Blemished Animals

Positive
Loving Abba
Conditional

This command can be connected to Exodus 12:3-5 (9).

#371. Leviticus 22:27 ~ Animals Are Acceptable for Sacrifice After 8 Days Old

Positive
Loving Abba
Conditional

This command can be connected to Exodus 12:3-5 (9).

#372. Leviticus 22:28 ~ Do Not Kill a Cow or Sheep with Their Offspring on the Same Day

Negative
Loving Abba
Conditional

#373. Leviticus 22:29 ~ A Sacrifice of Thanksgiving is For Your Acceptance

Positive
Loving Abba
Conditional

See #165 for more information.

#374. Leviticus 22:30 ~ A Sacrifice of Thanksgiving is to be Eaten on the Same Day Only

Positive
Loving Abba
Conditional

See #165 for more information.

#375. Leviticus 22:31 ~ To Guard Torah

Positive
Loving People
Unconditional

See #247 for more information.

#376. Leviticus 22:32 ~ Not to Profane What is Set-Apart

Negative
Loving Abba
Unconditional

This command is linked to various other commands. The people of Israel are set-apart (#218, #220, #270, #320, #337, & #571). How we behave and speak towards and/or about one another is important. When we speak negatively about someone within the body of believers, we are guilty of breaking this command. When we joke and have fun with one another, it should not be in a crude or tasteless way. There is no doubt that the Heavenly Father has a sense of humor, but jokingly saying that someone is ugly, stupid, or making similar comments makes it hard to see that individual as set-apart. If we see each other as set-apart and treat each other in that manner, the world will see that we are different.

The priesthood is set-apart (343 & 345). Because the Levite priesthood cannot fully function without the temple today, we can include congregation leaders as those identified as anointed from Adonai for this category. Hebrews 13:17 says, "*Obey your leaders and submit to them, for they watch on behalf of your souls, as those who will give account, that they may do this with joy, and not with groaning, for that would be unprofitable for you.*" Our spiritual leaders should be viewed as set-apart. Never speak badly, slander, argue with, or complain about leadership. If you cannot submit under your spiritual leader's authority, it is a problem. Either you struggle with submission, or you need to find another leader. However, if the problem is you, there will never be a leader you can follow until you address the person in the mirror.

Tithes and offerings are set-apart (360 & 462). This is for leadership. As leaders, you must be above reproach in how you manage the money given. As congregation leaders, you must be upright in handling the tithes and offerings. If people question you about it, make sure your books are in order. Of course, this does not mean that people have the right to say how leadership spends money; there is nothing in scripture that says how the tithes and offerings should be spent. There is nothing within the scriptures that suggests that the congregation should police such things.

For those of us who do not lead congregations, when we give our tithes and offerings, we are giving to Adonai, and that should be the end of it. If leadership uses the money unrighteously, that is between them and the Heavenly Father. Once again, there is absolutely nothing in the scriptures that suggests the people should police leaders in how they utilize tithes and offerings. If you question how the tithes and offerings are being mismanaged, ask your questions; if you are not satisfied with the answers, look for another congregation with anointed and above-reproach leadership. But also keep in mind that you may have submission issues.

Because Adonai is set apart (377), that means His voice, Torah, is set apart. Not only should we know Torah, but it is also important to know what He has identified as set apart so that we do not defile what He sees as important. The year of Jubilee is set apart (433); the uncovenanted cannot partake in what is set apart (363). If a man eats what is set apart by mistake, some things need to be done (367). When we understand that tithes and offerings are set apart, we take them more seriously.

#377. Leviticus 22:32-33 ~ The Heavenly Father is Set Apart

Positive
Loving Abba
Unconditional

NOTE: Leviticus 23 is where we see all the set-apart days of Adonai.

#378. Leviticus 23:3 ~ To Work 6 Days

Positive
Loving people
Unconditional

See #51 for more information.

#379. Leviticus 23:3 ~ To Rest on Shabbat

Positive
Loving Abba
Unconditional

See #50 for more information.

#380. Leviticus 23:5 ~ To Observe Passover at Its Appointed Time

Positive
Loving Abba
Unconditional

See #13 for more information.

#381. Leviticus 23:6 ~ To Observe the Feast of Unleavened Bread for 7 Days

Positive
Loving Abba
Unconditional

See #14 for more information.

#382. Leviticus 23:7 ~ The First Day of Unleavened Bread is a Shabbat

Positive
Loving Abba
Unconditional

See #15 for more information.

#383. Leviticus 23:8 ~ To Bring Sacrifices Every Day for Unleavened Bread

Positive
Loving People
Conditional

#384. Leviticus 23:8 ~ The 7th Day of Unleavened Bread is a Shabbat

Positive
Loving Abba
Unconditional

See #15 for more information.

#385. Leviticus 23:10 ~ To Observe the Feast of First Fruits

Positive
Loving Abba
Conditional

This command is about Israel expressing gratitude and faith by offering the initial spring portion of the harvest to the Heavenly Father, recognizing Him as the source of our blessings once we had settled in the Promised Land. Its meaning ties into themes of provision, worship, and trust. This command is conditional because it is tied to the land; the fruits provided should be from the land and observed on the Shabbat within the week of Unleavened Bread.

This command is tied to the next four commands (386-389). Some congregations make a memorial to this feast every year. Since we are not on the land nor have access to the storehouse of the Heavenly Father, additional offerings for the Shabbat during unleavened bread can spiritually fulfill this command each year. The 2nd tithe (640) can help meet this command. Depending on the timing, tax returns can work for this as well. Just like the 1st tithe (493), if it is done with the right heart, this is a form of worship.

#386. Leviticus 23:11 ~ To Wave the Sheaf on the Day After Shabbat for the Feast of First Fruits

Positive
Loving Abba
Conditional

#387. Leviticus 23:12 ~ An Ascending Offering for the Feast of First Fruits

Positive
Loving People
Conditional

#388. Leviticus 23:13 ~ The Grain Offering for the Feast of First Fruits

Positive
Loving People
Conditional

#389. Leviticus 23:14 ~ To Not Eat Bread, Roasted Grain, or Fresh Grain

Negative
Loving Abba
Conditional

This is to ensure that the first fruit offerings remain set apart. Once the first fruits are brought to the house of Adonai (128), then Israel may eat. Not eating bread can also be because this feast happens during the week of Unleavened Bread.

#390. Leviticus 23:15 ~ To Count the Weeks from the First to Shavuot (Feast of Weeks)

Positive
Loving Abba
Unconditional

Repeated in #671.

Shavuot is also known as Pentecost from its Greek adaptation. Within Judaism, it is believed that this is the day Moses first came down with the tablets. On that day, 3000 people were killed (Exodus 32:1-28). During the Shavuot of Acts 2:14-41, 3000 souls were added to the faith. Some look at this as a sign of restoration for Israel.

#391. Leviticus 23:16 ~ To Count 50 Days from the First Shabbat of Unleavened Bread to Shavuot

Positive
Loving Abba
Unconditional

There are debates as to when this count should begin. Some people believe the "first Shabbat" is the weekly Shabbat that falls during Unleavened Bread. This belief places Shavuot on Sundays perpetually. Others see the first day of Unleavened bread, which can also be considered the "first Shabbat of the week", as the day to begin counting the Omer. With this second belief, Shavuot can fall on any day of the week each year. During Yeshua's time on earth, the Pharisees and the Sadducees counted different days. We do not know if he ever addressed it; if so, it is not in any of the documents we have today.

#392. Leviticus 23:16 ~ To Bring New Grain Offerings to Shavuot

Positive
Loving People
Conditional

#393. Leviticus 23:17 ~ To Bring Two Wave Loaves for Shavuot

Positive
Loving Abba
Unconditional

#394. Leviticus 23:18 ~ To Bring 7 Lambs for Shavuot

Positive
Loving People
Conditional

#395. Leviticus 23:19 ~ To Do Sacrifices on Shavuot

Positive
Loving People
Conditional

#396. Leviticus 23:20 ~ For the Priest to Wave the Bread of the First Fruits for Shavuot

Positive
Loving Abba
Conditional

#397. Leviticus 23:21 ~ Shavuot is a Shabbat

Positive
Loving Abba
Unconditional

Judaism makes this a two-day Shabbat.

#398. Leviticus 23:22 ~ Do Not Reap the Corners or Glean Your Harvest for the Poor

Negative
Loving people
Unconditional

See #278 for more information.

#399. Leviticus 23:24 ~ To Observe the Feast of Trumpets

Positive
Loving Abba
Unconditional

This command is repeated in Numbers 29:1 (510). This feast begins the high holy days for Israel.

#400. Leviticus 23:25 ~ The Feast of Trumpets is a Shabbat

Positive
Loving Abba
Unconditional

#401. Leviticus 23:27 ~ To Observe Yom Kippur

Positive
Loving Abba
Unconditional

See command #240 for more information.

#402. Leviticus 23:27 ~ To Fast on Yom Kippur

Positive
Loving Abba
Unconditional

This command is repeated in #405.

There are a few days for Judaism when people fast, but this is the only fast commandment identified within Torah. It is a physical exercise for denying the flesh by not eating and/or drinking for that day. Some people cannot do without eating and/or drinking for medication purposes and other medical issues. If you are in that situation, then find another way to deny your flesh. What that looks like could be different from person to person. With command #240, we cover all the restrictions for Yom Kippur.

#403. Leviticus 23:28 ~ Yom Kippur is a Shabbat

Positive
Loving Abba
Unconditional

NOTE: Leviticus 23:29-30 shows us how important keeping Yom Kippur is for Israel.

#404. Leviticus 23:31 ~ Do No Work at All on Yom Kippur

Negative
Loving Abba
Unconditional

See #240 for more information.

#405. Leviticus 23:32 ~ To Fast on Yom Kippur

Positive
Loving Abba
Unconditional

See #240 & #402 for more information.

NOTE: In a careful review of Isaiah chapter 58, the Shabbat spoken of in Isaiah 58:13-14 is Yom Kippur. However, in the spirit of being Torah maximalists, it may not be a bad idea to apply this to all Shabbats.

#406. Isaiah 58:13-14 ~ Do Not Do Your Pleasure on Yom Kippur

Negative
Loving Abba
Unconditional

This command is repeated in Isaiah 58:13-14 (409) & Isaiah 58:13-14 (410).

On this day, unless an emergency occurs, all focus should be on Adonai. Do not play video games, watch sports, or engage in entertainment. If you must watch something, let it be Bible-focused. On this day, there is no internet surfing, social media scroll of doom on your phone/tablet, or talking about business, politics, TV shows, studying for school, or any of our interests or things you need to do on earth. All focus is on Adonai, repenting from our sins, and connecting to Him. As stated before, as those striving to be Torah maximalists, it would be good to develop this for all Shabbats.

#407. Isaiah 58:13-14 ~ To Call Yom Kippur a Delight

Positive
Loving Abba
Unconditional

#408. Isaiah 58:13-14 ~ To Esteem Yom Kippur

Positive
Loving Abba
Unconditional

#409. Isaiah 58:13-14 ~ To Not Do Your Desires on Yom Kippur

Negative
Loving Abba
Unconditional

See #406 for more information.

#410. Isaiah 58:13-14 ~ To Not Speak Your Own Words on Yom Kippur

Negative
Loving Abba
Unconditional

See #406 for more information.

#411. Leviticus 23:34 ~ To Observe the Feast of Sukkot

Positive
Loving Abba
Unconditional

See #143 for more information.

#412. Leviticus 23:35 ~ The First Day of Sukkot is a Shabbat

Positive
Loving Abba
Unconditional

See #143 for more information.

#413. Leviticus 23:36 ~ To Sacrifice 7 Days for Sukkot

Positive
Loving People
Conditional

#414. Leviticus 23:36 ~ The 8th Day of Sukkot is a Shabbat

Positive
Loving Abba
Unconditional

See #143 for more information.

The 8th day is also known as Shemini Atzeret. Traditionally, it is the day the Torah is reset back to Genesis 1:1 and the yearly Torah cycle begin anew for the following Shabbat. This also represents Revelation chapter 21.

#415. Leviticus 23:36 ~ To Sacrifice on the 8th Day of Sukkot

Positive
Loving People
Conditional

#416. Leviticus 23:39 ~ To Gather the Fruit of the Land for Sukkot

Positive
Loving People
Conditional

#417. Leviticus 23:39 ~ The 1st and 8th Day of Sukkot is a Shabbat

Positive
Loving Abba
Unconditional

See #143 for more information.

#418. Leviticus 23:40 ~ To Gather Good Trees, Branches, Palm of Trees, Twigs of Leafy Trees, and Willows for Sukkot

Positive
Loving Abba
Conditional

These are items expected to be collected from the land, which is why this command is conditional. However, it doesn't mean we cannot do a memorial exercise wherever we are in the world. Some people order these items from the land each year to keep this command.

#419. Leviticus 23:41 ~ To Celebrate Sukkot for 7 Days

Positive
Loving Abba
Unconditional

See #143 for more information.

#420. Leviticus 23:42 ~ To Dwell in Booths During Sukkot

Positive
Loving Abba
Unconditional

See #143 for more information.

Temporary dwellings today could be booths built in the backyard, travel trailers/5th wheels, RVs, tents, Hotels, Airbnb, VRBO, cabins, yachts, boats with cabins, or just about any place that can be viewed as a temporary dwelling. Ideally, it would be awesome to go to Israel and celebrate the feasts there, but most people cannot afford that. Around the world, many Messianic groups gather on camping grounds to follow this instruction. Some get together at convention centers and stay in hotels. I've heard congregations consider cruise ships or island getaways for this feast.

Some people have taught that living in booths is a reminder that Israel dwelt in the wilderness for 40 years, but that is debatable. The spring feasts of Passover, Unleavened Bread, the Feast of First Fruits, and Shavuot are all about things that have already happened. However, the Fall Feasts, or High Holy Days, all represent things that we are waiting to happen. We will hear trumpets when Yeshua returns. Yom Kippur represents Judgement Day. Sukkot represents the millennium reign, Shemini Atzeret represents the new beginning when we will have a new heaven and earth, and the Heavenly Father comes down with a New Jerusalem to dwell with mankind forever.

#421. Leviticus 24:2-4 ~ The High Priest's Duties with the Lamp Outside the Veil of Witness

Positive
Loving Abba
Conditional

#422. Leviticus 24:5-9 ~ Instructions for the Bread of the Tabernacle

Positive
Loving Abba
Conditional

#423. Leviticus 24:10-16 ~ Do Not Blaspheme the Name YHWH

Negative
Loving Abba
Unconditional

See #49 for more information.

#424. Leviticus 24:10-16 ~ To Execute the Ones Who Blaspheme the Name of the Heavenly Father

Positive
Loving Abba
Conditional

NOTE: In Leviticus 24:10-16, we see the proper steps for executing people within Israel. Contrary to popular belief, it was never meant to be a random act of a mob. It required a trial and at least two witnesses (687).

#425. Leviticus 24:17 ~ A Man Who Commits Murder Must Be Executed

Positive
Loving Abba
Conditional

See #56 for more information.

#426. Leviticus 24:18 ~ If a Man Kills a Beast That Belongs to Someone Else, They Must Replace the Animal

Positive
Loving People
Unconditional

This command is repeated in #428.

#427. Leviticus 24:19-20 ~ If a Man Strikes a Man and Leaves Lasting Bodily Injury, Punishment cannot be beyond the Injury

Negative
Loving People
Unconditional

See #85 for more information.

#428. Leviticus 24:21 If a Man Kills a Beast that Belongs to Someone Else, They Must Replace the Animal

Positive
Loving People
Unconditional

First seen in #426. The fact that this teaching is repeated so close to each other is a strong sign that the Heavenly Father desires His people to take full responsibility for our actions when we do wrong to others, a true example of loving one another.

#429. Leviticus 24:21 ~ A man who Murders Another Man Must be executed

Positive
Loving People
Conditional

See #56 for more information.

#430. Leviticus 25:2-7 ~ The 7th Year Shabbat of the Land

Positive
Loving People
Conditional

Begins on Yom Kippur; see #432.

#431. Leviticus 25:8 ~ 7 Times 7 Years is the Year of Jubilee

Positive
Loving People
Conditional

The year of Jubilee is when all debts are forgiven, Hebrew slaves can be set free, property and houses seized by another tribe can be repurchased, and the land gets a break from farming activities. It is unclear exactly when Israel lost track of the year of Jubilee, but many believe it started with the Babylonian captivity. It is unclear if we ever got back on track after that point. It does not appear that Israel was following this command during the Roman occupation in the first century.

Today, some people believe that the year of Jubilee was restarted in 1948, when the world government of Israel was re-established; without solid proof, this is merely wishful thinking. Additionally, they do not observe this practice in the land. Because there were never solid dates marked for when Israel kept this command, there is no way to know when the year of Jubilee is today. However, whenever the right situation arises, we can individually keep the spirit of the year of Jubilee when people owe us.

#432. Leviticus 25:9 ~ To Sound the Trumpet on Yom Kippur for the Year of Jubilee

Positive
Loving Abba
Conditional

The year of Jubilee begins on Yom Kippur. This shows us that Yom Kippur is the beginning of the year for Israel, while the 1st of Nisan in the spring begins the calendar of months.

#433. Leviticus 25:10 ~ The Year of Jubilee is Set Apart

Positive
Loving People
Conditional

#434. Leviticus 25:10 ~ The Year of Jubilee is the Year Israelite Slaves Are Set Free

Positive
Loving People
Conditional

This would also include slaves from other countries who covenanted with the Heavenly Father.

#435. Leviticus 25:11-12 ~ Do Not Sow or Reap That Which Grows by Itself or Gather from Untended Vines During the Year of Jubilee

Negative
Loving Abba
Conditional

#436. Leviticus 25:13 ~ For Every Hebrew Slave to Return to Their Property

Positive
Loving People
Conditional

#437. Leviticus 25:14-16 ~ To Be Above Reproach in Buying and Selling Due to the Jubilee Year

Positive
Loving People
Unconditional

The Year of Jubilee occurred every 50 years; it was a time when land returned to its original owners or their heirs (Leviticus 25:10-13). Because land ownership was temporary until the next Jubilee, the price of land was to be determined by the number of years remaining until the Jubilee. The command not to "take advantage of each other" emphasizes ethical conduct in business dealings. It reveals the Heavenly Father's concern for justice, ensuring neither party exploits the other's vulnerability or ignorance for this transaction.

#438. Leviticus 25:17 ~ To Not Cheat One Another

Negative
Loving People
Conditional

This command is specifically for the Year of Jubilee; however, its spiritual principle can apply to anything we do. As covenanted people of Israel, we are expected to be above reproach in anything that we do because we represent the Heavenly Father. Our conduct in the world reflects upon His Name.

#439. Leviticus 25:18-22 ~ To Keep the Commands for the Year of Jubilee

Positive
Loving People
Conditional

#440. Leviticus 25:23 ~ The Land Belongs to the Heavenly Father and Cannot be Sold

Negative
Loving Abba
Unconditional

#441. Leviticus 25:24 ~ To Redeem the Land

Positive
Loving People
Conditional

#442. Leviticus 25:25-28 ~ Instructions to Redeem Land Sold

Positive
Loving People
Conditional

#443. Leviticus 25:29-30 ~ Instructions to Redeem a House in a Walled City

Positive
Loving People
Conditional

#444. Leviticus 25:31 ~ Instructions to Redeem Houses of Villages

Positive
Loving People
Conditional

#445. Leviticus 25:32-34 ~ Instructions for Redeeming Levite Property

Positive
Loving People
Conditional

#446. Leviticus 25:35 ~ To Help an Israelite Who Has Become Poor

Positive
Loving People
Unconditional

This is another command that shows an expectation of financial strength among the people of Israel. Today, we must be careful when trying to obey this command. Just because someone says they are Messianic or covenanted doesn't mean much. Are they in the proper covenant relationship with the Heavenly Father? You have the right to find out what caused their financial ruin; this information is useful to determine the best way to help them; otherwise, they can simply be taking advantage of you. Use proper discernment in such situations.

#447. Leviticus 25:36-37 ~ To Not Profit from an Israelite Who Has Become Poor

Positive
Loving People
Unconditional

#448. Leviticus 25:39-41 ~ Instructions for a Hebrew Who Sells Himself as a Servant

Negative
Loving People
Conditional

#449. Leviticus 25:42 ~ To Not Sell Hebrews as Slaves

Negative
Loving People
Conditional

#450. Leviticus 25:43 ~ Do Not Rule Harshly Over Hebrew Servants

Negative
Loving People
Conditional

For most people in civilized countries, this command means nothing because slavery is a thing of the past. Unfortunately, slavery is still a legal practice in small parts of the world.

#451. Leviticus 25:44-46 ~ Instructions for Non-Hebrew Slaves

Positive
Loving Abba
Conditional

#452. Leviticus 25:47-55 ~ Instructions to Redeem a Hebrew Sold to a Non-Hebrew

Positive
Loving People
Conditional

Non-covenanted people within the land are expected to keep Torah while living in the land. This command is not speaking about Hebrew slaves sold to other countries, a practice not allowed according to Torah; this command is for a situation where a non-covenanted person who lives within the land buys a slave.

#453. Leviticus 26:1 ~ Do Not Make Idols

Negative
Loving Abba
Unconditional

See #48 for more information.

#454. Leviticus 26:1 ~ Do Not Set Up Carved Images or Pillars

Negative
Loving Abba
Unconditional

See #48 for more information.

#455. Leviticus 26:1 ~ Do Not Place Stone Images (For worship)

Negative
Loving Abba
Unconditional

See #48 for more information.

#456. Leviticus 26:2 ~ To Guard the Shabbats

Positive
Loving Abba
Unconditional

See #50 for more information.

#457. Leviticus 26:2 ~ To Respect the Set Apart Place

Positive
Loving Abba
Unconditional

NOTE: Leviticus 26:3-13, blessings for obeying the Heavenly Father. Leviticus 26:14-39, the curses for disobeying the Heavenly Father. Leviticus 26:40-45, The good news of the Bible. The good news message does not change throughout the entire Bible.

#458. Leviticus 27:1-28 ~ Instructions to Estimate the Value of a Promise

Positive
Loving People
Conditional

In today's world, this is like determining the collateral value of a loan.

#459. Leviticus 27:29 ~ Those Under the Ban Cannot be Ransomed/Redeemed and Are to be Executed

Positive
Loving Abba
Conditional

Someone who is under the ban is subject to the death penalty. Such individuals cannot be redeemed, ransomed, or work it off. Based on what Yeshua says in Matthew 12:22-32, those who blaspheme the set-apart Spirit can also fall under this category.

#460. Leviticus 27:30 ~ Tithe Belongs to the Heavenly Father

Positive
Loving Abba
Unconditional

When we tithe, we are not tithing to organizations or people. We tithe unto Adonai. What leadership does with the money is between them and the Heavenly Father. Consider this first if you suspect that the leadership is mismanaging the money. As stated before, it is possible that you need to grow in trust and submission to your leadership. If your suspicions prove correct, look for a congregation with leadership you can trust. If you cannot trust leaders with money, you will never truly submit to their authority. That is a problem because it undermines the vertical structure of the kingdom.

#461. Leviticus 27:31 ~ To Add 1/5 to Redeemed Tithe

Positive
Loving People
Unconditional

According to the Jewish sages, this command is connected to the second tithe and Sukkot. Back then, tithing was animals and/or produce. Once the tithe was given, if you did not have resources for the feast, you could redeem your tithe for its coin value so you could spend it on the feast only. An additional 1/5 would be given to Levites for this service.

#462. Leviticus 27:32 ~ The Tithe from Herd or Flock is Set Apart to the Heavenly Father

Positive
Loving Abba
Unconditional

The Industrial Revolution changed how most people work. Today, many of us do not tend to herd or flocks, and we do not farm; instead, we own businesses, have careers, or jobs, and our tithes are monetary. That does not make them less set-apart. When we tithe, we still do it from the heart to put Adonai first in our finances and trust in His words. This is a heart check category, and it is a hard one for many to overcome. When it comes to money, it is hard not to be selfish, especially if you are not in a place of financial strength and every penny counts. If you are tithing for the blessings or the challenge that the Heavenly Father made in Malachi 3:10, you could have the wrong motive. When you can tithe and/or make offerings out of gratitude, that is a good sign of overcoming the world. When it comes to tithing, the heart matters; it is the difference between making it a chore or an act of worship.

#463. Leviticus 27:33 ~ To Not Inquire the Condition of the Tithe

Negative
Loving The Father
Conditional

Once the tithe is given, it is no longer your concern. We give to Adonai, not people or organizations. If you believe leadership is mismanaging the money, look for another congregation with leadership you can trust. How can you truly submit to a spiritual authority if you cannot trust them with money? Before questioning leadership about finances, look within; it could be that you need to grow in trusting people or submitting to leadership. When it comes to tithes, do not make the mistake of thinking that a congregation or the Heavenly Father owes you anything. Tithing should never become a tool of entitlement, a chore, or seen as a common bill. It is an act of gratefulness and a way to place the Heavenly Father first in your finances. As the Author and Perfecter of our lives, He allows us to have the comprehension and skills to support ourselves.

#464. Leviticus 27:33 ~ To Not Exchange

Negative
Loving Abba
Conditional

This command speaks of not exchanging the tithe from the flock or herd. Because of this command, such practices were most likely frowned upon, and probably the reason why I couldn't find any solid information on it.

#465. Leviticus 27:33 ~ If it is Exchanged

Negative
Loving Abba
Conditional

This command is for when people get an exchange of the tithe from the flock or herd. As stated before, I could not find any solid information on this practice. It was most likely frowned upon based on Command #464, or something seldom done in dire situations.

#466. Numbers 3:6-10 ~ The Duties of the Levites

Positive
Loving People
Conditional

#467. Numbers 3:10 ~ To Execute Those That Should Not Come Near

Positive
Loving Abba
Conditional

#468. Numbers 5:6-10 ~ Instructions for Confessing Sins and Paying Restitution

Positive
Loving Abba and People
Unconditional

#469. Numbers 5:11-31 ~ Instructions to Test if a Wife Committed Adultery

Positive
Loving Abba
Conditional

#470. Numbers 6:1-21 ~ Instructions for a Nazirite Vow

Positive
Loving Abba
Conditional

This is what Paul helped with in Acts 21:20-26. This command gives us the most detailed information we have on Nazirite vows. We do not know what they are for or when to make one. These verses are not presented as an introduction to this act, which leads to the idea that this was a common practice at the time, like salt covenants. It is most likely that Judah stopped this practice when the temple was destroyed in 70 AD.

#471. Numbers 6:22-27 ~ Aaron's/The High Priest's Blessing Upon Israel

Positive
Loving People
Unconditional

#472. Numbers 8:24-26 ~ Levites Work Until 50, Then Retire

Positive
Loving People
Conditional

This is an excellent goal for everyone. To work so that you can retire at 50. Most people who turn 50 can still enjoy life. Do not think of retirement as the world does. We are designed to be productive until our bodies give out. Retirement should be an opportunity to focus full-time on the productive things you want to do to contribute to society and/or your congregation.

#473. Numbers 9:2-3 ~ To Observe Passover at its Appointed Time

Positive
Loving Abba
Unconditional

See #13 for more information.

#474. Numbers 9:10-12 ~ To Observe the Alternate Date of Passover if Needed

Positive
Loving Abba
Unconditional

This is not an optional day; it is an alternate day if you cannot observe Passover on the 14th of Nisan with a legitimate reason. The next command clearly states that we are to observe Passover at its appointed time. The people who would use this day are those unclean and cannot be clean by the time of the feast, people who suffer from an illness, hospitalization, death in the family, or other serious life reasons that would prevent them from keeping Passover on the 14th of Nisan.

#475. Numbers 9:13 ~ To Observe Passover at its Appointed Time

Positive
Loving Abba
Unconditional

See #13 for more information.

#476. Numbers 9:14 ~ Instructions for Non-Hebrews to Observe the Instructions of Passover

Positive
Loving Abba
Unconditional

This is not a conflicting command, as some people would believe. If a non-covenanted person wants to observe the Passover, they need to follow the requirements, such as Exodus 12:48. Once again, this is the only feast not open to the public.

#477. Numbers 9:14 ~ One Torah for All

Positive
Loving Abba
Unconditional

See #30 for more information.

NOTE: Numbers 11:16-20, complaining is the same as rejecting the Heavenly Father.

NOTE: Numbers 12:6-8, the Heavenly Father speaks to Moses plainly.

NOTE: Numbers 12:9-15, leprosy connected to La Shon Hara, the evil tongue.

#478. Numbers 15:2-5 & 11-12 ~ Instructions for Lamb Sacrifices

Positive
Loving Abba
Conditional

#479. Numbers 15:6-7 & 11-12 ~ Instructions for Ram Sacrifices

Positive
Loving Abba
Conditional

#480. Numbers 15:8-12 ~ Instructions for Bull Sacrifices

Positive
Loving Abba
Conditional

#481. Numbers 15:13-16 ~ One Torah for All

Positive
Loving Abba
Unconditional

See #30 for more information. Moses wrote this command 3 times. The concept of "One Torah for All" makes it impossible to believe that the Heavenly Father has different expectations for people joining Israel from the nations.

#482. Numbers 15:22-26 ~ Instructions for When Israel Sins Corporately by Mistake

Positive
Loving Abba
Conditional

#483. Numbers 15:27-28 ~ Instructions for Individuals Who Sin by Mistake

Positive
Loving Abba
Conditional

#484. Numbers 15:29-31 ~ Do Not Sin on Purpose

Negative
Loving Abba
Unconditional

To sin on purpose is rebellion. It is people making a conscious choice to put Adonai in a status that is less than set-apart. To sin on purpose is to declare that what you want is more important than the Heavenly Father, or it states that you know better than Him. This is why there are no provisions within Torah for sinning on purpose. When you choose to sin, there are no sacrifices that cover for that. People who sin on purpose place themselves under the ban (459). Many people believe that Yeshua's death on the cross covers all sins; there is no reason to believe that rebellion is one of those things covered.

In contrast, sinning by mistake involves coercion, temptation, being misinformed, deception, possibly forced, or committing a sin without even knowing you've done it. It is the difference between why David was forgiven and why Saul lost the kingdom. This is a very interesting topic because it begs the question, what happens to the Christians who are taught that Torah is done away with? No one truly knows, but I believe that the Heavenly Father's plan is wise, fair, and just. He will handle the situation accordingly.

NOTE: Numbers 15:32-36 show us an example of intentional sinning.

#485. Numbers 15:38-40 ~ Instructions to Wear Tzitzit (Tassels)

Positive
Loving People
Unconditional

Repeated in Deuteronomy 22:12 (749).

Over the years, I've had conversations with "Messianic" believers who think they do not need to wear the tassels because they are "filled with the Set-Apart Spirit". However, the purpose of the tassels and the role of the Set-Apart Spirit are two different things. The Set-Apart Spirit guides us in all truths (John 16:13). When you are filled with the Set-Apart Spirit, you will be convicted about sin, righteousness, and judgments (John 16:8). The tassels are about remembering the commands of the Heavenly Father (Numbers 15:39). Here is a question that most people do not think about regarding the tassels: Are the tassels for you to remember, or to help the people around you remember?

The place where tassels are worn on the body isn't somewhere we typically look at throughout the day. Once we put them on, unless we walk by a mirror, your hands happen to graze them, or you move to a position where you can see them, they are pretty much "set it and forget it". As you go throughout your day, it is easy to forget you have them on; however, everyone around you can see them. This command is about loving people because as you wear tassels, people around you see them, and it helps them to remember. Of course, this is only true if you are in a community of people who honor Torah, for everyone else, they are a mystery and can open doors to verbally share your faith.

If you truly are filled with the Set-Apart Spirit, you'd be moved to keep this command from within. Unfortunately, within the Messianic or Hebrew Roots community, it is far more common for people not to wear tassels because they value their appearance more than the Heavenly Father. Some people make the excuse that tassels should be on the corners of garments, not on belt loops, suggesting that the Heavenly Father would have overlooked changing human fashion; but ultimately, does that really matter? Others would say you have to make it yourself, which is not a difficult task (749), and what about the people who cannot make them because of handicaps? Wearing them is the most important part of this command.

#486. Numbers 15:40 ~ Remember and Do the Commands of the Heavenly Father

Positive
Loving Abba
Unconditional

This command is one reason why yearly Torah cycle readings are beneficial. With each passing cycle and as we grow spiritually each year, Torah reveals new insights and lessons, deepening our understanding with each cycle. If you are not a part of a congregation that does the Torah cycle, leave and find one.

#487. Numbers 18:1 ~ The Levites Bear the Sins Against the Set Apart Place and the Priesthood

Positive
Loving Abba
Unconditional

#488. Numbers 18:7 ~ For the Levites to Guard the Priesthood

Positive
Loving Abba
Unconditional

#489. Numbers 18:7 ~ No Stranger is Allowed to Come Near

Negative
Loving Abba
Unconditional

This command is speaking about the Tent of Appointment; See Numbers 18:22.

#490. Numbers 18:8-15 & 18-21 & 24 ~ All Offerings Belong to the Priesthood

Positive
Loving People
Unconditional

This command is connected to Leviticus 27:33 (463). Sadly, it is not unheard of to hear people feeling entitled to get their tithes back, or for people who believe they are entitled to benevolence because they tithe. Tithing does not lead to you having an emergency fund. It does not work that way. If your congregation has the resources to help you out with benevolence, if needed, that is great! If not, it shouldn't matter. Once it is given, that is it. The priests were free to do whatever they wanted with the offerings. The same thing applies today when we tithe. As stated with previous commands, if you cannot trust that your leaders are using the tithes properly, either you have trust issues, or you need to find leadership you can trust.

#491. Numbers 18:16-17 ~ Instructions for Ransom

Positive
Loving Abba
Unconditional

Every firstborn male child in Israel belongs to the Heavenly Father. Judaism teaches that this is a reminder of how Elohim spared the Israelites' firstborn during the Passover (Exodus 12). Instead of being dedicated to tabernacle service (Scriptures hint that this was the original plan before the golden calf issue), these children were "redeemed" (bought back) by paying five shekels of silver to the priests when the child was one month old. The redemption price (about 100-140 grams of silver by today's estimates) was paid to the Levites, who served in place of the firstborn (See Numbers 3:12-13 for more content). This act acknowledges the Heavenly Father's sovereignty over life while allowing families to retain their children. The "sanctuary shekel" ensured a standardized measure for fairness. This teaching reflects the same principle of fairness and stewardship seen in Leviticus 25:14-16, where transactions (like land sales) were regulated to prevent exploitation. The fixed price ensures no one is overcharged or cheated in fulfilling a sacred duty, it also promotes the idea that we are all equal. This command is unconditional because it is not tied to anything that would prevent us from doing it today. The reason most people do not do it is that most congregations do not administer it.

#492. Numbers 18:22-23 ~ Only Levites Come Near the Tent of Appointment

Positive
Loving Abba
Unconditional

#493. Numbers 18:26-28 ~ To Tithe 10% (1st Tithe)

Positive
Loving Abba & People
Unconditional

This command was directed to the Levites because they were not producing like everyone else. Their daily work was devoted to the ministry, serving Israel and the Heavenly Father full-time. Although this command is directed at the Levites, it is not just for Levites. Abraham gives us precedence in Genesis 14:20 when He gave a 10% tithe to Melchizedek, and his grandson Jacob pledged a 10% tithe to Adonai in Genesis 28:22. Both examples show that the 10% tithe was something commonly understood way before Israel left Egypt, and of course, neither Abraham nor Jacob was Levite.

This command is directly connected to Malachi 3:10, a verse also pointed to the priesthood of that time (Start at Malachi 2:1 for the complete thought), it is highly abused in mainstream religion today. However, life has proven that the challenge given in Malachi 3:10 is open to anyone. Many wealthy people have publicly claimed that consistently giving 10% of their money to a church, synagogue, or the poor is the key to their financial success. This is the first of three tithes we are expected to give within the Torah. The 2nd tithe is seen in #642, and the 3rd tithe is seen in #646.

Unfortunately, many who first come into the Torah lifestyle are not capable of tithing 10%, let alone 30% of their income at the beginning of their walk. Allow this command to be the start of a healthy financial motivator for you to become financially strong. If you are motivated to make more money to tithe properly, that is something that the Heavenly Father can get behind. In the meantime, if you are struggling financially and cannot tithe 10%, start with offerings for your 1st, 2nd, and 3rd tithes until you can do the full 1st tithe; then 1st tithe and offerings for 2nd tithe until you can do 1st and 2nd tithe; and so on until you can do a full tithe for all three and comfortably live off of 70% of your income. All 3 tithes serve a different purpose, designed for your benefit. Very few people can make quick adjustments to fix their finances right away; for most people, it can take anywhere from 3 months to 3 years, but it can be done with the proper motivation.

#494. Numbers 18:29-32 ~ For the Levites to Give the Best Offerings to the Heavenly Father

Positive
Loving Abba
Conditional

This is something that was lacking in Malachi chapters 2-3.

#495. Numbers 19:11 ~ Touching a Dead Body Makes You Unclean for 7 Days

Negative
Loving Abba
Unconditional

#496. Numbers 19:12 ~ To Wash Yourself on the 3rd Day if You Touch the Dead

Positive
Loving Abba
Unconditional

This command instructs the washing of the body on the third day after contact with a dead body. Even if you wash every day, it is that third day that begins the purification process. In this command, we have a direct connection to Yeshua, who was dead for 3 days and 3 nights (Matthew

12:40). After his resurrection, Yeshua told Mary Magdalene, "Do not hold on to Me, for I have not yet ascended to My Father. But go to My brothers and say to them, 'I am ascending to My Father and your Father, and to My Elohim and your Elohim (John 20:17)." According to Acts 1:3, Yeshua stayed with the Apostles for 40 days demonstrating his teaching for going above and beyond for this command.

#497. Numbers 19:13 ~ Not Washing Yourself After Touching the Dead on the 3rd Day is a Sin

Negative
Loving Abba
Unconditional

Repeated in command #500.

#498. Numbers 19:14-15 & 17-19 & 21-22 ~ Instructions for People Who Live in a House Where Someone Dies

Positive
Loving Abba
Conditional

#499. Numbers 19:16 ~ Touching the Dead

Negative
Loving Abba
Unconditional

#500. Numbers 19:20 ~ Not Washing Yourself After Touching the Dead on the 3rd Day is a Sin

Negative
Loving Abba
Unconditional

First seen in #497.

#501. Numbers 28:2-8 ~ Instructions for Daily Offerings

Positive
Loving Abba
Conditional

#502. Numbers 28:9-10 ~ Instructions for Shabbat Offerings

Positive
Loving Abba
Conditional

#503. Numbers 28:11-15 ~ Instructions for Monthly Offerings

Positive
Loving Abba
Conditional

#504. Numbers 28:16 ~ To Observe Passover on its Appointed Time

Positive
Loving Abba
Unconditional

See #13 for more information.

#505. Numbers 28:17 ~ To Observe the Feast of Unleavened Bread on its Appointed Time

Positive
Loving Abba
Unconditional

See #14 for more information.

#506. Numbers 28:18 ~ The First Day of Unleavened Bread is a Shabbat

Positive
Loving Abba
Unconditional

See #15 for more information.

#507. Numbers 28:19-24 ~ Instructions for Unleavened Bread Offerings

Positive
Loving People
Conditional

#508. Numbers 28:25 ~ The 7th Day of Unleavened Bread is a Shabbat

Positive
Loving Abba
Unconditional

See #15 for more information.

#509. Numbers 28:26-31 ~ Instructions for Shavuot Offerings

Positive
Loving Abba
Conditional

#510. Numbers 29:1 ~ To Observe the Feast of Trumpets

Positive
Loving Abba
Unconditional

First seen in #399.

#511. Numbers 29:2-6 ~ Instructions for Feast of Trumpets Offerings

Positive
Loving Abba
Conditional

#512. Numbers 29:7 ~ To Observe Yom Kippur

Positive
Loving Abba
Unconditional

See #240 for more information.

#513. Numbers 29:8-11 ~ Instructions for Yom Kippur Offerings

Positive
Loving Abba
Conditional

#514. Numbers 29:12 ~ To Observe the Feast of Sukkot

Positive
Loving Abba
Unconditional

See #143 for more information.

#515. Numbers 29:13-40 ~ Instructions for Sukkot Offerings

Positive
Loving Abba
Conditional

#516. Numbers 30:2 ~ For Men to Keep Their Vows to the Heavenly Father

Positive
Loving Abba
Unconditional

This command is connected to:

- Leviticus 3:1-5 (165)
- Leviticus 5:4 (178)
- Matthew 5:33-37 (833)

A vow made to Adonai or in His name is taken extremely seriously because it takes on the Authority and power that comes with His name. When Adonai has fulfilled His part of the vow, a peace offering is expected as a public display of gratitude for Adonai keeping His word (165). Including Adonai in a vow should not be taken lightly or rashly (178). Vows that include Adonai are so serious that they are optional (772). As covenanted people, the Heavenly Father takes our vows seriously. However, people have abused this. In addressing this command, Yeshua discourages including Adonai in vows (836), directing us to let our "Yes" be "Yes" and our "No" be "No" (Matthew 5:37).

#517. Numbers 30:3-16 ~ Instructions for When a Woman Makes a Vow

Positive
Loving Abba
Unconditional

#518. Numbers 35:1-8 ~ Cities for Levites

Positive
Loving People
Conditional

#519. Numbers 35:9-34 ~ Cities of Refuge

Positive
Loving People
Conditional

See #76 for more information.

NOTE: Numbers 36 speaks of the marriage of female Heirs so that the land that belongs to one tribe stays within that tribe.

#520. Deuteronomy 4:1 ~ To Listen to Moses

Positive
Loving Abba
Unconditional

Also see Exodus 19:9.

#521. Deuteronomy 4:2 ~ To Not Alter the Words of Torah

Negative
Loving Abba
Unconditional

Commands #520 and #521 are foundational characteristics of Yeshua. Throughout the books of Matthew, Mark, Luke, and John, Yeshua honors and stands by the words written through Moses. Some people believe that Yeshua stood against Jewish teachings and the Torah, but that is not an accurate view. Yeshua only spoke against Jewish teachings that contradicted or canceled what Moses wrote, and he exposed the hypocrisy within their teachings. The best place to see an example of Yeshua living by this command is Matthew 4:1-11.

When Satan tried to make Yeshua abuse his authority (Matthew 4:3), Yeshua replied with Deuteronomy 8:3. When Satan twisted Psalms 91:11-12 to get Yeshua to test the Heavenly Father (Matthew 4:6), Yeshua fired back with Deuteronomy 6:16. When Satan tried to get Yeshua to worship him (Matthew 4:9), Yeshua used Deuteronomy 6:13 to fight against his offer. In Matthew 4:1-11, Yeshua shows us that we can depend on the words of Moses to fight the enemy, another important running theme throughout the Bible. Matthew 4:1-11 shows us a very important message that many people ignore.

#522. Deuteronomy 4:6 ~ To Guard Torah

Positive
Loving Abba
Unconditional

See #247 for more information.

#523. Deuteronomy 4:6 ~ For Torah to be Our Wisdom and Understanding

Positive
Loving Abba
Unconditional

This is another crucial command within Torah. This instruction is at the core of what being "Born Again" is truly all about. Before we came to Yeshua, we lived by what we thought was right and wrong. Through Yeshua's guiding words and his example of how we should live, Torah becomes our wisdom and understanding. Torah is the knowledge that transforms us to the likeness of Yeshua. This is why Paul said, "*Don't be conformed to this world, but be transformed by the renewing of your mind, so that you may prove what is the good, well-pleasing, and perfect will of the Heavenly Father* (Romans 12:2)." Paul was not referring to what most people call the "New Testament", that was nothing but a bunch of letters (most that he wrote) floating around until the late 2nd century, some of it wasn't even constructed when Paul died.

#524. Deuteronomy 4:9 ~ To Carefully Guard Yourself

Positive
Loving Abba
Unconditional

This teaching shows that we must be careful not to stray from the previous command (523).

#525. Deuteronomy 4:9 ~ Do Not Forget Torah

Positive
Loving Abba
Unconditional

It is repeated in:

- Deuteronomy 4:15 (528)
- Deuteronomy 4:23 (530)

This is another command that shows us that the Heavenly Father has no plans for Israel to deviate from Torah. People who teach that Torah has expired are not anointed nor appointed by our One True Heavenly Father.

#526. Deuteronomy 4:9 ~ To Teach Your Children and Grandchildren About Torah

Positive
Loving People
Unconditional

This instruction is repeated in:

- Deuteronomy 6:7 (559)
- Deuteronomy 6:20-24 (559)
- Deuteronomy 11:19 (594)

Also see #21 for more information.

#527. Deuteronomy 4:10 ~ To Fear the Heavenly Father

Positive
Loving Abba
Unconditional

See #287 for more information.

#528. Deuteronomy 4:15 ~ To Carefully Guard Yourself

Positive
Loving Abba
Unconditional

See #525 for more information.

#529. Deuteronomy 4:16-19 ~ Do Not Worship Idols

Negative
Loving Abba
Unconditional

See #48 for more information.

#530. Deuteronomy 4:23 ~ To Guard Yourself from Forgetting Torah

Positive
Loving Abba
Unconditional

See #247 and #525 for more information. Another example of the idea that the Heavenly Father will not stray away from Torah.

#531. Deuteronomy 4:23 ~ Do Not Forget the Covenant

Negative
Loving Abba
Unconditional

See Exodus 19:5-7. Another affirmation showing that the Heavenly Father will never deviate from what He had Moses write.

NOTE: Deuteronomy 4:24-31 is another example of the good news.

#532. Deuteronomy 4:35 ~ The Heavenly Father Has No Equal

Negative
Loving Abba
Unconditional

This is a teaching that Yeshua strongly advocated throughout his ministry. Look at the temptation in the wilderness (Matthew 4:10, Luke 4:8). If you compare how the enemy communicated with Elohim in the book of Job versus how he communicates with Yeshua, even the enemy does not see Yeshua equal to the Heavenly Father. Other examples where Yeshua emphasizes that the Heavenly Father is above all are found in the greatest commandment teaching (Matthew 22:37-38, Mark 12:29-30), the Lord's Prayer (Matthew 6:9-13, Luke 11:2-4), and Yeshua's teaching on hypocrisy (Matthew 6:1-6). More examples can be found in John 14:28, John 5:30, John 6:38, John 12:49-50, and Mark 10:18. Within all these instructions, Yeshua makes it very clear that the Heavenly Father is above all with no equals!

#533. Deuteronomy 4:40 ~ To Guard Torah

Positive
Loving Abba
Unconditional

See #247 for more information.

#534. Deuteronomy 4:41-43 ~ Cities of Refuge

Positive
Loving People
Conditional

See #76 for more information.

#535. Deuteronomy 5:1 ~ To Learn Torah

Positive
Loving Abba
Unconditional

#536. Deuteronomy 5:1 ~ To Guard and Do Torah

Positive
Loving Abba
Unconditional

See #247 for more information.

#537. Deuteronomy 5:6 ~ To Acknowledge YHWH Who Brought Israel out of Egypt

Positive
Loving Abba
Unconditional

See #38 for more information.

#538. Deuteronomy 5:7 ~ To Worship YHWH Alone

Positive
Loving Abba
Unconditional

#539. Deuteronomy 5:8-9 ~ Do Not Create Carved Images to Worship

Negative
Loving Abba
Unconditional

See #48 for more information.

NOTE: Deuteronomy 5:9-10: To not follow the Heavenly Father's commands is hating Him, and to keep His commands is loving Him. This doesn't change throughout the entire scriptures.

#540. Deuteronomy 5:11 ~ Do Not Disgrace the Name of YHWH

Negative
Loving Abba
Unconditional

See #49 for more information.

#541. Deuteronomy 5:12 ~ To Guard the Weekly Shabbat

Positive
Loving Abba
Unconditional

See #50 for more information.

#542. Deuteronomy 5:13-14 ~ To Work 6 Days and Rest on Shabbat

Positive
Loving People
Unconditional

See #51 and #52 for more information.

#543. Deuteronomy 5:15 ~ To Remember That We Were Slaves in Egypt and the Heavenly Father Freed Us

Positive
Loving Abba
Unconditional

Repeated in:

- Deuteronomy 15:15 (650)
- Deuteronomy 24:18 (789)
- Deuteronomy 24:22 (793)

Also, see #38 for more information.

#544. Deuteronomy 5:16 ~ To Respect Your Parents

Positive
Loving People
Unconditional

See #55 for more information.

#545. Deuteronomy 5:17 ~ Do Not Murder

Negative
Loving People
Unconditional

See #56 for more information.

#546. Deuteronomy 5:18 ~ Do Not Commit Adultery

Negative
Loving People
Unconditional

See #57 for more information.

#547. Deuteronomy 5:19 ~ Do Not Steal

Negative
Loving People
Unconditional

Repeat of #58.

#548. Deuteronomy 5:20 ~ Do not Lie Against Someone

Negative
Loving People
Unconditional

See #59 for more information.

#549. Deuteronomy 5:21 ~ Do Not Covet or Desire What Belongs to Someone Else

Negative
Loving People
Unconditional

See #60 for more information.

#550. Deuteronomy 5:29 ~ To Fear the Heavenly Father

Positive
Loving Abba
Unconditional

See #287 for more information.

#551. Deuteronomy 5:29 ~ To Guard Torah

Positive
Loving The Father
Unconditional

See #247 for more information.

#552. Deuteronomy 5:32 ~ To Not Deviate from Torah

Negative
Loving The Father
Unconditional

This was told directly to Moses, but it applies to all of us. This command is also another reminder that the Heavenly Father has never had plans for His people to move away from Torah. A lesson Yeshua teaches throughout Matthew, Mark, Luke, and John.

#553. Deuteronomy 5:33 ~ To Walk in a Way that Flows Perfectly with Torah

Positive
Loving Abba
Unconditional

This command is directed at Moses, but it can apply to all of us.

#554. Deuteronomy 6:2 ~ To Fear the Heavenly Father

Positive
Loving Abba
Unconditional

See #287 for more information.

#555. Deuteronomy 6:2 ~ To Guard Torah

Positive
Loving Abba
Unconditional

See #247 for more information.

#556. Deuteronomy 6:3 ~ To Hear and Do Torah

Positive
Loving People
Unconditional

In Acts Chapter 15, we see a debate on whether those from the nations should be circumcised when they first come to the faith. James ends the debate by instructing them to avoid the four common pagan practices of that time so they can go to a Synagogue on Shabbat and follow Moses

Choose Life

(See Acts 15:1-21 for full context). This reinforces Torah as the foundation of our faith and allows the believers from the nations to keep this command and grow in the faith at their own pace. The idea that those coming from the nations should walk a different way is a man-made teaching that is rendered void by commands #30 (Exodus 12:49), #477 (Numbers 9:14), and #481 (Numbers 15:13-16).

#557. Deuteronomy 6:5 ~ To Love the Heavenly Father with Everything You Are

Positive
Loving Abba
Unconditional

This commandment is impossible to keep without submitting to Torah. See Deuteronomy 6:5-6, Deuteronomy 11:1, Joshua 22:5, John 14:15, John 14:21, John 15:10, 1st John 5:2-3, 2nd John 1:6, Romans 13:8-10, and Galatians 5:14.

#558. Deuteronomy 6:6 ~ For Torah to be in Your Heart

Positive
Loving Abba
Unconditional

Something that Yeshua demonstrated perfectly.

#559. Deuteronomy 6:7 ~ To Teach Your Children Torah

Positive
Loving People
Unconditional

See #21 for more information.

#560. Deuteronomy 6:7-8 ~ To Always Think About Torah

Positive
Loving Father & People
Unconditional

Torah is not a religion; it is a covenant that changes us from within by redirecting how we think. It shifts our thinking from the ways of the world to the ways of the Heavenly Father. Torah shapes us into human beings as Elohim defines what humans look like. The more we think about Torah, the more we become in sync with Yeshua, and ultimately, Adonai.

Within spiritual Judaism, evolution is not taught; however, there is a concept of de-evolution. Sin tugs at the desires of the flesh. Just like animals that behave based on how they feel, we do the same thing when we sin. Sin feeds on our baser instincts, which come from the desires of the flesh. This is why sin is emotionally charged, not intellectual. Torah is the tool used to get us to behave like humans according to the Heavenly Father's view. Outside of Torah, we behave like animals.

#561. Deuteronomy 6:9 ~ To Have Torah on Your Doorposts and Gates (Mezuzahs)

Positive
Loving Abba
Unconditional

A mezuzah is a small, parchment scroll inscribed with specific Hebrew verses from the Torah, typically Deuteronomy 6:4-9 and 11:13-21, which include the Shema prayer. It's placed in a protective case and affixed to the doorposts of homes, often at a slight angle (Jewish tradition). Mezuzahs can be purchased online. The purpose of the mezuzah is to remind us of Torah when we leave our house and when we return. To make sure that we don't forget about them in our comings and goings, Judah has developed a habit of touching and/or making a gesture of kissing them as they come and go. This is not a part of Torah directly, but with the right heart, it can be a good thing.

#562. Deuteronomy 6:13 ~ To Fear the Heavenly Father

Positive
Loving Abba
Unconditional

See #287 for more information.

#563. Deuteronomy 6:13 ~ To Serve the Heavenly Father

Positive
Loving People
Unconditional

See #132 for more information.

#564. Deuteronomy 6:13 ~ To Swear by the Name YHWH

Positive
Loving Abba
Unconditional

This command is talking about making oaths only in YHWH's Name, and it flows with commands #47 & #49. This command is not mandatory; it is not something we must do, as we will see with #769 and #833.

#565. Deuteronomy 6:14 ~ Do Not Seek After Other Gods

Negative
Loving Abba
Unconditional

See #131 for more information.

#566. Deuteronomy 6:16 ~ Do Not Test the Heavenly Father

Negative
Loving Abba
Unconditional

The testing at Massah can be seen in Exodus 17:1-7. After everything that Adonai did to free Israel from Egypt, shortly after going into the wilderness, Israel began to complain of thirst, asking Moses, "Why have you brought us up out of Egypt, to kill us, our children, and our livestock with thirst?" (V3). Israel didn't understand the type of relationship Adonai seeks, and they didn't realize that all they needed to do was ask, and it would be given to them (850). The only exception to this command is Malachi 3:10, where Adonai challenges the priests to test Him in the giving of the 10% tithe. A challenge that many have testified to be effective.

#567. Deuteronomy 6:17 ~ To Guard the Commands of the Heavenly Father

Positive
Loving Abba & People
Unconditional

See #247 for more information.

#568. Deuteronomy 6:18 ~ To Do What is Right in the Eyes of the Heavenly Father

Positive
Loving Abba
Unconditional

Also see Deuteronomy 13:4 (615)

Some people may think this command is for the exodus generation only because it says, "*that you may go in and possess the good land which Adonai swore to your fathers, to thrust out all your enemies from before you, as Yahweh has spoken. (Verses 18-19)*" However, this command also applies to us today. We are currently in dispersion, and as part of the restoration of Israel, there will be a greater exodus where all of Israel will be in the land. In the meantime, wherever we are, Adonai expects His people to live according to Torah and discern what is good and what is not. To do what is right in the eyes of the Heavenly Father is to walk after Him and fulfill His desire of how humans should behave (See Genesis 1:26). No matter where we are in the world, keeping Torah, what is right in His eyes, makes us law-abiding citizens of His kingdom.

#569. Deuteronomy 6:20-24 ~ To Explain to Children Why We Keep Torah

Positive
Loving People
Unconditional

Seen in command #526. Also see command #21 for more information.

#570. Deuteronomy 6:25 ~ Torah is Our Righteousness

Positive
Loving People
Unconditional

Torah defines what righteousness and sin look like for the people of Israel. This is something that Paul teaches when he said, "*What shall we say then? Is the law sin? May it never be! However, I wouldn't have known sin, except through the law. For I wouldn't have known coveting, unless the law had said, 'You shall not covet'* (Romans 7:7)." Pay close attention to the words of this command, it does not say that Torah makes us righteous, it says that Torah is our righteousness. Don't allow Torah observance to fill you up with pride. Even if we keep Torah perfectly, we all have things of the flesh that we struggle with; we all have room for spiritual growth. Keeping Torah is never a reason to feel better than anyone else because within our corruptible flesh lurks all kinds of evil waiting to spring out when we let our guard down. This is why Yeshua says in Mark 10:18, "*No one is good except one—Elohim.*"

NOTE: Deuteronomy Chapter 7 explains, in detail, the relationship between Israel and the Heavenly Father.

#571. Deuteronomy 7:6 ~ To Be Set Apart for the Heavenly Father

Positive
Loving Abba
Unconditional

See #218 for more information.

NOTE: Deuteronomy 7:9-10: Another example that connects loving the Heavenly Father with keeping His commands.

#572. Deuteronomy 7:11 ~ To Guard Torah

Positive
Loving People
Unconditional

See #247 for more information.

NOTE: Deuteronomy 7:12-13; when we guard Torah, the Heavenly Father guards the covenant of Exodus 19:5.

#573. Deuteronomy 8:1 ~ Be Careful to do Everything that the Heavenly Father Commands

Positive
Loving People
Unconditional

See #44 for more information.

#574. Deuteronomy 8:6 ~ To Guard the Commands

Positive
Loving People
Unconditional

See #247 for more information.

#575. Deuteronomy 8:6 ~ To Walk in the Ways of the Heavenly Father

Positive
Loving People
Unconditional

This instruction is repeated in:

- Deuteronomy 10:12 (579)
- Deuteronomy 13:4 (615)
- Deuteronomy 30:16 (809)

Torah is the way of the Heavenly Father. All the commands from the feasts, to how we deal with each other, how we conduct business, and more, are all His ways. As we practically study Torah, it becomes easier to understand the spirituality behind the commands and become more aligned with Yeshua and the Heavenly Father. Yeshua kept the commands perfectly, walking in the ways of the Heavenly Father, showing us what keeping this instruction looks like, and we are to follow in his example (See #872). Knowing the voice of the Heavenly Father and walking in His ways is how we can identify the enemy's attacks/deceptions and how we can effectively resist the desires of the flesh (See Galatians 5:16-17, Romans 7:18-25, Romans 8:5-13, 1st Corinthians 9:27, Ephesians 6:12, 1st Peter 2:11, Matthew 26:41, Psalms 119:11, and Proverbs 4:23). When we walk in all the ways of the Heavenly Father, we are constantly alert to the thoughts in our minds, the things we hear, and the things we see. This is how we can always catch what goes against Torah around us and within us.

#576. Deuteronomy 8:6 ~ To Fear the Heavenly Father

Positive
Loving Abba
Unconditional

See #287 for more information.

#577. Deuteronomy 8:11 ~ Be Careful Not to Forget the Heavenly Father's Commands

Negative
Loving Abba
Unconditional

See #44 for more information.

NOTE: Deuteronomy 8:12-18: All blessings come from the Heavenly Father; always give Him the glory when good fortune comes your way in anything.

#578. Deuteronomy 10:12 ~ To Fear the Heavenly Father

Positive
Loving Abba
Unconditional

See #287 for more information.

#579. Deuteronomy 10:12 ~ To Walk in All the Ways of the Heavenly Father

Positive
Loving People
Unconditional

This command encourages a life that flows with Torah. A life where we are fully aware of what always works with or against the voice of our Heavenly Father all around us, so that we can make choices pleasing the Heavenly Father in all situations. To properly keep this command, we need to know the Heavenly Father's instructions, understanding what pertains to us and what doesn't. It is essential to examine each command and understand the surrounding conditions, which makes it easier to determine why we should practice some commands and not others. We must seek to find the spiritual meaning behind each command and allow it to change us from within. In other words, we need practical knowledge of Torah, not just intellectual knowledge.

#580. Deuteronomy 10:12 ~ To Love the Heavenly Father

Positive
Loving Abba
Unconditional

This instruction is repeated in:

Deuteronomy 11:1 (589)

- Deuteronomy 11:13 (591)
- Deuteronomy 30:16 (808)
- Deuteronomy 30:20 (813)

How do you love a Being that you cannot physically see, hear, or touch? We do so by honoring Adonai through His commands. In Exodus 20:6, we see that when we keep the instructions of the Heavenly Father, we love Him. Yeshua encourages this by saying that his family listens to the teachings of the Father and does them (Luke 8:20-21). Yeshua identifies the two greatest commands within Torah as Deuteronomy 6:5 and

Leviticus 19:18 because when we love Adonai properly, we will love our neighbors. Keeping Torah as our way to love Adonai is reinforced throughout the Bible, most clearly in 1st John 5:1-5, which shows us that loving Adonai is also how we overcome the world.

#581. Deuteronomy 10:12 ~ Serve the Elohim with Everything That You Are

Positive
Loving People
Unconditional

See #132 for more information.

#582. Deuteronomy 10:13 ~ To Guard the Commands of the Heavenly Father

Positive
Loving People
Unconditional

See #247 for more information.

#583. Deuteronomy 10:16 ~ To Circumcise the Foreskin of Your Heart

Positive
Loving Abba
Unconditional

In this command, Moses uses a metaphorical term to convey a spiritual idea. "*Circumcise the foreskin of your heart*" refers to conditioning our hearts to be in favor of the voice of our Heavenly Father and not fight against it. This command urges us to purify our inner selves. The physical circumcision only happens once, but this is a constant circumcision of devotion to our Elohim, submitting our will to His from within repeatedly. The phrase "*be no more stiff-necked*" warns against stubbornness or rebellion from the heart, calling for our humility and obedience to the voice of Elohim, to fight against our own will and completely submit to the ways of our Heavenly Father. As we study Torah, especially if we are new to this walk, we see things in a way we've never thought about before and run into commands that challenge our old beliefs. While dealing with another situation, Yeshua says something key to this subject.

> *So Yeshua said, "Do you also still not understand? Don't you understand that whatever goes into the mouth passes into the belly, and then out of the body? But the things which proceed out of the mouth come out of the heart, and they defile the man. For out of the heart come evil thoughts, murders, adulteries, sexual sins, thefts, false testimony, and blasphemies. These are the things which defile the man; but to eat with unwashed hands doesn't defile the man."* - Matthew 15:16-20

Mainstream religion regularly teaches that all temptations are from Satan and/or demons, but that is not always the case. The enemy does not need to be all-knowing or omnipresent because we all have hearts connected to the desires of the flesh. This is why Yeshua said that we must die to ourselves daily (Luke 9:23). Torah is the solution to that problem! All praises to the Heavenly Father who gives us Torah and fills us with His Set-Apart Spirit, giving us the tools to subdue the heart and the desires of the flesh from within!

This teaching is exactly what Yeshua was talking about in John 4:23. Circumcising the foreskin of our hearts is where the rubber meets the road: Do we stand on what we believe is right and wrong? Do we submit to the will of our flesh, which is driven by emotions? Or do we let it all go, trust in Yeshua's ways and words, and submit to the will of the Father through His Torah? That is what it means to circumcise the foreskin of the heart. This is what Paul was talking about in Romans 2:12-29. When our hearts are circumcised unto Adonai, we will submit to Torah properly and die to our old self. This command is a main reason why we should never subscribe to the idea that Torah is "done away with," that "Yeshua fulfilled the Torah, so we don't have to," or the concept that there are "new commands" for "New Testament believers." Such concepts spit in the face of everything that the Heavenly Father is all about. As stated before, unlike the physical circumcision that only happens once, circumcising the foreskin of our hearts is something we do every day until we draw our last breath, until our souls leave this world because the enemy, people around us, the government and life in general, will constantly test us in this.

#584. Deuteronomy 10:19 ~ To Love the Non-Israelite

Positive
Loving people
Unconditional

Israel is supposed to be the bridge that fills the gap between Yeshua and the people of the world. As Israel, we love the world when we keep Torah because by doing so, we properly advertise our One True Elohim. This is how we draw people to Him. Living a Torah observant lifestyle is the best way to evangelize the world and show love to everyone around us. This is how we love each other as Yeshua loves us (855).

#585. Deuteronomy 10:20 ~ To Fear the Heavenly Father

Positive
Loving Abba
Unconditional

See #287 for more information.

#586. Deuteronomy 10:20 ~ To Serve the Heavenly Father

Positive
Loving People
Unconditional

See #132 for more information.

#587. Deuteronomy 10:20 ~ To Cling to the Heavenly Father

Positive
Loving Abba
Unconditional

Repeated in:

- Deuteronomy 13:4 (620)
- Deuteronomy 30:20 (815)

The goal of life is to connect with the Heavenly Father; this was Yeshua's ultimate purpose on earth for all humanity. Through Torah, we can develop a proper moral and ethical character that pleases the Heavenly Father and brings us into accord with Him (See Amos 3:3). When we perfectly love and fear Adonai, we reach the apex of human spirituality. This concept in Judaism is called "*deveikut*," which is how we can keep this command. What we do on earth matters to the Heavenly Father. By living according to Torah, we advocate for His balance and order in the universe. It is how we ultimately cling to Him.

#588. Deuteronomy 10:20 ~ To Swear by the Name of YHWH

Positive
Loving Abba
Unconditional

First seen in #564.

#589. Deuteronomy 11:1 ~ To Love the Heavenly Father

Positive
Loving Abba
Unconditional

See #580 for more information.

#590. Deuteronomy 11:8 ~ To Guard All the Commands

Positive
Loving People
Unconditional

See #247 for more information.

#591. Deuteronomy 11:13 ~ To Love Elohim with Everything That You Are

Positive
Loving Abba
Unconditional

See #580 for more information.

#592. Deuteronomy 11:16 ~ Be Careful Not to Turn Away from the Heavenly Father and Serve Other Gods

Negative
Loving Abba
Unconditional

See #131 for more information.

#593. Deuteronomy 11:18 ~ To Have Torah in Your Mind and Soul

Positive
Loving Abba
Unconditional

As stated before, Torah is the vehicle used to transform us from people of the world to people like Yeshua. Torah is not a religion; it is a covenant and a process that changes us from within. The end goal of Torah is to get us to think and act more like Yeshua and ultimately the Heavenly Father as we progress through this walk. This is what the born-again process is all about. Once Torah fully occupies your mind and soul, that is when you've met the requirement to fulfill this command. This is not just a command; it is also an internal goal to be reached.

#594. Deuteronomy 11:19 ~ To Teach Torah to the Children

Positive
Loving People
Unconditional

First seen in #526. Also see #21 for more information.

#595. Deuteronomy 11:20 ~ To Have Torah on Your Doorposts and Gates (Mezuzahs)

Positive
Loving Abba
Unconditional

First seen in #561.

NOTE: Deuteronomy 11:22: Another example connecting keeping the commands and loving the Heavenly Father.

NOTE: Deuteronomy 11:26-28: Blessings for keeping Torah, Curses for breaking Torah.

#596. Deuteronomy 12:5-7 ~ To Sacrifice at the Place Where the Heavenly Father Chooses

Positive
Loving People
Conditional

See #241 for more information.

#597. Deuteronomy 12:8 ~ Do Not Do What is Right in Your Own Eyes

Negative
Loving Abba
Unconditional

We keep this command when we allow the commands of Adonai to dictate what is right and wrong in the world. Torah provides that change of perspective and focus that those in the world do not get. This also prevents us from personally judging others because we only support the judgments of Adonai. We do not seek out what we believe is right or wrong; we look to what Elohim says on the subject, and we allow that to determine what is right or wrong. If we run into something that is not covered within Torah, that is when we pray and allow the Set Apart Spirit to do its thing. Also, see Judges 17:6 & 21:25.

#598. Deuteronomy 12:11 ~ To Sacrifice Where the Heavenly Father Chooses

Positive
Loving Abba
Conditional

See #241 for more information.

#599. Deuteronomy 12:13-14 ~ Only Sacrifice Where the Heavenly Father Accepts Sacrifices

Negative
Loving The Father
Unconditional

See #241 for more information.

#600. Deuteronomy 12:15 ~ Those Clean and Unclean May Eat of What is Sacrificed

Positive
Loving People
Conditional

Repeated in Deuteronomy 12:22 (605).

#601. Deuteronomy 12:16 ~ Do Not Consume Blood

Negative
Loving Abba
Unconditional

See #5 for more information.

#602. Deuteronomy 12:17-18 ~ To Eat the Sacrifices Vowed Before the Heavenly Father

Positive
Loving Abba
Conditional

See #165 for more information.

#603. Deuteronomy 12:19 ~ Do Not Neglect the Levites

Negative
Loving People
Conditional

Of course, this command is for a situation when the Levites function to serve Israel full-time. But if we are searching for the spiritual meaning behind this command, to some extent, there could be situations where this would apply today, which can make this command unconditional. From a more obvious standpoint, this can be viewed as a call to support our spiritual leaders.

#604. Deuteronomy 12:21 ~ Sacrificing Within Israel, When the Place the Heavenly Father Chooses is Too Far

Positive
Loving People
Conditional

Earlier in this chapter, the Heavenly Father instructed us to offer sacrifices only at the place He chooses. This ensures proper worship and avoids idolatry. At the very least, everyone was still expected to go to Jerusalem 3 times a year. Some sacrifices had nothing to do with spiritual motivations and were not needed for worship purposes. This teaching distinguishes between sacrificial offerings, which must be made at a certain location, and sacrifices for the consumption of meat in everyday meals and other things. The latter is allowed locally if it follows all the instructions about eating meat, such as draining the blood (Deuteronomy 12:23-25 and Leviticus 17:10-14) and so on.

#605. Deuteronomy 12:22 ~ The Clean and Unclean Can Eat When Sacrificing Within the Land

Positive
Loving People
Conditional

#606. Deuteronomy 12:23-25 ~ Do Not Consume Blood

Negative
Loving Abba
Unconditional

See #5 for more information.

#607. Deuteronomy 12:26 ~ The Set Apart Gift and Vowed Offering Must Only Go to the Place Where the Heavenly Father Chooses

Positive
Loving Abba
Conditional

See #165 for more information.

#608. Deuteronomy 12:27 ~ Make Ascending Offerings at the Slaughter Place of the Heavenly Father

Positive
Loving Abba
Conditional

See #241 for more information.

#609. Deuteronomy 12:28 ~ To Guard the Commands of the Heavenly Father

Positive
Loving People
Unconditional

See #247 for more information.

#610. Deuteronomy 12:28 ~ To Obey the Commands of the Heavenly Father

Positive
Loving People
Unconditional

See #248 for more information.

#611. Deuteronomy 12:30 ~ Do Not Seek Other Gods or Learn Their Ways

Negative
Loving Abba
Unconditional

See #131 for more information.

#612. Deuteronomy 12:32 ~ To Guard What Moses Says

Positive
Loving Abba
Unconditional

See #247 for more information. Also see Exodus 19:9 and the example of Yeshua in Matthew 4:1-11.

#613. Deuteronomy 12:32 ~ Do Not Add to or Take Away from What Moses Wrote

Negative
Loving Abba
Unconditional

This is the command that Yeshua was defending when he mostly debated with the Pharisees of his time. Yeshua's debates were never against Torah or Judaism, but against the elements that add, alter, or take away from what Moses wrote. Some of those same elements are still practiced today in Judaism.

#614. Deuteronomy 13:1-3 ~ Do Not Listen to Anyone Who Leads You Away from the Heavenly Father's Commands

Negative
Loving Abba
Unconditional

This command makes it impossible to believe that Torah would ever be "done away" with. It is also one of the biggest obstacles that Yeshua faced when dealing with the religious leaders of his time. The biggest benefit of believing in YHWH is that He does not change! That is the oak that our faith rests upon. If the Heavenly Father ever walked away from Torah, there would be no security in this faith. If the Heavenly Father ever turned His back on Judah, what would make Christianity think He would not turn His back on them? This command shows us that Torah is the anchor of our Faith. The commands that Moses wrote are carved in a substance that is far stronger than stone and are bound by the laws of the universe. It is because of this command that we know the Heavenly Father will never change the mark.

#615. Deuteronomy 13:4 ~ To Walk After the Heavenly Father

Positive
Loving Abba
Unconditional

See #570 and #577 for more information.

#616. Deuteronomy 13:4 ~ To Fear the Heavenly Father

Positive
Loving Abba
Unconditional

See #287 for more information.

#617. Deuteronomy 13:4 ~ To Guard the Commands of the Heavenly Father

Positive
Loving People
Unconditional

See #247 for more information.

#618. Deuteronomy 13:4 ~ To Obey the Voice of the Heavenly Father

Positive
Loving Abba
Unconditional

See #44 for more information. Also see Exodus 19:5.

#619. Deuteronomy 13:4 ~ To Serve the Heavenly Father

Positive
Loving People
Unconditional

See #132 for more information.

#620. Deuteronomy 13:4 ~ To Cling to the Heavenly Father

Positive
Loving Abba
Unconditional

See #589 for more information.

#621. Deuteronomy 13:5 ~ To Execute the Prophet or Dreamer of Dreams, The One Who Leads You Away from Following the Heavenly Father

Positive
Loving Abba
Conditional

#622. Deuteronomy 13:6-8 ~ Do Not Listen to Anyone Who Says to Worship Another God

Negative
Loving Abba
Unconditional

This can easily include doing what is known to other gods. Many holidays celebrated in the world have pagan origins. It doesn't matter if the Catholic Church appropriated them to "glorify" Elohim; they still have pagan origins. Based on the commands of Torah, there is no situation where the Heavenly Father would be pleased with His people appropriating traditions or holidays that started from false gods. Following holidays and traditions from pagan sources is a dangerous practice we must resist early in the walk. Another thing to look for is people who present Elohim in a way that is out of character, which also breaks this command. Torah establishes the character of our Heavenly

Father; any teaching that cancels or modifies just one command comes from a false god. Meditate on Yeshua's example in Matthew 4:1-11 and how he deals with the enemy.

#623. Deuteronomy 13:9-11 ~ To Execute Those Who Try to Entice You to Worship Other Gods

Positive
Loving Abba
Conditional

#624. Deuteronomy 13:12-18 ~ If You Hear a City Has Turned Away from the Heavenly Father

Positive
Loving Abba
Conditional

It is important to note that this does not refer to cities of the world. This command specifically refers to a city within the land of Biblical Israel. Some might argue that this can pertain to the world government known as Israel, established in 1948, but that government does not submit to Torah; this command is illegal according to their laws, otherwise, we would have seen this command take place.

#625. Deuteronomy 14:1 ~ Do Not Cut Yourself for the Dead

Negative
Loving Abba
Unconditional

First seen in #306.

#626. Deuteronomy 14:1 ~ Do Not Shave the Front of Your Head for the Dead

Negative
Loving Abba
Unconditional

#627. Deuteronomy 14:3 ~ Do Not Eat What is Abominable

Negative
Loving Abba
Unconditional

See #221 for more information. Also see commands 204, 205, 214, & 215 for what makes you abominable.

#628. Deuteronomy 14:4-7 ~ Animals That Are Good for Food and Not Good for Food

Positive
Loving Abba
Unconditional

See Leviticus chapter 11 & #200 for more information.

#629. Deuteronomy 14:8 ~ Do Not Eat Pig

Negative
Loving Abba
Unconditional

When this command was first given, not eating pork was very clear and easy to keep. Today, this instruction is harder than most people think and requires constant due diligence on our part to keep. On the surface, we know this command means no pork bacon, pork chops, or pork ribs.

However, today, there are many things we do not even think about that contain pork. Most beef sausages are in cased in pork products. The cheapest hotdogs are made with beef, chicken, and pork. Many Italian restaurants mix beef and pork in their meatballs.

While in the grocery store, look for the kosher symbols, a "U" inside a circle (Ⓤ), a "K" inside a circle, a "K" inside a stylized letter "K" or star-like shape, a "K" inside a star, a "cRc" in a distinctive logo, sometimes with a triangle around it, and the letters "MK" (Montreal Kosher) in a circle or stylized design. Not all "K" on products are kosher! A plain "K" without a circle or specific design is not a reliable kosher certification, because it's not regulated and could be used by any manufacturer. Here are a few more things to consider when transitioning to not eating pork.

Gelatin: Often comes from pork skin or bones, gelatin is used in foods like gummy candies, marshmallows, Jell-O, and some yogurts (Yoplait, Activia, Dannon and usually store brand yogurt), Greek yogurt is usually safe. It's also in non-food items like capsules for medications and supplements. Not all gelatin is bad, when it comes to gelatin, there are 3 kinds: Porcine (Pork), Bovine (Cow), and Fish. If you are looking into a product made with gelatin, sometimes you'll have to dig deep into finding out which type of gelatin it is talking about.

Lard: Rendered pork fat is used in cooking and baking, especially in pie crusts, biscuits, and traditional recipes like tamales. Look for kosher symbols wherever possible. It can be a part of processed food like refried beans or various snacks. Not all lard is made with pork such as Beef Tallow, Mutton Tallow, Duck or Goose Fat, Chicken Schmaltz, vegetable-based "lard", and vegetable shortening (Crisco). Here are some more things to consider.

- Sausage Casings: Many sausages use natural casings made from pork intestines, though this is less surprising to those familiar with traditional sausage-making.

- Bone Broth and Stocks: Pork bones are used in some commercial broths, soups, and ramen bases, often unlabeled as specifically pork based. If you go to a ramen or Pho restaurant, you need to ask what kind of broth they are using.

- Cosmetics and Personal Care Products: Pork-derived ingredients like collagen or glycerin (sometimes from pork fat) appear in creams, lotions, soaps, and even toothpaste.

- Medical Products: Porcine heart valves are used in some heart surgeries, and pork-derived heparin, a blood thinner, is extracted from pig intestines.

- Pet Food: Pork by-products, like organs or trimmings, are common in dog and cat food, often listed vaguely as "meat by-products."

- Fertilizers and Industrial Products: Pork by-products can be processed into fertilizers, animal feed supplements, or even industrial lubricants.

Many items involve by-products from the pork industry, making them less obvious to consumers. Always check labels or contact manufacturers if needed to make sure you are keeping this instruction properly. Because pork is in so much of what we use daily, this instruction can take a while to master.

Some bread products are made with lard. Lard is used in various breads for its rich flavor and tenderizing properties. Here are some breads commonly made with lard that you might not immediately associate with it:

- Tortillas (Mexican): Traditional corn and flour tortillas, especially in Mexico and parts of Latin America, often use lard for a soft, pliable texture and authentic taste.
- Biscuits (Southern U.S.): Many Southern-style buttermilk biscuits incorporate lard for a flaky, tender crumb, a staple in American comfort food.
- Cornbread (Southern U.S.): Some traditional cornbread recipes, particularly in the South, use lard to enhance moisture and richness.
- Tamale Dough (Masa): The masa for tamales, a Latin American dish, frequently includes lard to achieve a light, fluffy texture when steamed.
- Soda Bread (Irish): Certain regional Irish soda bread recipes use lard for a softer texture, though butter is more common today.
- Pan de Muerto (Mexican): This Day of the Dead bread sometimes includes lard for a tender, slightly sweet crumb.
- Cuban Bread: Used in Cuban sandwiches, this bread often contains lard, giving it a soft interior and crisp crust.
- Bolillos (Mexican): These crusty Mexican rolls, like French bread, traditionally use lard for flavor and texture.
- Frybread (Native American): While often fried in lard, some recipes also incorporate it into the dough for added richness.
- Empanada Dough (Latin American): Some empanada recipes use lard in the dough for a flaky, tender pastry encasing savory or sweet fillings.

If you like any of these things, it is best that you learn to make them yourself because if you go to a restaurant or store to buy such products, chances are they are most likely made with pork. Lard is used in breadmaking and is rooted in worldly traditions, especially in regions where pork is a dietary staple. Modern recipes might substitute butter or vegetable shortening, but lard remains key for authenticity in many of the food products we are exposed to. For us to properly avoid eating pork today, we need to check ingredient lists, ask bakers, and even manufacturers, as lard can be listed vaguely or omitted in casual recipes. For this command, it is best to avoid it if you cannot be 100% sure. When it comes to not eating pork, we want to make sure that we are as confident as Peter was in Acts chapter 10. If you discover that you've eaten pork by mistake, don't beat yourself up for it: Just learn from it, repent, and move on. As stated before, it can take a while to master this command and that is primarily due to no fault of our own.

#630. Deuteronomy 14:8 ~ Do Not Touch the Dead Carcass of a Pig

Negative
Loving Abba
Unconditional

#631. Deuteronomy 14:9 ~ What Can Be Eaten from the Waters

Positive
Loving Abba
Unconditional

See #203 for more information.

#632. Deuteronomy 14:10 ~ Whatever does not have fins and scales from the waters is not for food

Negative
Loving Abba
Unconditional

See #221 for more information.

#633. Deuteronomy 14:11 ~ Clean Birds for Food

Positive
Loving Abba
Unconditional

See #221 for more information. Leviticus 11:13-19 shows us the birds to avoid eating.

#634. Deuteronomy 14:12-18 ~ Birds That Are Not for Food

Negative
Loving Abba
Unconditional

See #205 for more information.

#635. Deuteronomy 14:19 ~ Insects That Fly Are Not for Food

Negative
Loving Abba
Unconditional

See #221 for more information.

#636. Deuteronomy 14:20 ~ Clean Birds That Are for Food

Positive
Loving Abba
Unconditional

See Leviticus 11:13-19 for birds that are not food.

#637. Deuteronomy 14:21 ~ Do Not Eat What Dies Naturally

Negative
Loving Abba
Unconditional

See #112 for more information.

#638. Deuteronomy 14:21 ~ To Sell What Dies Naturally to the Non-Covenanted and Foreigners

Positive
Loving People
Unconditional

See #112 for more information.

#639. Deuteronomy 14:21 ~ Do Not Cook a Young Goat in Its Mother's Milk

Negative
Loving Abba
Unconditional

See #129 for more information.

#640. Deuteronomy 14:22 ~ To Do the Yearly Tithe (The 2nd Tithe)

Positive
Loving People
Unconditional

The 2nd tithe, also known as the festival tithe, or Ma'aser Sheni, is for you to have the resources to celebrate the feasts. Unlike the regular tithe given to our congregations each time we get paid, this tithe is placed in an account that you have 100% control of, and these funds are used only for the feasts, mainly Passover, Shavuot, and Sukkot. This 2nd tithe builds from Sukkot to Sukkot. When the feast of Sukkot is done, if anything is left over, that is the 2nd tithe offering (643). Like the first tithe is 10%, the 2nd tithe is supposed to be likewise from each paycheck. The goal is 10% of the gross, not net, for all three tithes. If you cannot do the full 10% at first, make an offering within your means until you can do the full 10% for all 3 tithes.

#641. Deuteronomy 14:23 ~ To Sacrifice Only Where the Heavenly Father Chooses for Grain Offerings During Sukkot

Positive
Loving Abba
Conditional

See #241 for more information.

#642. Deuteronomy 14:24 ~ To Use Up the 2nd Tithe for the Feast of Sukkot

Positive
Loving People
Unconditional

See #640 for more information.

#643. Deuteronomy 14:27 ~ To Give the Remainder of the 2nd Tithes to the Priesthood

Positive
Loving People
Unconditional

See #640 for more information.

#644. Deuteronomy 14:28-29 ~ To Give a 3rd Tithe of Benevolence Every 3 Years

Positive
Loving People
Unconditional

The 3rd tithe can be viewed as the tithe of personal wealth. It is expected that you tithe every three years for benevolence from this tithe (803). Just like the 2nd tithe, this is expected to be given during Sukkot. A 10% tithe means that this 3rd tithe should come from 10% of something. Ideally, you can take 10% of your paycheck and place it into an account, let it grow, and empty that account out every three years or take the 10% from there, maybe make it a life-saving account; however, the parable of the Talents (Matthew 25:14-30) seems to discourage the idea of just tucking the money away somewhere.

When the words of this command were first spoken, 10% meant from the herd, flock, grains, fruits, and/or vegetables. Today, most people are not farmers nor tend to flock or herd, so we must conform to modern resources for this command. This 3rd tithe can come from money you invest. Start putting money in a money market, CD, start buying stocks in a long-term investment strategy, even day trading, swing trading, and such, get into dividend stock investing, or other kinds of investments, and use those sources for the 3rd tithe every three years. Make it a goal to have that resource grow so you can give more each time.

Whatever type of investments you get into, the goal is to make profit, and it is from those profits that you can give the 3rd tithe. Just that focus alone can get you far when it comes to gaining financial strength.

This 3rd tithe easily places us in a position to build financial strength and stability. If you are saving and investing to have a 3rd tithe, that is a righteous goal; it should motivate you to get your finances in order. During those 3 years, this money can be used to pay off debts and for extreme emergencies. This 3rd tithe can provide your own personal benevolence resource not only for yourself, but for others in need around you. There are various ways to righteously handle this 3rd tithe. The 3rd tithe is for the poor, and throughout the scriptures, it is easy to see that the Heavenly Father has a heart for the poor. If you run into someone who is in need, this 3rd account can help. Keeping this instruction helps us focus on the poor like the Heavenly Father does and it also elevates us to financial strength by default. If all you do is set your financial goals so that you can fully do the 1st, 2nd, and 3rd tithes, that alone can elevate you to financial strength.

Although we've only spoken about monetary assets for the 3rd tithe, it doesn't have to be that. When you buy clothes, get some extra and place them on the side. In that 3rd year, buy canned goods and food that does not spoil quickly, and start piling them up at the beginning of the year. You can collect various items to give to homeless shelters every 3 years. Do not give them to thrift stores or the salvation army because they will most likely be sold for profit and that is not what this 3rd tithe is about. This 3rd tithe is for the sole purpose of helping the poor!

#645. Deuteronomy 15:1-3 ~ To Release Debts Every 7 Years for Those Covenanted

Positive
Loving Abba
Unconditional

See #431 for more information.

NOTE: Deuteronomy 15:4-6: This is not a commandment, but it is important to note that the Heavenly Father desires that there should be no poverty within the body of believers if we live within the boundaries of Torah. The system of 1st, 2nd, and 3rd tithes can bring you out of poverty, provide financial stability, and more.

#646. Deuteronomy 15:7-8 ~ To Help the Covenanted Poor

Positive
Loving People
Unconditional

See #446 for more information.

#647. Deuteronomy 15:9-11 ~ Do Not Withhold from Giving to the Poor Due to the Coming of the Sabbatical Year

Negative
Loving People
Conditional

During the sabbatical year, the ground is not to be disturbed, which means no farming. This could quickly drive people to hoard food instead of trusting the Heavenly Father to provide for that year. If people had done this, the poor of Israel would have suffered the most.

#648. Deuteronomy 15:12 ~ If a Covenanted Man or Woman Is Sold, They Serve 6 Years and Are Freed on the 7th Year.

Positive
Loving People
Unconditional

#649. Deuteronomy 15:13-14 ~ If a Covenanted Enslaved Man is Freed, Send Them Away with Riches

Positive
Loving People
Conditional

Slavery is a by-product of a world full of sinful people. During the Mesopotamian era, slavery was a constant possibility due to nations fighting over resources and other reasons. World history does not have a shortage of horrific slavery situations all around the globe. However, the Heavenly Father found a positive use for such a barbaric system. This command reveals something about slavery in Israel that most people overlook. For Israel, slavery was used to help people get out of poverty and/or financial ruin. In the courts, slavery could be a way to pay off a debt or restitution for a crime. Poor families would sell their daughters into slavery so that their status in society could be elevated. It is also possible that sons were sold into slavery to help them succeed in life.

One of the benefits of being a slave in this situation is that you get the opportunity to watch the habits and practices of a wealthy individual. Not only do you learn the skills of managing money, but you are also set free with riches of your own to manage! Think about Joseph in the book of Genesis. His brothers tended the flock while he stayed at his father's side. That is how he gained the skills to be successful in

Egypt. Another wisdom from this command is that it was a great deterrent to prevent people from wanting to enslave their fellow Israelites. Giving away wealth every 7 years to slaves you free is a guaranteed way to fall into financial ruin if you acquire a lot of them.

#650. Deuteronomy 15:15 ~ To Remember That We Were Slaves in Egypt

Positive
Loving The Father
Unconditional

See #38 for more information.

#651. Deuteronomy 15:16-17 ~ If a Covenanted Slave Chooses to Stay on the Sabbatical Year

Positive
Loving People
Conditional

#652. Deuteronomy 15:18 ~ To Rejoice When You Set a Covenanted Slave Free

Positive
Loving People
Conditional

#653. Deuteronomy 15:19 ~ The Firstborn Males of the Herd or Flock are Set Apart

Positive
Loving Abba
Conditional

See #31 for more information.

#654. Deuteronomy 15:20 ~ To Eat the Set Apart Firstborn at the Place Where the Heavenly Father Chooses

Positive
Loving Abba
Conditional

See #241 for more information.

#655. Deuteronomy 15:21 ~ To Not Sacrifice a Firstborn from the Flock or Herd with a Defect Before the Heavenly Father

Negative
Loving Abba
Conditional

#656. Deuteronomy 15:22 ~ To Sacrifice and Eat the Firstborn from the Flock or Herd Within Israel's Borders

Positive
Loving People
Conditional

#657. Deuteronomy 15:22 ~ Those Clean and Unclean May Eat of the Defected Firstborn of the Flock or Herd

Positive
Loving People
Conditional

Defected animals are not unclean; they are not fit to be sacrificed to the Heavenly Father. They may still be eaten.

#658. Deuteronomy 15:23 ~ Do Not Consume the Blood of the Defected Firstborn of the Flock or Herd

Negative
Loving Abba
Unconditional

See #5 for more information.

#659. Deuteronomy 16:1 ~ To Guard the New Moon

Positive
Loving Abba
Unconditional

See #8 for more information.

#660. Deuteronomy 16:1 ~ To Observe Passover

Positive
Loving Abba
Unconditional

See #13 for more information.

#661. Deuteronomy 16:2 ~ To Slaughter the Passover Lamb, Where the Heavenly Father Chooses to Place His Name

Positive
Loving Abba
Conditional

See #241 for more information.

#662. Deuteronomy 16:3 ~ Do Not Eat Leavened Bread with the Passover Meal

Negative
Loving Abba
Unconditional

See #145 for more information.

#663. Deuteronomy 16:3 ~ To Eat Unleavened Bread for 7 Days

Positive
Loving The Father
Unconditional

See #33 for more information.

#664. Deuteronomy 16:4 ~ No Leavened Bread Should Be Seen on Your Property for 7 Days

Negative
Loving Abba
Unconditional

See #18 for more information.

#665. Deuteronomy 16:4 ~ No Remains of the Passover Meat by the Next Morning

Negative
Loving Abba
Conditional

See #25 & #26 for more information.

#666. Deuteronomy 16:5-6 ~ To Only Sacrifice the Passover Lamb Where the Heavenly Father Chooses to Make His Name Dwell

Positive
Loving Abba
Conditional

See #241 for more information.

#667. Deuteronomy 16:7 ~ To Roast the Passover Lamb

Positive
Loving Abba
Conditional

#668. Deuteronomy 16:7 ~ To Return Home the Next Night of Passover

Positive
Loving People
Conditional

This command is marked conditional because we only do a memorial to Passover today, and most people around the world cannot afford to go to the land for the feast every year. However, feasts such as Passover and Sukkot are feasts of hospitality. If you are a part of a congregation that honors this, then you are blessed.

#669. Deuteronomy 16:8 ~ To Eat Unleavened Bread During the Week of Unleavened Bread

Positive
Loving Abba
Unconditional

See #33 for more information.

#670. Deuteronomy 16:8 ~ The 7th Day of Unleavened Bread is a Shabbat

Positive
Loving Abba
Unconditional

See #15 for more information.

#671. Deuteronomy 16:9 ~ To Count 7 Weeks to Shavuot

Positive
Loving Abba
Unconditional

See #390 for more information.

#672. Deuteronomy 16:10-11 ~ To Observe the Feast of First Fruits, Where the Heavenly Father Chooses

Positive
Loving Abba
Conditional

#673. Deuteronomy 16:12 ~ To Remember That You Were Slaves in Egypt During the Feast of Shavuot

Positive
Loving Abba
Unconditional

See #38 for more information.

#674. Deuteronomy 16:13-14 ~ To Observe the Feast of Sukkot with Rejoicing

Positive
Loving Abba
Unconditional

See #143 for more information.

#675. Deuteronomy 16:15 ~ To Observe Sukkot Where the Heavenly Father Chooses

Positive
Loving Abba
Conditional

#676. Deuteronomy 16:16 ~ To Appear Before the Heavenly Father 3 Times a Year at the Location He Chooses

Positive
Loving Abba
Conditional

See #125 for more information.

#677. Deuteronomy 16:16-17 ~ To Not Appear Before the Heavenly Father at the 3 Appointed Times Empty-Handed

Negative
Loving People
Unconditional

See #125 and #642 for more information. The 2nd tithe makes this command a no-brainer.

#678. Deuteronomy 16:18 ~ To Appoint Judges and Officers to Judge Israel

Positive
Loving People
Conditional

This command is tied to:

- Deuteronomy 17:8-9 (689)
- Deuteronomy 17:10-11 (690)
- Deuteronomy 17:12-13 (691)
- Deuteronomy 25:1 (794)

Once again, Torah is the constitution of Israel that is supposed to control a specific land which belongs to the Heavenly Father. Like any other country, there needs to be a judicial system in place to maintain law and order. To some degree, congregational leaders can fill this role when there are disputes among congregation members, but ultimately, this cannot be properly done today. No matter how these judges are selected, the Heavenly Father allows them to be, so their judgments must be respected because they represent Adonai (See Romans 13:1).

#679. Deuteronomy 16:19 ~ Judges and Officers Are Not Allowed to Distort the Right Rulings of Torah

Negative
Loving People
Conditional

This is where we see that Israel is not restored anywhere in the world today. No government in the entire world is entirely devoted to Torah, not even the world government known as Israel today. When Yeshua returns, there will be a government with judges who honor Torah fully. That will be the real Biblical Kingdom of Israel.

#680. Deuteronomy 16:19 ~ Judges and Officers Are Not Allowed to Show Partiality

Negative
Loving People
Conditional

#681. Deuteronomy 16:19 ~ Judges and Officers Are Not Allowed to Take Bribes

Negative
Loving people
Conditional

#682. Deuteronomy 16:19 ~ Judges and Officers Are to Follow Righteousness Alone

Positive
Loving People
Unconditional

Also see Deuteronomy 6:25. Just like command 681, this is another command that we can see is not happening anywhere in the world. Within every government, some upright individuals believe in the honor of their government, but we know that there are corrupt people in the same positions.

#683. Deuteronomy 16:21 ~ Do Not Plant a Tree (Idol) Near the Slaughter Place of the Heavenly Father

Negative
Loving Abba
Unconditional

See command #48 for more information. The word used is Ashĕrah. You can read more about Asherah on the World History Encyclopedia website.

#684. Deuteronomy 16:22 ~ Do Not Erect Pillars for Worship

Negative
Loving Abba
Unconditional

See #48 for more information.

#685. Deuteronomy 17:1 ~ Do Not Slaughter Defective Animals to the Heavenly Father

Negative
Loving Abba
Conditional

It is impossible to view the Heavenly Father as set-apart but sacrifice defective animals to Him. That is called an oxymoron. If we truly want to honor the Father, we give Him our best in everything. We put Him first. That is what He desires in everything we do concerning Him.

#686. Deuteronomy 17:2-5 ~ Instructions for When Someone Is Guilty of Idolatry

Positive
Loving Abba
Conditional

#687. Deuteronomy 17:6 ~ Two or More Witnesses Are Needed for the Death Penalty

Positive
Loving Abba
Conditional

#688. Deuteronomy 17:7 ~ Witnesses Are the First to Throw Stones

Positive
Loving Abba
Conditional

There is a lot of wisdom in commands #687 and #688. There are very few extreme situations where the average human being would truly want someone to die. Unlike most people in the world, I suspect that stoning people were very uncommon within Israel. Not too many people would want that on their conscious.

#689. Deuteronomy 17:8-9 ~ Go to the Levites and Judges for Hard Issues

Positive
Loving Abba
Conditional

See #680 for more information.

#690. Deuteronomy 17:10-11 ~ To Follow the Judgments of the Levite and the Judge

Positive
Loving Abba
Conditional

See #678 for more information.

#691. Deuteronomy 17:12-13 ~ To Publicly Execute the Individual Who Does Not Listen to the Judgment of the Levite and/or the Judge

Positive
Loving Abba
Conditional

See #680 for more information.

#692. Deuteronomy 17:15 ~ The Heavenly Father Selects the Kings of Israel

Positive
Loving Abba
Unconditional

#693. Deuteronomy 17:15 ~ Only an Israelite Can Be King Over Israel

Positive
Loving People
Conditional

#694. Deuteronomy 17:16 ~ A King of Israel Is Not to Increase Horses for Himself

Negative
Loving Abba
Conditional

Although Yeshua did not come as King during His first arrival, he still demonstrated the heart of this command. If he wanted to, Joseph and Mary could have had riches beyond their wildest dreams. Yeshua could have amassed wealth, but he didn't even have a place to call home (Matthew 8:20, Luke 9:58). When Yeshua returns as King, we will not need to worry about him doing anything for selfish gains.

#695. Deuteronomy 17:16 ~ A King of Israel is Not Allowed to Cause the People of Israel to Return to Egypt to Increase Horses

Negative
Loving Abba
Conditional

The command warns against leading the people back to Egypt to acquire horses. Egypt was a major source of horses in the ancient Near East, but it was also the land where Israel had been enslaved. Returning to Egypt for trade or alliances would symbolize a reversal of the Heavenly Father's deliverance and a lack of faith in His provision. Back then, accumulating many horses indicated a reliance on military might rather than trust in Elohim for protection and victory. This command pushes the kings of Israel to depend on Adonai instead of worldly power or foreign alliances.

#696. Deuteronomy 17:17 ~ A King of Israel is Not to Increase Wives for Himself

Negative
Loving Abba
Conditional

This command, along with Command #697 and Command #699, shows how the king of Israel is not supposed to abuse their position for personal gain. Something we can look forward to when Yeshua returns and officially becomes King of a fully restored biblical Israel.

#697. Deuteronomy 17:17 ~ A King of Israel is Not to Increase Silver and Gold for Himself

Negative
Loving People
Conditional

#698. Deuteronomy 17:18 ~ A King of Israel Must Write a Copy of Torah for Himself

Positive
Loving Abba
Conditional (Unconditional)

This command is conditional because it is directed to the kings of Israel. However, I strongly recommend that all who covenant with Adonai do it. In ancient times, only the wealthy and powerful had copies of scriptures. Today, with the internet at our fingertips, most people can do this command. Personally speaking, compiling this list of commands has been life changing. These next few commands are for kings, those who lead the people of Israel. They set an example for everyone else to follow.

#699. Deuteronomy 17:19 ~ A King of Israel Must Always Keep His Own Personal Copy of Torah with Him

Positive
Loving Abba
Conditional (Unconditional)

#700. Deuteronomy 17:19 ~ A King of Israel Must Read His Personally Written Copy of Torah Every Day

Positive
Loving Abba
Conditional (Unconditional)

This was only given to the kings because at that time, the kings had easy access to the scriptures, while most people did not. With the invention of the printing press, access to the scriptures became much easier. With the progression of the internet, access to the scriptures is practically at will for most people worldwide. If Torah were first presented today, there is no doubt that this command would be directed to all of Israel.

#701. Deuteronomy 17:19 ~ A King of Israel Must Fear the Heavenly Father

Positive
Loving Abba
Conditional (Unconditional)

This command can also be viewed as unconditional because all Israel is instructed to fear the Heavenly Father (287). If this command is already given to all of Israel, why would the Heavenly Father direct this to the kings? When Israel first heard these words, Egypt was still a world power and had great influence. The Pharaohs were often viewed as gods.

This was why the Pharaoh felt he had the authority to reject YHWH's request to free Israel. The Heavenly Father does not want the kings of Israel to let their positions go to their heads like the Pharaohs did.

We see examples of this command playing out through David in 2 Samuel 16:5-13. David had the authority to execute Shimei, but at that moment, he trusted in the Heavenly Father. Yeshua also gives us an example of fearing the Heavenly Father in Luke 22:42, Mark 14:36, Matthew 26:39, and Matthew 26:53. In these verses, Yeshua submits to the Heavenly Father instead of utilizing his divine authority.

#702. Deuteronomy 17:19-20 ~ A King of Israel Must Guard Torah

Positive
Loving Abba
Conditional (Unconditional)

This is another command given to all Israel but also directed to the kings of Israel. Through commands #696 to #703, the Heavenly Father reveals to all of Israel that a proper king will not deviate from Torah nor use his position for selfish gains. It is almost as if the Heavenly Father is empowering the people to look out for and rebel against evil kings; unfortunately, history shows that the people of Israel didn't get that message, which is why the prophets were raised to call the people back to righteousness.

Just like in Deuteronomy 13:1-4, a true king of Israel should not lead the people away from Torah. David (2 Samuel, 1 Kings 2, 1 Chronicles) is known as a good king of Israel, and Solomon (1 Kings 1– 11, 2 Chronicles 1–9) was also considered a good king of Israel. From Judah, we have Asa (1 Kings 15:9-24, 2 Chronicles 14–16) and Hezekiah (2 Kings 18–20, 2 Chronicles 29–32), who were considered good kings because they led the people back to Torah.

When Yeshua returns, just like the good kings before him, he will not deviate from Torah and will rule with an iron scepter (See Psalms 2:9, Revelation 2:27, and Revelation 19:15), something that mainstream religion either ignores or minimizes. Ruling with an "iron scepter" or "rod of iron" does not mean that Yeshua will return as a mean person. Unlike when humans rule with an "iron fist" that usually leads to tyranny, Yeshua's "iron" rule will be perfect, fair, and aligned with the Heavenly Father's will, as seen in his role as judge in Revelation 19:11-16. His judgments and rules will be based on Torah. If Yeshua does come up with any new commands, it is guaranteed that his commands will not contradict Torah or cancel anything that Moses said, such as his command in #855; how can we be confident in this? Yeshua already told us what greatness within the kingdom will look like (Matthew 5:19), and only our perfect and good Heavenly Father will be greater than Yeshua.

#703. Deuteronomy 18:1 ~ The Levites Can Eat the Offerings Made to the Heavenly Father

Positive
Loving People
Conditional

#704. Deuteronomy 18:2 ~ The Heavenly Father is the Inheritance of the Levites

Positive
Loving People
Conditional

Unlike all the other tribes, the Levites do not have land. Many people think that when we are in the forever Israel Kingdom, we will all praise the Heavenly Father 24/7. We will be praising the Father, but it is suspected that we will be busy doing other things as well. The Levites will serve the Heavenly Father 24/7. We do not know what He plans for us to do, but knowing the Heavenly Father, it will be productive, fulfilling, and enjoyable.

#705. Deuteronomy 18:3 ~ Of the Slaughters of the Heavenly Father, The People Are to Give the Levites the Shoulder, Cheeks, and Stomach

Positive
Loving People
Conditional

#706. Deuteronomy 18:4-5 ~ To Give the First Fruits of the Grain to the Levites

Positive
Loving People
Conditional

#707. Deuteronomy 18:4-5 ~ To Give Your New Wine to the Levites

Positive
Loving People
Conditional

#708. Deuteronomy 18:4-5 ~ To Give Your Oil to the Levites

Positive
Loving People
Conditional

#709. Deuteronomy 18:4-5 ~ To Give the First of the Fleece of Your Sheep to the Levites

Positive
Loving People
Conditional

#710. Deuteronomy 18:6-8 ~ When a Levite Goes to Where the Heavenly Father Chooses to Serve

Positive
Loving People
Conditional

#711. Deuteronomy 18:10-11 ~ Do Not Make Your Children Pass Through the Fire

Negative
Loving People
Unconditional

See #264 for more information.

#712. Deuteronomy 18:10-11 ~ Do Not Practice Divination

Negative
Loving Abba
Unconditional

Divination: The practice of seeking knowledge of the future, hidden truths, or divine will through supernatural, mystical, or occult means. In the context of the Bible and broader cultural history, there are various methods to interpret signs, omens, or spiritual messages. Divination is often associated with fortune-telling, interpreting omens, consulting spirits, or using objects (e.g., casting lots, reading entrails) to gain insight. It's consistently condemned in the Bible as a pagan practice. This command shows us that the Heavenly Father would never speak to His people through such means. The Heavenly Father consistently communicates through anointed people that He appoints, and it is our job to find His anointed and appointed people. We know how to spot them because they are the ones not teaching against Torah and encouraging people to follow the voice of Elohim.

#713-714. Deuteronomy 18:10-11 ~ Do Not Use Magic/ Do Not Interpret Omens/ Do Not Practice Sorcery

Negative
Loving Abba
Unconditional

See #303 for more information.

#715. Deuteronomy 18:13-14 ~ To Be Perfect Before the Heavenly Father

Positive
Loving Abba
Unconditional

The word for "perfect or blameless" in this command comes from the Hebrew word תָּמִים (tāmîm – H8549) and it means; complete, whole, entire, sound, healthful, unimpaired, innocent, having integrity; the Heavenly Father sees the use of magic, divination, sorcery, and such as going in the opposite direction of tāmîm. In Context: To be "perfect" in this statement is to follow the previous four commands, which once again solidifies that our One True Elohim does not communicate to His people through such methods: Never. People who use such methods usually tell you otherwise, but do not believe it. They are either communicating with evil spirits or making it up.

#716. Deuteronomy 18:15 & 19 ~ To Follow the Prophet (Anointed one) of the Heavenly Father

Positive
Loving Abba
Unconditional

See #130 for more information.

#717. Deuteronomy 18:20-22 ~ False Prophets Must be Executed

Positive
Loving Abba
Conditional

#718. Deuteronomy 19:2-3 & 7 ~ To Create 3 Cities of Refuge for People Who Murder by Mistake

Positive
Loving People
Conditional

See #76 for more information.

#719. Deuteronomy 19:4-6 ~ Defining Who the City of Refuge is for and Why

Positive
Loving People
Conditional

See #76 for more information.

#720. Deuteronomy 19:8-10 ~ To Add More Cities of Refuge as the Borders of Israel Increase

Positive
Loving People
Conditional

See #76 for more information.

#721. Deuteronomy 19:11-13 ~ A City of Refuge Will Not protect one who murders on purpose

Negative
Loving People
Conditional

See #76 for more information.

#722. Deuteronomy 19:15 ~ Judgements Cannot Be Made on One Witness Alone

Negative
Loving People
Conditional

#723. Deuteronomy 19:16-21 ~ How to Deal with False Witnesses

Positive
Loving People
Conditional

#724. Deuteronomy 20:1 ~ Not to Fear Your Enemies in Battle

Positive
Loving Abba
Conditional

David shows this command is not just for the Exodus generation; see 1st Samuel chapter 17.

#725. Deuteronomy 20:2-4 ~ For the Levite Priesthood to Encourage Israel Before a Battle

Positive
Loving People
Conditional

#726. Deuteronomy 20:5 ~ A Man Who Built a New House Cannot go out to War

Negative
Loving People
Conditional

#727. Deuteronomy 20:6 ~ A man who plants a vineyard and has not used it yet, cannot go out to war

Negative
Loving People
Conditional

#728. Deuteronomy 20:7 ~ A Man Who is Engaged to be Wed Cannot go out to War

Negative
Loving People
Conditional

#729. Deuteronomy 20:8 ~ The Fearful Cannot go out to War

Negative
Loving People
Conditional

#730. Deuteronomy 20:9 ~ Officers Appoint Command Divisions for War

Positive
Loving People
Conditional

#731. Deuteronomy 20:10-11 & 15 ~ To Make a Call for Peace Before War for Cities Far from the Land

Positive
Loving People
Conditional

#732. Deuteronomy 20:10-11 ~ If Peace is Received, the People Will Become Laborers

Positive
Loving People
Conditional

#733. Deuteronomy 20:12-14 ~ If Peace is Not Received

Positive
Loving Abba
Conditional

#734. Deuteronomy 20:19-20 ~ During Times of War, do not Destroy Trees That Bear Fruit

Negative
Loving People
Conditional

#735. Deuteronomy 21:1-9 ~ Instructions for Unsolved Murders

Positive
Loving People
Conditional

#736. Deuteronomy 21:15-17 ~ Rights of the Firstborn

Positive
Loving People
Conditional

#737. Deuteronomy 21:18-21 ~ To Execute a Rebellious Son

Positive
Loving People
Conditional

This instruction does not clearly define what a rebellious son looks like. It must be something more than just not listening to their parents;

otherwise, Israel would not have survived to this day and no human being would have hope. There is no such thing as a child who never rebels against their parents. According to Jewish history, this command has never been put into practice. This may be for a situation when a child begins to worship a false god.

#738. Deuteronomy 21:22-23 ~ Do Not Allow a Body to Hang Overnight

Negative
Loving People
Conditional

The Pharisees of Yeshua's time seemed to diminish the importance of this command. They were concerned because the following day was the 1st of Unleavened Bread, a roaming Shabbat (John 19:31). It is possible that if it weren't for the 1st day of Unleavened Bread, they would have allowed Yeshua's body to stay there for days. It was the Romans' way of doing things. This command also shows that hanging could have been a judgment for the death penalty in Israel.

#739. Deuteronomy 22:1 ~ To Return a Straying Sheep or Ox to Your Brother

Positive
Loving People
Unconditional

Commands 739-741 show a common theme of Torah. The Heavenly Father does not want us to gain at the expense of another's loss. If you find something lost, do what you can to find the owner and return it. If that fails, take it to the police. I remember watching a video on social media where someone was telling a story of when they needed money, and as they were walking down the street, they saw someone drop a wallet with money in it. That person picked it up and walked away praising "god" for the "blessing". That was not a blessing from the Heavenly Father; it could have been a test from above, or temptation from the enemy. Regardless of what was happening, spiritually, he failed.

#740. Deuteronomy 22:2 ~ To Take Care of What is Lost Until the Owner Comes for It

Positive
Loving People
Unconditional

See #739 for more information.

#741. Deuteronomy 22:3 ~ Do Not Hide Lost Items for Yourself

Negative
Loving People
Unconditional

#742. Deuteronomy 22:4 ~ To Help Your Brother with Their Donkey in Need

Positive
Loving people
Unconditional

This command encourages us to help people; it is not about the donkey. Since we are currently in dispersion, this command is not limited to covenanted people in need; it can apply to anyone you see needing help. Yeshua only ministered to the Jewish community, but when non-Jewish individuals sought help from him, he helped them too. The Canaanite Woman (Matthew 15:21-28, Mark 7:24-30), the Roman Centurion

(Matthew 8:5-13, Luke 7:1-10), the Samaritan Woman at the Well (John 4:1-42); none of these people were Jewish, and Yeshua helped them. There is also the healing of the Demon-Possessed Man in the Gerasene area (Mark 5:1-20, Luke 8:26-39). The region of the Gerasene was a Gentile area, so it is safe to believe that the demon-possessed man was not Jewish.

#743. Deuteronomy 22:5 ~ Men and Women Do Not Cross-Dress

Negative
Loving Abba
Unconditional

I often wonder if this counts when it comes to entertainment as well. It is not unheard of for actors to cross-dress for a movie or TV role for the sake of entertainment. Some people within the Messianic faith would say such films or shows are a sin because of this command, while others would disagree.

#744. Deuteronomy 22:6-7 ~ When You Find a Nest of Birds with Mother and Eggs or a Mother with Younglings

Positive
Loving Abba
Unconditional

#745. Deuteronomy 22:8 ~ Build a Parapet on Your Roof

Positive
Loving People
Conditional

In ancient times, people would rent out their roofs for people to live. A parapet is a fence on the roof to prevent people from falling off by accident. This command is conditional because it is for the Land. Technically, it can be unconditional if you own a home. Honestly, does anyone in the world rent out their roofs today?

#746. Deuteronomy 22:9 ~ Not to Sow Two Different Kinds of Seeds in a Vineyard

Negative
Loving Abba
Unconditional

See #299 for more information.

#747. Deuteronomy 22:10 ~ Not to Plow an Ox and Donkey Together

Negative
Loving Abba
Unconditional

From a practical standpoint, yoking an ox and a donkey together would cause nothing but problems because the stronger ox would overpower the donkey, leading to uneven plowing and/or injury to one or both animals. However, this is something that anyone in ancient times would have clearly understood. This command is most likely an old idiom, which led scholars to search for spiritual understanding behind this instruction.

Many biblical scholars interpret this instruction as a broader principle of separation and purity. Torah often emphasize maintaining distinctions, for example, not mixing different types of seeds (Leviticus 19:19) or fabrics (Deuteronomy 22:11). Yoking an ox (a "clean" animal) with a donkey (an "unclean" animal) could symbolize the importance of avoiding unequal or incompatible partnerships in this world, whether in marriage, business, or spiritual matters. Paul drew inspiration from this command in 2nd Corinthians 6:14, when he warned against being "unequally yoked" with unbelievers.

#748. Deuteronomy 22:11 ~ Do Not Put on Garments with Wool and Linen Together

Negative
Loving Abba
Unconditional

See #300 for more information.

#749. Deuteronomy 22:12 ~ To Make Tassels (Tzitzit) For Your Garments

Positive
Loving People
Unconditional

See #485 for more information. Normally, wherever you buy Tzitzits, you can also find kits to make them yourself, making this command relatively easy for anyone to keep. There are also videos online showing you how to tie them in various ways.

#750. Deuteronomy 22:13-19 ~ When a Man Wrongfully Accuses His Wife of Not Being a Maiden

Positive
Loving People
Conditional

#751. Deuteronomy 22:20-21 ~ When a Man Rightfully Accuses His Wife of Not Being a Maiden

Positive
Loving Abba
Conditional

#752. Deuteronomy 22:22 ~ Men Having Sexual Relations with Married Women is Adultery; Both Must Be Executed

Positive
Loving People
Conditional

See #57 for more information.

#753. Deuteronomy 22:23-24 ~ If an Engaged Woman Sleeps with Another Man, Both Must Be Executed

Positive
Loving People
Conditional

See #57 for more information.

#754. Deuteronomy 22:25-27 ~ A Man Who Rapes an Engaged Woman Must Be Executed

Positive
Loving People
Conditional

#755. Deuteronomy 22:28-29 ~ Instructions for a Man Who Sleeps with a Maiden Who Is Not Engaged

Positive
Loving People
Unconditional

This teaching is unconditional because it does not require a court system to impose; however, if you are in a Torah-honoring community with anointed and appointed leadership, and all parties agree to the Heavenly Father's judgment, it can be upheld. In this situation, it does not appear that either the maiden or the man sinned directly; however, this command gives room to correct the situation and not bring shame to either of them. Based on the wording of this command, it is unclear if it counts if the woman is not a maiden. This command is for a woman who has never had sex before. Since the daughters of Israel are forbidden to whore (#308 & #346) this command seems to protect the women of Israel far more than the men.

#756. Deuteronomy 22:30 ~ Men Do Not Sleep with Their Father's Wife

Negative
Loving People
Unconditional

First seen in Leviticus 18:8 (251).

#757. Deuteronomy 22:30 ~ Not to Uncover Your Father's Skirt

Negative
Loving People
Unconditional

First seen in #251. Relating to inappropriate sexual relations with the father's wife, see the previous command.

#758. Deuteronomy 23:1 ~People Born Because of an Abominable Union Cannot Enter the Community of Israel

Negative
Loving Abba
Unconditional

This could be connected to commands #333 and #334. If it is not an immediate situation or a situation spawned from within Israel, then command #45 shows the exception to the rule.

#759. Deuteronomy 23:3-4 ~ Ammonites and Moabites Shall Not Enter the Assembly of Israel

Negative
Loving Abba
Unconditional

The reason is in verse 5.

#760. Deuteronomy 23:6 ~ Do Not Seek Peace nor Goodwill with Ammonites and Moabites

Negative
Loving Abba
Unconditional

The reason is in verse 5.

#761. Deuteronomy 23:7 ~ Do Not Hate the Edomite or the Egyptians

Negative
Loving People
Unconditional

#762. Deuteronomy 23:9-14 ~ Instructions on How to Keep the Camp Clean During War

Positive
Loving Abba
Conditional

#763. Deuteronomy 23:15-16 ~ Instructions for When a Slave Flees to You

Positive
Loving People
Conditional

The wording does not exclude foreign slaves.

#764. Deuteronomy 23:17 ~ Prostitution is Not Allowed in Israel

Negative
Loving Abba
Unconditional

#765. Deuteronomy 23:18 ~ Do Not Give a Vowed Offering from Sinful Profits

Negative
Loving Abba
Unconditional

#766. Deuteronomy 23:19 ~ Do Not Lend to Your Brother with Interest

Negative
Loving People
Unconditional

#767. Deuteronomy 23:20 ~ Can Lend to Foreigners with Interest

Positive
Loving Abba
Unconditional

#768. Deuteronomy 23:21 ~ To Quickly Pay a Vow to the Heavenly Father

Positive
Loving Abba
Conditional

See #165 for more information.

#769. Deuteronomy 23:22 ~ Vowing to the Heavenly Father is Optional

Positive
Loving Abba
Unconditional

See #516 and #833 for more information.

#770. Deuteronomy 23:23 ~ To Do What You Say You Will Do

Positive
Loving People
Unconditional

Repeated in Matthew 5:33-37 (833). Also see command #516 for more information.

#771. Deuteronomy 23:24 ~ Instructions When Eating in a Vineyard

Positive
Loving Abba
Conditional

This is conditional because it talks about vineyards on the land; however, it can also be unconditional and customary outside of the land.

#772. Deuteronomy 23:25 ~ Instructions to Eat Grain in a Field

Positive
Loving The Father
Unconditional

#773. Deuteronomy 24:1-4 ~ Instructions on Divorce

Positive
Loving People
Unconditional

The WEB says, "some unseemly thing in her", The TS2009 version uses the term, "matter of uncoveredness". Depending on the Bible version you use, Deuteronomy 24:1-4 can be ambiguous or more distinct. The word for uncovered or unseemly comes from the Hebrew word עֶרְוָה ('ervâ – H6172), and it means nakedness, nudity, shame, indecency, exposed, or figuratively used as undefended, and pudenda, which implies shameful exposure. The Hebrew word 'ervâ points us to infidelity. This supports what Yeshua says in #834.

#774. Deuteronomy 24:5 ~ Men Are Exempt from War in the First Year of Marriage

Negative
Loving People
Conditional

#775. Deuteronomy 24:6 ~ Do Not Take a Life in a Pledge

Negative
Loving People
Unconditional

This seems like an odd command, possibly because we are about 3400 years removed from when these words were first spoken. If you pledge to take someone's life, then you are planning to murder, which makes you guilty of breaking #56. I suspect that there were certain situations where people thought this was a legitimate thing to do. The only thing that makes sense for this teaching today is when someone is assigned the role of a "Blood Avenger" (See #76 for more information).

Despite the name, the Blood Avenger is not John Wick! They couldn't just kill someone accused of murder; there were rules they needed to follow. If they found the alleged murderer in a refuge city, there had to be a trial. If that accused individual was found innocent, there was nothing more for the Blood Avenger to do because, according to #690, Israel should listen to a judge of Israel. If a Blood Avenger pledged to take someone's life before the official trial took place, they would be guilty of breaking this command, and it would be worse if the accused is found innocent because more than one command would be broken.

#776. Deuteronomy 24:7 ~ Kidnappers Should Be Executed

Positive
Loving People
Conditional

First seen in #79.

#777. Deuteronomy 24:8 ~ To Carefully Follow the Priests in an Outbreak of Leprosy

Positive
Loving Abba
Unconditional

#778. Deuteronomy 24:9 ~ Remember What the Heavenly Father Did to the Egyptians When We Came out of Egypt

Positive
Loving Abba
Unconditional

This command is usually covered in the Torah cycles and the Passover Sedar.

#779. Deuteronomy 24:10-11 ~ When You Lend to Your Brother, Do Not Be Aggressive to Get Back

Negative
Loving People
Unconditional

An underlying theme of Torah is that we should be a financially strong people. One of the most common causes of broken friendships and severed family ties is lending money simply because it's there, without realizing that we couldn't afford it. We should never lend needed money; it's a recipe for disaster. As citizens of Israel, lending should be from a position of financial strength. If the person borrowing the money says they will pay it back at a certain time, that is between them and the Heavenly Father; from a borrower's standpoint, it shouldn't matter if the money is returned or when, because you don't need it! If the loan cannot be paid back when promised or can never be paid back, it shouldn't affect you in the least. This makes it easy to keep the spirit of the year of Jubilee alive and forgive their debt if needed. The idea of being financially strong is also perpetuated in Matthew 5:42 (836) when Yeshua instructs us to lend when people ask. If you cannot meet command #836 because you do not have the money to lend, that is a strong sign that you are not where you should be financially; it should motivate you to aim higher.

A word of caution: When you lend money from a position of financial strength, it is easy to forget the transaction; however, if the other person cannot pay you back, they can have an opposite reaction and suffer guilt for not being able to pay you back. Some people avoid certain congregations because they cannot pay back a loan and often subconsciously create some form of drama to justify walking away. When you lend, let the other person know there is no pressure, even assure them that if they can't pay it back, it's ok. This is mercy that flows perfectly with various commands within Torah. Of course, this is only talking about personal loans. Business loans are different; nonetheless, there should still be a level of mercy in those situations as well when it is done within the body of believers.

#780. Deuteronomy 24:12-13 ~ To Return a Poor Man's Pledge Right Away

Positive
Loving People
Unconditional

During this time, it was common for poor people to lend their cloaks as collateral if they needed to borrow something or get a loan. Their cloaks were usually the only way to stay warm at night, making them valuable for collateral. If they couldn't return the item borrowed or pay back the loan as promised, this command calls for the borrower to show compassion and return the cloak to ensure that the lender's basic needs are still met.

#781. Deuteronomy 24:14 ~ To Pay the Poor Promptly

Positive
Loving People
Unconditional

#782. Deuteronomy 24:15 ~ Do Not Delay in Giving the Poor Their Wages

Negative
Loving People
Unconditional

#783. Deuteronomy 24:16 ~ Fathers Are Not Responsible for the Sins of Their Sons

Negative
Loving People
Unconditional

#784. Deuteronomy 24:16 ~ Sons Are Not Responsible for the Sins of Their Fathers

Negative
Loving People
Unconditional

Commands #783 and #784 render the doctrine of "original sin" useless. While it is true that sin came into the world through Adam, none of us are being punished due to Adam's sins. We are all responsible only for the sins that we commit. When people stand before Elohim on the Day of Judgment, He will not address what Adam did, what their grandfathers did, or what their fathers did. On the Day of Judgment, every individual will be judged based on their own actions.

#785. Deuteronomy 24:17 ~ Do Not Distort Justice for the Stranger

Negative
Loving People
Conditional

#786. Deuteronomy 24:17 ~ Do Not Distort Justice for the Fatherless

Negative
Loving People
Unconditional

#787. Deuteronomy 24:17 ~ Do Not Take the Garment of a Widow

Negative
Loving People
Unconditional

#788. Deuteronomy 24:18 ~ To Remember That the People of Israel Were Slaves in Egypt

Positive
Loving Abba
Unconditional

See #38 for more information.

#789. Deuteronomy 24:18 ~ To Remember That the Heavenly Father Ransomed Israel from Egypt

Positive
Loving Abba
Unconditional

#790. Deuteronomy 24:19 ~ To Leave Some Produce in Your Fields for Strangers, the Fatherless, and Widows

Positive
Loving People
Unconditional

See #278 for more information.

#791. Deuteronomy 24:20 ~ To Leave Some Olives for the Stranger, the Fatherless, and the Widows

Positive
Loving People
Unconditional

See #278 for more information.

#792. Deuteronomy 24:21 ~ To Leave Some Grapes in Your Vineyard for Strangers, the Fatherless, and the Widow

Positive
Loving People
Unconditional

See #278 for more information.

#793. Deuteronomy 24:22 ~ To Remember That We Were Slaves in Egypt

Positive
Loving Abba
Unconditional

See #38 for more information.

#794. Deuteronomy 25:1 ~ For Men to go to a Judge for Disputes

Positive
Loving Abba
Unconditional

See #678 for more information.

#795. Deuteronomy 25:2-3 ~ Instructions for Wrongdoers to be Struck According to the Judge's Ruling

Positive
Loving People
Conditional

When Yeshua said, *"But I tell you, don't resist him who is evil; but whoever strikes you on your right cheek, turn to him the other also* (Matthew 5:39)." This command is what he was addressing. It fits the theme of wrongdoers going above and beyond in restitution (See #93 & #834).

#796. Deuteronomy 25:4 ~ To Not Muzzle an Ox While it's Threshing

Positive
Loving Abba
Unconditional

#797. Deuteronomy 25:5-6 ~ Duties of a Husband's Brother

Positive
Loving People
Conditional

This is one of those rare commands that most people just do not run into. I've never heard of a woman who would want to do this in today's age. This was obviously a thing during biblical times, but humanity has moved away from such things. There is a reference for this command in Genesis chapter 38. There are few cultures in the world today where this takes place, and even rarer situations in America where a woman marries the brother of her husband who has passed away. This command can be unconditional because it doesn't require a court to implement, but if the brother refuses, there is nothing that can be done about it today. The punishment is in the next command. Even though there is no death penalty involved, there is no government to enforce it either. If the brother is not willing to marry her, he is most likely not sticking around for what is to come in command #798. Also, if the brother is married, that would be a legitimate reason to reject this setup since polygamy is outlawed in most countries today. That is why this command is conditional.

#798. Deuteronomy 25:7-10 ~ If the Husband's Brother Refuses His Duties

Positive
Loving People
Unconditional

#799. Deuteronomy 25:11-12 ~ Women Are Not Allowed to Damage Men's Genitals

Negative
Loving People
Unconditional

#800. Deuteronomy 25:13-15 ~ To Have Perfect and Right Weights for Business Transactions

Positive
Loving People
Unconditional

#801. Deuteronomy 25:14-15 ~ To Have Perfect and Right Measures for Business Transactions

Positive
Loving People
Unconditional

#802. Deuteronomy 25:17-19 ~ To Remember What Amalek Did While Israel Was Coming Out of Egypt

Positive
Loving Abba
Unconditional

Possibly detailed in the missing book of wars mentioned in Numbers 21:14.

#803. Deuteronomy 26:12-19 ~ When Giving the 3rd Tithe

Positive
Loving People
Unconditional

See #644 for more information.

#804. Deuteronomy 27:1 ~ To Guard all of Torah

Positive
Loving People
Unconditional

See #247 for more information.

#805. Deuteronomy 27:10 ~ To Obey the Voice of the Heavenly Father

Positive
Loving People
Unconditional

See #44 for more information.

NOTE: Deuteronomy 27:11-26 The Curses from Mount Ebal

NOTE: Deuteronomy 28:1-14 Blessings for obeying the Heavenly Father

NOTE: Deuteronomy 28:15-68 Curses for disobeying the Heavenly Father

NOTE: Deuteronomy 29:4 People need eyes to see and ears to hear the Heavenly Father. This is what we should pray for ourselves and those in the world

#806. Deuteronomy 29:9 ~ To Guard the Words of the Covenant

Positive
Loving Abba
Unconditional

See #247 for more information.

#807. Deuteronomy 29:9 ~ To Do the Words of the Covenant

Positive
Loving Abba
Unconditional

This book is designed to help us meet this command. Every command of Torah originated from the voice of our Heavenly Father. The words of the covenant are found in the following scripture verses:

> *Now therefore, if you will indeed obey my voice, and keep my covenant, then you shall be my own possession from among all peoples; for all the earth is mine; and you shall be to me a kingdom of priests, and a holy nation. These are the words which you shall speak to the children of Israel.*
> – Exodus 19:5-6

To do the words of the covenant is to know Torah to the best of our ability, so we can establish Torah wherever we are (Romans 3:31). Obeying His voice is to keep His commands. We cannot meet the requirements of this instruction without knowing all the teachings of the Heavenly Father.

NOTE: Deuteronomy 29:14-15 is connected to Exodus 19:9 for Israel to believe in Moses forever.

NOTE: Deuteronomy 30:1-10 The good news.

#808. Deuteronomy 30:16 ~ To Love the Heavenly Father

Positive
Loving Abba
Unconditional

See #580 for more information.

#809. Deuteronomy 30:16 ~ To Walk in the Ways of the Heavenly Father

Positive
Loving People
Unconditional

See #575 for more information.

#810. Deuteronomy 30:16 ~ To Guard the Commands of the Heavenly Father

Positive
Loving Abba
Unconditional

See command #247 for more information.

#811. Deuteronomy 30:16 ~ To Guard the Right Rulings of the Heavenly Father

Positive
Loving People
Unconditional

See #247 for more information.

#812. Deuteronomy 30:19 ~ To Choose Life

Positive
Loving Abba
Unconditional

Choosing Torah is choosing life. This command is a reference to Yeshua, who said that he is the way, the truth, and the *life* (John 14:6). Yeshua never sinned (2nd Corinthians 5:21, Hebrews 4:15, 1st Peter 2:22, & 1st John 3:5), and since Torah defines what sin is (Romans 7:7, Deuteronomy 6:25), that means Yeshua kept Torah perfectly. We are expected to follow in Yeshua's footsteps (1st John 2:6 & 1st Peter 2:21). When we walk like Yeshua, keeping Torah perfectly as he demonstrated (or at least doing everything possible to do so), we are choosing life, and the reward is that we too will resurrect from the dead, just like he did (See Romans 6:1-14).

Very early in this book, I said, "This is not a Messianic apologetics book." For this command, I will make the only exception to that rule. When Moses wrote Deuteronomy 30:19, there is no doubt that his message is for us to keep Torah; it is how we choose life. Contrary to what most people believe, it is not difficult to choose life, to keep Torah (Deuteronomy 30:11).

We are almost at the end of our Torah list; so far, has there been any commandment presented that is difficult to keep? When it comes to the Torah lifestyle, the difficulties come from our desires for control and the people around us who do not understand or agree with total submission to the Heavenly Father. Torah is relatively logical, mostly easy to understand, and not hard to do. However, today it is common to hear people discourage the Torah way of life because "we have already messed up!" Such people will usually say, "No one can keep the law." What does that mean?

Choose Life

This is a statement often heard from people who discourage the Torah lifestyle. However, this seemingly straightforward comment is not as straightforward as most people think. Even though people say it with good intentions, it is a statement fueled by the enemy of mankind. When people say those words, the scripture they are most likely thinking of is, *"for all have sinned, and fall short of the glory of God"* (Romans 3:23).

When Paul wrote those words, what was he saying? Was he saying, "Well, we all mess up, so why bother trying?" Of course not! At the end of that chapter (verse 31), he also writes, *"Do we then nullify Torah through faith? May it never be! No, we establish Torah."* But in contrast, when people say, "No one can keep the law!" it seems like their attitude is more in the spirit of, "Why bother trying?" What if Torah is not about directly living sin-free? What if there was a greater goal behind the teachings of the Heavenly Father written by Moses and the Prophets?

If Torah was about not sinning, why are there contingency plans embedded in Torah for when people sin by mistake? For example, Numbers 15:22-28, and Deuteronomy 19:2-3 & 7. In 1st John 2:1, we read, *"My little children, I write these things to you so that you may not sin. If anyone sins, we have a Counselor with the Father, Yeshua Messiah, the righteous."* For the citizens of Israel, sin should not be a common part of our lives, sin shouldn't define who we are, but we still deal with desires of the flesh in a world filled with sin and sinful people all around us. Even the most well-tempered of us can get triggered with rage by selfish, inconsiderate individuals. However, the Heavenly Father is truly an understanding Father.

Abraham sinned, and the Heavenly Father still said that Abraham obeyed His voice, and kept His requirements, commandments, statutes, and laws (Genesis 26:5). David sinned in ways that most people wouldn't! He arranged to have a man killed after finding out that he had gotten the man's wife pregnant (2nd Samuel Chapter 11). David begged the Heavenly Father to build the temple, but the request was rejected because David was a man of war, his hands were stained with a lot of blood (2 Samuel 7:1-17 & 1 Chronicles 17:1-15). In the accounts of David, we see his highs and his lows, we even see some of his poor choices, but despite all that, after the death of David, Elohim still says to Solomon, "*And if you walk in my ways, keeping my statutes and my commandments, as your father David walked, then I will lengthen your days* (1 Kings 3:14)." Also see 1 Kings 11:34 & 2 Chronicles 7:17-18.

It is a no-brainer to see that our Elohim does not want us to sin, but He also understands the struggles we face in this world, the temptations and snares set by our enemy, and the desires of the flesh we must fight every second of every day. Ultimately, Torah is about Adonai's people staying away from sin, but most importantly, Torah is about us developing a perfect heart towards our Heavenly Father. Through that perfect heart, our transgressions are removed as far as the east is from the west (Psalms 103:11-12). He knows that we stumble and fall, but as we stumble and fall, we get back up, repent, and continue to draw closer to Him (Proverbs 24:16).

"No one can keep the law?" Then how do you explain Zacharias and Elizabeth in Luke 1:6? "No one can keep the Law?" How do you explain Job? In Mark 2:17, Yeshua said, "*Those who are healthy have no need for a physician, but those who are sick. I came not to call the righteous, but sinners to repentance* (Also see Matthew 9:12-13, and Luke 5:31-32)." That statement alone makes it clear that not everyone in Israel was messing up Torah. The statement, "No one can keep the law," is a very deceptive and evil statement, born from the belly of demons, designed to discourage people from walking like Yeshua and draw close to the Heavenly Father.

Despite our struggles, the Heavenly Father is our greatest supporter. Otherwise, He would not say things such as, "*Come now, and let's reason together," says YHWH: "Though your sins be as scarlet, they shall be as white as snow. Though they be red like crimson, they shall be as wool. If you are willing and obedient, you shall eat the good of the land; but if you refuse and rebel, you shall be devoured with the sword; for the mouth of Yahweh has spoken it* (Isaiah 1:18-20)."

#813. Deuteronomy 30:20 ~ To Love the Heavenly Father

Positive
Loving Abba
Unconditional

See #580 for more information.

#814. Deuteronomy 30:20 ~ To Obey the Voice of the Heavenly Father

Positive
Loving Abba
Unconditional

See #44 for more information.

#815. Deuteronomy 30:20 ~ To Cling to the Heavenly Father

Positive
Loving Abba
Unconditional

See #587 for more information.

#816. Deuteronomy 31:10-13 ~ To Read All of Torah to the Congregation of Israel Every 7 Years

Positive
Loving People
Unconditional

With yearly Torah cycles today, thanks to our Jewish brothers, this command is well taken care of as we read Genesis, Exodus, Leviticus, Numbers, and Deuteronomy every year. Some congregations even do the whole book of Deuteronomy every year for the week of Sukkot. If you are not a part of a congregation that reads the Torah year-round, or at least on the 3-year cycle, you need to find another congregation.

NOTE: Deuteronomy 31:16 When you die, you sleep. The Heavenly Father gathers all of Israel when we die; Deuteronomy 32:49-50. There is no detailed explanation of what that means, but the scriptures hint at the idea that when humans die, something different happens to those who believe in the Heavenly Father, which is why Abraham, Moses, and all the great men of the Bible are not dead. Also see what Yeshua says in Luke 20:34-38.

#817. Deuteronomy 32:46-47 ~ To Know the Final Song of Moses

Positive
Loving Abba
Unconditional

See Deuteronomy 32:1-43.

NOTE: Deuteronomy 33: The final blessings of Moses.

#818. 2nd Chronicles 15:2 ~ To Seek Adonai

Positive
Loving Abba
Unconditional

Knowing His voice is the only way to seek the Heavenly Father properly. In Luke 17:20-21, Yeshua said the following: *"Elohim's Kingdom doesn't come with observation; neither will they say, 'Look, here!' or, 'Look, there!' for behold, Elohim's Kingdom is within you."*

Throughout this book, I have said that Torah is about changing you from within. In command #812, I stated that the goal of Torah is to develop the perfect heart towards our Heavenly Father. In Matthew 5:8, Yeshua also says, *"Blessed are the pure in heart, for they shall see Elohim."* The world cannot see Elohim because they are looking with their physical eyes. Every command of Elohim is a map that leads us to see Him from within. It is only through Torah, understanding Torah as He wants it to be understood, allowing Torah to change us from within, that we can see Him.

#819. Psalms 119:142 ~ Torah is Righteousness and Truth Forever

Positive
Loving People
Unconditional

#820. Proverbs 6:16-19 ~ 7 Things the Heavenly Father Hates

Negative
Loving Abba
Unconditional

- Arrogant eyes
- Lying tongue
- Hands that shed innocent blood
- Heart that devises wicked schemes
- Feet that are swift in running to mischief
- False witness who utters lies
- He who sows discord among brothers

These are things we all should know very well. The world calls these "7 deadly sins". People who do these things on a regular basis are not people filled with the Set-Apart Spirit of our Elohim. The overall spirit of Torah draws us in the opposite direction of these things.

#821. Proverbs 10:4 ~ Do Not Be Lazy

Negative
Loving People
Unconditional

#822. Proverbs 14:30 ~ Do Not Envy

Negative
Loving Abba
Unconditional

See Psalms 37:1, Proverbs 24:19-20, Ecclesiastes 4:4, Galatians 5:26, Proverbs 6:6, 13:4, 24:33-34, and 2nd Thessalonians 3:10.

#823. Proverbs 28:25 ~ Do Not Be Greedy

Negative
Loving Abba
Unconditional

See Ecclesiastes 5:10.

#824. Ecclesiastes 12:13 ~ To Obey the Commands of Adonai

Positive
Loving Abba
Unconditional

The words of Ecclesiastes 12:13 bring us full circle to Genesis 12:1-3.

#825. Isaiah 8:20 ~ To Teach Torah and the Testimony

Positive
Loving Abba
Unconditional

See Matthew 5:19.

#826. Isaiah 51:7 ~ To Not Fear Man

Negative
Loving Abba
Unconditional

See Matthew 10:28.

#827. Jeremiah 9:23-24 ~ Do Not Be Prideful

Negative
Loving People
Unconditional

See Proverbs 16:16-18, Romans 12:16, 1st Corinthians 13:4, & Galatians 6:3.

Pride spoils Torah! We are not chosen because we are better than everyone else. Keeping Torah sets us apart from the world for our

Heavenly Father, but it doesn't elevate us above anyone. Keeping Torah does not make us better than other people! Those who keep Torah, thinking that they are better than others, turn Torah into a religion, and Torah is not a religion; it is a covenant that changes us from within. No matter how close we draw to Elohim in this world, we are still in corruptible bodies with the ability to perform all kinds of evil. What is the point of looking down upon rapists, pedophiles, murderers, thieves, con men, and so on? The only difference is that we've chosen to believe in the ways of the Heavenly Father, but once again, we are still capable of doing such things and more. This is why we can never be better than anyone else in this world. Paul masterfully explains this dilemma in Romans 7:7-25.

#828. Matthew 5:19 ~ To Teach and Do Torah

Positive
Loving Abba
Unconditional

#829. Matthew 5:21-26 ~ To Avoid Anger

Negative
Loving People
Unconditional

See Job 5:2 and #56 for more information.

#830. Matthew 5:27-28 ~ Do Not Lust After Other People

Negative
Loving People
Unconditional

See command #60 for more information. When reviewing this command, we often focus on men wanting women who belong to someone else. This command can also be for women lusting after men they should not have. The best example is Joseph and Potiphar's wife in Genesis 39:1-20.

#831. Matthew 5:29-30 ~ To Fight Against Your Weaknesses

Positive
Loving Abba
Unconditional

See #4 for more information.

#832. Matthew 5:31-32 ~ To Only Divorce for Sexual Immorality

Positive
Loving People
Unconditional

First seen in:
- Deuteronomy 24:1-4 (773)

This instruction is repeated in:
- Matthew 19:9

According to command #773, the only reason to divorce is if the woman was not a virgin at the time of marriage; this is considered sexual immorality within Israel, and it also alludes to the idea that the woman deceived about her virginity. This can be a serious sin if the woman is marrying a Levite (Leviticus 21:13-14). In today's world, marrying a virgin is rare. If you get married knowing your bride is not a virgin, you void the right to use this command as an excuse for divorce. In Exodus 21:10 (73), if a man is not happy with his wife, he could marry another, with guidelines on what to do and not do in that situation, and if he fails to meet those guidelines, the 1st wife can leave (74).

This book does not promote polygamy! We are simply covering all bases. While it is true that Torah does not discourage polygamy, there is nothing within Torah that says you must have more than one wife either. It is suspected that the Heavenly Father didn't condemn it because of how humanity was at the time, and that it could have been something that many of the men of Israel couldn't resist.

The Heavenly Father hates divorce (See Malachi 2:14-16). While sexual immorality is a reason for divorce, the command does not state that you must get a divorce in that situation. Divorce is allowed because of our spiritual immaturity.

Today, divorce is quite common. People part ways for various reasons, which undermines the sanctity of marriage. As Israelites, we should find a way to make it work as we grow from within, even if our spouse doesn't take the same spiritual path. If you find yourself in a situation where divorce seems like the only option, heed the words of Yeshua in Matthew 19:9. Unless the other person moves on to engage in sexual relations with others, are you prepared to embrace the single lifestyle? One final point to consider: When studying the commands in the writings of Moses, it seems that only men could initiate a divorce. In Matthew 19:9, if a man marries another, that is also considered adultery, implying that a woman can likewise initiate a divorce and move on. While the writings of Moses may not address this, it does not contradict, nor are there any indications within Moses' writings that the Heavenly Father is opposed to it either.

#833. Matthew 5:33-37 ~ How to Approach Oaths

Negative
Loving People
Unconditional

First seen in:

* Deuteronomy 23:23 (770)

Also see #516 for more information.

#834. Matthew 5:38-39 ~ Not to Retaliate

Negative
Loving People
Unconditional

See #85 for more information.

#835. Matthew 5:40-41 ~ To Go Above Court-Ordered Restitution if You Lose a Trial

Positive
Loving People
Unconditional

See command #93.

#836. Matthew 5:42 ~ To Lend When Asked

Positive
Loving People
Unconditional

See #779 for more information.

#837. Matthew 5:43-48 ~ To Love Your Enemies

Positive
Loving People
Unconditional

See Romans 12:19-20 (858), and Proverbs 25:21.

#838. Matthew 6:1-4 ~ To Not Give for Vanity

Negative
Loving Abba
Unconditional

#839. Matthew 6:5-15 ~ How to Pray

Positive
Loving Abba
Unconditional

Many people recite this prayer verbatim, but it may be more of the anatomy of how a prayer should be structured.

#840. Matthew 6:16-18 ~ Do Not Fast for Vanity

Negative
Loving Abba
Unconditional

Of course this is talking about fasting for spiritual purposes. Today, many people fast more for health reasons, those do not count for this command.

#841. Matthew 6:19-21 ~ To Lay Up Treasures in Heaven

Positive
Loving Abba
Unconditional

For this teaching, Yeshua directs us to prioritize living for the Heavenly Father's kingdom more than worldly pursuits. It follows giving, prayer, and fasting, emphasizing sincerity in faith over appearances. Reflect on what you prioritize—wealth and status, or faith and service unto the Heavenly Father. Invest in what lasts: relationships, kindness, and devotion to the Heavenly Father. It's a call to trust in Abba's provisions and seek eternal rewards over temporary gains in everything we do.

#842. Matthew 6:22-23 ~ Be Careful of What You Expose Yourself To

Positive
Loving Abba
Unconditional

#843. Matthew 6:24 ~ Avoid Personification of Wealth

Negative
Loving Abba
Unconditional

Many people believe that money is the root of all evil, but the Bible says it is the love of money that is the root of all evil (1st Timothy 6:10). However, we need money to survive, and often throughout the scriptures, blessings from above and wealth seem to coincide. In this world, we can't avoid money, so how can we approach this command from a healthy, spiritual, and righteous point of view?

Torah for Modern Messiah Believers

Money is like a power tool, such as a chainsaw or jack hammer. If you respect money, and treat it with caution, it will do what it is supposed to do. When you handle money carelessly, just like a chainsaw, or jack hammer, you can hurt yourself and everyone around you. Many people struggle financially because they do not respect the money they get and/or do not believe in themselves to aim higher financially. Thanks to mainstream religion and the media, some people have a love/hate relationship with money. Many people romanticize about having money, but at the same time, they subconsciously believe that having too much money is bad.

With examples like Abraham, Joseph, David, and what the Heavenly Father says in Deuteronomy 28:1-14, our Elohim has no problem with His people becoming wealthy. As stated throughout this book, our Heavenly Father wants us to prosper in everything good that we do. When we look at the tithing system He has established, He wants us to be financially strong. There is nothing wrong with aiming for high paying jobs or owning a business. There is nothing wrong with aiming to be financially independent or even wealthy.

Personification or love for wealth comes when people do not care if other are effected negatively, as long as they make money. Making money at the expense of others' misfortune, taking advantage of people's lack of knowledge, or gaining an unfair advantage of a system in a way that others could go to jail if they did it. It's the mechanic that finds all kinds of problems that was never there before, the medical expert that wants to take full advantage of the health insurance system to make as much money as possible, the car salesman that doesn't tell you everything that is wrong with the car, that lawyer trying to convince you that you can get millions, when all you really need is a few thousand, or that gas stations that gouge prices during a natural disaster. Of course, all this also includes anytime someone lies, cheats, or steals, to get money.

It is clear in the Bible that the Heavenly Fathers wants to bless His people in all kinds of ways, but He wants to do it through our hard and righteous works. He wants us to prosper in win-win situations where we get fair and honest pay while others get their money's worth. When we make money, no one gets the short end of the stick, everyone walks away happy. Unfortunately, in this world there are many ways to gain money at the expense of others. Fortunately, there are many ways to gain money in ways that no one is screwed over and that is what the Heavenly Father loves to see from His people.

#844. Matthew 6:25-34 ~ Do Not Be Anxious

Negative
Loving Abba
Unconditional

Also see Philippians 4:6. This command can be easier for some than others. If you suffer from anxiety, do everything you can to seek help. Usually, anxiety is a fear of something that may or may not come to pass. Anxiety causes social and mental stress. Trust and focus on the Heavenly Father is the solution that Yeshua presents in this command. If you cannot do that, once again, seek help from a professional who can lead you to that point.

#845. Matthew 7:1-5 ~ Not to Judge

Negative
Loving People
Unconditional

See #293-#294 for more information. We do not personally judge. We submit to the Heavenly Father's judgments written by Moses and establish those judgments wherever we live (Romans 3:31, also see John 5:45-47).

#846. Matthew 7:6 ~ Do Not Waste Time with People Who Will Not Listen

Negative
Loving People
Unconditional

#847. Matthew 7:7-11 ~ To Ask the Heavenly Father What You Want

Positive
Loving The Father
Unconditional

#848. Matthew 7:12 ~ Treat Others as You'd Like to be Treated

Positive
Loving People
Unconditional

Known as the "golden rule" in the world, this command comes from Leviticus 19:18. It talks about not taking revenge; however, it is likely that the verse right before it makes the complete thought.

> *"You shall not hate your brother in your heart. You shall surely rebuke your neighbor, and not bear sin because of him. You shall not take vengeance, nor bear any grudge against the children of your people; but you shall love your neighbor as yourself. I am Yahweh." - Leviticus 19:17-18*

#849. Matthew 7:13-14 ~ Enter the Narrow Gate

Positive
Loving Abba
Unconditional

When you think about it, the narrow gate is Torah, not just doing Torah, but striving to let Torah be absorbed in who you are, to understand Torah as the Heavenly Father intends it to be understood from within. The narrow road is getting Torah absorbed into your character. Spiritual Judaism does not follow what Moses wrote exactly. Judaism does not have it all wrong, but they created a whole system based on commentaries of Torah and placed those commentaries on an equal level to what Moses wrote. It is why we see Yeshua butting heads with the Pharisee leaders of his time.

Thanks to Catholicism and its efforts to distinguish itself from Judaism, Torah has become taboo for most Christians around the world, with ministries that strongly oppose Torah for a false "grace" doctrine. Yeshua teaches us that what Moses wrote is trustworthy, and he lived it perfectly. We must be careful in guarding his words and following how he lives, because his life and words show us the true narrow road.

The mechanics of Torah is not the hard part. In its simplest form, Torah is just a list of things to do and things not to do. The actual work comes from what is going on within as you do or don't do. Anyone can choose not to work on Saturdays, what is going on within as you do so? Are you making that day set-apart to the Heavenly Father or doing things that take away from focusing on Him? That is where the spiritual growth in the command comes in. Anyone can stop eating pork and shrimp, but do you still desire to eat such things within, or do you get sick at the thought of it? That is where the spiritual growth from such teachings comes in. Doing Torah is how you enter the narrow road;

allowing Torah to transform you from within is the engine and fuel that gives you the power to travel down that road.

#850. Matthew 7:15-20 ~ To Be Aware of False Prophets

Positive
Loving Abba
Unconditional

The easiest way to identify false prophets today is to identify the people who discourage living by Torah (see Deuteronomy 13:1-4). Another way to identify false prophets is to recognize the hypocrites, those who say the right things but don't do them (see Matthew 23:1-36).

#851. Matthew 11:25-26 ~ To Forgive

Positive
Loving People (self)
Unconditional

Forgiveness is not about the people who have done you wrong. Forgiveness is for your peace of mind. When we fail to forgive people, we get emotionally stuck in that traumatizing situation that hurts us, unable to progress and move forward. Forgiveness allows us to move on from that point of hurt so we can grow and heal. Forgiveness does not mean forgetting or exposing yourself to more pain, but it also allows you to see if that person has repented and changed from what they did to hurt you.

#852. Matthew 7:24-27 ~ To Hear and Do What Yeshua Says in the Sermon on the Mount

Positive
Loving The Father
Unconditional

The Sermon on the Mount is in Matthew Chapters 5-7 and covers commands 830-852. This sermon is the foundation of Yeshua's teachings in the books of Matthew, Mark, Luke, and John. Almost everything he teaches past Matthew chapter 7 can point us back to something he says in the Sermon on the Mount. Nothing that Yeshua taught was of his own words (See John 14:23-24); everything spoken on the Sermon on the Mount came from the Heavenly Father. The Sermon on the Mount was to a Jewish audience from Galilee, Decapolis, Jerusalem, Judea, and beyond the Jordan (Matthew 4:25). At that time, all those cities were almost exclusively Jewish communities, so it is safe to believe that there were no, or very few, Gentiles in the crowd. Everything that Yeshua said in Matthew chapters 5-7 was to a Jewish audience first and then for anyone else who would believe in him (see John 4:22 & Romans 1:16).

Here is a quick breakdown of the sermon on the mount: The beatitudes/Salt and Light – Matthew 5:2-16: Yeshua starts by blessing the poor in spirit, those who mourn, the gentle, those who hunger and thirst for righteousness, the merciful, the pure of heart, the peacemakers, those persecuted for righteousness' sake, and for his sake. When we look at all these attributes, they are all things that the Heavenly Father has praised in the Bible and things we see in Yeshua. Most of the beatitude attributes are characteristics of the Heavenly Father. The people described in the beatitudes are the same people Yeshua calls "light of the world and salt of the earth."

Torah for Modern Messiah Believers

In Matthew 5:17-20, Yeshua says that he did not come to undo, destroy, or end Torah or the prophets, but to fulfill them. In this section, we see that it is easier for the heavens and earth to be destroyed than for one stroke from Torah or the prophets to fail before all is done. We are still waiting for prophecies to be fulfilled. He says that people who do and teach what is in Torah will be great in the kingdom, and those who do the opposite will not be regarded well. So far, everything that Yeshua has said was without any controversy, but from verse 20, Yeshua begins tearing apart the scribes and Pharisees.

In Matthew 5:21-48, Yeshua begins to correct erroneous teachings from the scribes and Pharisees. Yeshua doesn't stop there. In Matthew 6:1-18, he continues to attack their public displays of giving, praying, and fasting, showing us that such things should be private and not for public glory. For Matthew 6:19-24, Yeshua has us setting our hearts towards the kingdom, and because we are covenanted people with the Heavenly Father, he tells us not to be anxious in Matthew 6:25-34. Keeping Torah comes with promises (See Deuteronomy 28:1-14). Even when we go through troubles in this life, we can still have peace knowing that He is on our side and that things will work out. Just remember Joseph and all that he went through.

Yeshua tells us not to judge others in Matthew 7:1-6; when you think about it, there is no need to. Our judgments are relics of the old flesh we left behind when we decided to covenant with the Heavenly Father. As Israel, we live off the Heavenly Father's judgments; all He teaches is right and wrong. It is essential for spiritual growth that we learn to separate our judgments from Torah and allow the commands of Torah to prevail.

Yeshua teaches us to ask our Heavenly Father for the things we want (Matthew 7:7-11), to treat others as we would like to be treated (Matthew 7:12), to go through the narrow gate (Matthew 7:13-14), and to watch out for false prophets based on what they do (Matthew 7:15-

20). This is the other side of what we learn in Deuteronomy 13:1-4, which teaches us to watch for what they say. Some false prophets might say the right things but do the wrong things; in other words, they are hypocrites. In Matthew 7:21-23, Yeshua says that he does not have a relationship with people who do not live by the Torah. These are the words that this instruction tells us to pay close attention to and to follow.

#853. Luke 6:42 ~ Avoid Hypocrisy

Negative
Loving Abba
Unconditional

Have you ever seen an adult with a lit cigarette in their hand telling kids not to smoke? Yeshua is talking about this. Throughout Matthew, Mark, Luke, and John, he continues to expose the Pharisees as hypocrites and examples of what we should not follow. When you think about it, hypocrisy is an insult to the Heavenly Father because hypocrites pimp the words of Abba to make themselves look good to other people instead of using the words of our Elohim to get right with Him from within. How others view them is far more important than what the Heavenly Father thinks of them. People who are true to the Heavenly Father focus more on the inside than the outside.

Yeshua's words on hypocrisy should be taken very seriously. His message on hypocrisy is not just him telling off the Pharisees; they are also a strong warning to those who follow him. This faith must be done from within. This walk is not about looking good on the outside, this faith is all about the Heavenly Father seeing you clean on the inside! You can fool everyone around you, but you cannot fool the One who is able to see what is really going on within. This alone is the reason why we should listen to Paul when he says, "*work out your own salvation with fear and trembling* (Philippians 2:12)."

#854. Luke 9:35 ~ To listen to Yeshua (Also see John 3:36)

Positive
Loving Abba
Unconditional

This command seems simple to follow, but when we look at the world, maybe it is not so easy. So many people claim to believe in Yeshua worldwide, and yet they ignore what he teaches for doctrines that fly in the face of everything he stands for. When we truly start paying attention to Yeshua and what he said, the covenant relationship with the Heavenly Father becomes the natural progression in our walk. Yet, the enemy has fooled so many people into thinking that if you believe in Yeshua, Torah is void, and that cannot be further from the truth. It is Genesis 3:1-6 on a constant repeat, and it will not end until humanity gets to Revelation chapter 21.

#855. John 13:34 ~ To Love One Another as Yeshua Loves

Positive
Loving People
Unconditional

See 1st John 3:16, 5:1-3, and 2nd John 1:4-6.

How did Yeshua love the disciples, Israel, everyone who lived, is currently living, and will live? When that question is asked, the knee-jerk answer is usually, "He died on the cross for us!" That is only a sliver of the actual answer. Think about it. Had Yeshua sinned just once, the cross would be meaningless and without power. Had Yeshua spoken one thing falsely, the cross would be meaningless and without power. What Yeshua did and said before getting to that cross is the source of all the power and love. Once this is understood, it becomes easy to see that the cross was not where Yeshua's love is. The love that Yeshua displayed was in his perfect obedience to the Heavenly Father before he got to the cross, even up to his last breath! That is how he loves all of Israel and everyone in the world. That is how he wants us to love each other and the Heavenly Father.

#856. John 14:12 ~ To Imitate Yeshua

Positive
Loving People
Unconditional

#857. John 14:15 ~ To Guard the Commands of Yeshua

Positive
Loving People
Unconditional

See #247 for more information.

#858. Romans 12:19 ~ Do Not Seek Revenge

Negative
Loving People
Unconditional

Paul Quotes from Deuteronomy 32:35, Moses' final song.

#859. 1st Corinthians 5:7-8 ~ To Keep the Passover Feast

Positive
Loving Abba
Unconditional

See #13 for more information.

#860. 2nd Corinthians 6:14 ~ Avoid Being Unequally Yoked with Non-Covenanted People

Negative
Loving People
Unconditional

See #747 for more information.

#861. 2nd Corinthians 10:3-5 ~ To Fight Thoughts That Are Against Torah

Positive
Loving Abba
Unconditional

See #4, #60, and #831 for more information.

#862. Ephesians 4:1-6 ~ For the Body of Believers to be Unified

Positive
Loving People
Unconditional

#863. Colossians 3:5-9 ~ Do Not Do as Those in the Flesh

Negative
Loving Abba
Unconditional

#864. Colossians 3:17 ~ To Work as if Unto Yeshua

Positive
Loving People
Unconditional

Also see Colossians 3:23, Ecclesiastes 9:10.

#865. 1st Timothy 4:16 ~ To Watch What You Say and Do Carefully

Positive
Loving People
Unconditional

#866. 1st Timothy 5:8 ~ To Provide for Your Family

Positive
Loving People
Unconditional

#867. 1st Timothy 6:9-10 ~ Do Not Love Money

Negative
Loving Abba
Unconditional

#868. 2nd Timothy 2:22 ~ To Avoid Lust

Negative
Loving People
Unconditional

See commands #60 and #830.

#869. 2nd Timothy 2:22 ~ To Seek Righteousness

Positive
Loving Abba
Unconditional

#870. 1st John 2:6 ~ To Walk as Messiah Walks

Positive
Loving People
Unconditional

See #577 for more information.

#871. James 1:19-20 ~ Seek Understanding More Than to be Understood

Positive
Loving People
Unconditional

#872. James 2:10 ~ To Live by All of Torah

Positive
Loving Abba
Unconditional

See #248 for more information.

This is one of the most misinterpreted verses in the Bible. Many people think that James is saying that when you break one command, you break them all. Here is the complete thought.

> *My brothers, don't hold the faith of our Lord Yeshua,*
> *Messiah of glory, with partiality. If a man with a*

gold ring, in fine clothing, comes into your synagogue, and a poor man in filthy clothing also comes in, and you pay special attention to him who wears the fine clothing, and say, "Sit here in a good place;" and you tell the poor man, "Stand there," or "Sit by my footstool;" haven't you shown partiality among yourselves, and become judges with evil thoughts? Listen, my beloved brothers. Didn't Elohim choose those poor in this world to be rich in faith and heirs of the Kingdom that he promised to those who love him? You have dishonored the poor man. Don't the rich oppress you and personally drag you before the courts? Don't they blaspheme the honorable name by which you are called? However, if you fulfill the royal law, according to the Scripture, "You shall love your neighbor as yourself," you do well, but if you show partiality, you commit sin, being convicted by the law as transgressors. For whoever keeps the whole law and yet stumbles in one point, he has become guilty of all. For he who said, "Do not commit adultery," also said, "Do not commit murder." Now, if you do not commit adultery, but murder, you have become a transgressor of the law. - James 2:1-11

James is saying that we cannot pick and choose commands to keep. The command they were ignoring is #289. The covenant says, "*Now therefore, if you will indeed obey my voice, and keep my covenant, then you shall be my own possession from among all peoples; for all the earth is mine; and you shall be to me a kingdom of priests, and a holy nation. (45)*" In those words, there is no option to pick and choose which of the Father's commands we should keep. We keep all of them. The ones we can keep, we do; the ones we cannot keep, we should still know them, so we are always alert to sin around us. When James spoke those words, favoritism was the subject, a concept that strongly goes against Torah and something people still struggle with today.

#873. 1ˢᵗ John 4:1 ~ To Test Every Spirit

Positive
Loving Abba
Unconditional

There are 3 Biblical ways to fulfill this command, and all 3 ways work together:

- Deuteronomy 13:1-3 (614)
- Luke 9:35 (854)
- 1ˢᵗ John 2:6 (870)

The instructions of the Heavenly Father, written by Moses, are universally absolute. Yeshua verbally honored, defended, and encouraged what Moses and the prophets wrote. Yeshua lived by Torah perfectly.

- Torah
- The words spoken by Yeshua
- And the life of Yeshua

Those 3 witnesses are an ironclad union of woven perfection: Anything that speaks contrary to those 3 witnesses is not from above. Unfortunately, there isn't a shortage of people who "believe" in Yeshua but do not follow Torah, Yeshua's words (at least not all or most of his words), or how Yeshua lived. That is the very definition of the word oxymoron.

#874. Revelation 12:17 ~ To Believe in Yeshua and Keep Torah

Positive
Loving Abba
Unconditional

The biggest thing people overlook in this verse is that the beast identifies its enemies as people who believe in Yeshua and keep the covenant relationship with the Heavenly Father.

#875. Revelation 14:12 ~ To keep the Torah of the Heavenly Father and Believe in Yeshua

Positive
Loving Abba
Unconditional

> *"If anyone worships the beast and his image, and receives a mark on his forehead, or on his hand, he also will drink of the wine of the wrath of God, which is prepared unmixed in the cup of his anger. He will be tormented with fire and sulfur in the presence of the holy angels, and in the presence of the Lamb. The smoke of their torment goes up forever and ever. They have no rest day or night, those who worship the beast and his image, and whoever receives the mark of his name. Here is the perseverance of the saints, those who keep the commandments of Elohim, and the faith of Yeshua."*
>
> - Revelation 14:9-12

The angel who spoke the words above warned us about worshipping the beast. Then, he reaffirmed the beast's enemies by identifying the believers in the same way the beast identifies its enemies in the previous command.

Choose Life

Conclusion:

Now that we've gone through all these commands, what's next? How do we perfectly fuse the Torah lifestyle, faith in Yeshua, worship of the Father, the writings of Paul, and all the other letters written by the Apostles? Let's go back to Genesis.

> *YHWH Elohim commanded the man, saying, "You may freely eat of every tree of the garden; but you shall not eat of the tree of the knowledge of good and evil; for in the day that you eat of it, you will surely die."* – Genesis 2:16-17

What we read in Genesis 2:16-17 is not just a command. The Heavenly Father introduces a universal law of nature that affects all humanity. When we disobey the Heavenly Father, death will cling to our lives. This is what Paul is trying to teach us in Romans 6:23, as he also provides the solution.

In the next chapter, Adam chooses to break the command of the Heavenly Father and eat the fruit he was told not to eat. Shortly after, Elohim addresses Adam, Eve, and the serpent. Along with punishments, the Heavenly Father also gave humanity its very first prophetic gospel message.

> *I will put hostility between you and the woman, and between your offspring and her offspring. He will bruise your head, and you will bruise his heel.* – Genesis 3:15

Choose Life

For the first time, we see a prophecy of someone who will defeat the enemy. This is the plan to save humanity from death and undo the damage done by the serpent. Another important message was given here, but we will return to this verse to tell the rest.

In Genesis 3:21, we see that Elohim makes garments of animal skins for Adam and Eve. From what we know of sacrifices, it is safe to assume that this sacrifice was also to cover the sins of Adam and Eve, in other words, forgiveness.

In Genesis 3:22, the Heavenly Father kicks Adam and Eve out of the garden. Many people think this was a continuation of the punishments, but it was an act of love, mercy, and compassion. Adam and Eve were kicked out of the garden so that they would not eat of the tree of life, which would make them, possibly all of us, live in a fallen state forever with no hope of ever being perfectly restored to the Heavenly Father ever again. That is ultimate mercy.

From this point, we see the Heavenly Father communicating with a line of men who have chosen to go against the grain of what everyone else is doing to follow Abba and do things His way. Eventually, we get to Moses, whom the Heavenly Father has selected to lead the most unique revolution the world has ever known. It is important to point out that from Genesis chapter 3 to Moses, we have seen forgiveness of sins, grace, and mercy from the Heavenly Father. Despite the Heavenly Father's forgiveness of sin, His mercy, love, and favor (grace), none of this could take away death, which is where Yeshua comes in.

In John 5:46, Yeshua said, *"For if you believed Moses, you would believe me; for he wrote about me."* Where exactly does Moses write about Yeshua? Everywhere. Every commandment exposes a characteristic of Yeshua. Torah is Yeshua's ID card. Torah is how we can identify The Messiah and get in sync with him. If Yeshua sinned or lied once, we would know that he is not the one true son of the Heavenly Father. Let's get back to the second part of Genesis 3:15.

Torah for Modern Messiah Believers

Aside from the prophecy of a Messiah who will defeat the enemy, the Heavenly Father also says that the enemy will bruise the heel of the Messiah; this is a metaphor. If your heel is bruised, you cannot walk straight. Yeshua came and lived a specific Hebrew life that was dedicated to the words of Abba written by Moses and the prophets. This is how we should also walk as we follow him. However, almost all the people who claim to believe in the central figure of Matthew, Mark, Luke, and John reject the words of Yeshua and how he lived. Everyone loves the idea of salvation, but many people hate the idea of conforming to the commands of our Elohim. Ultimately, they reject the core of who Yeshua is: Torah. Many claim to believe in him, but do not walk as he walked. If your heel is bruised, you will not walk straight. Thanks to false doctrines, the heel of Yeshua is bruised, and the awkward walk from the bruised heel is seen in everyone who claims to believe in him but does not walk as he walks.

We continuously observe the bruising of Yeshua's heel all around us. We have seen it since Mount Sinai, when the golden calf was made. Anytime Israel walked away from Torah, the heels of Yeshua were getting bruised. Anytime you hear someone say something like, "The Law is done away with!" You are listening to Yeshua's heel getting bruised. Whenever you see a bunch of Christians blessing the pork they are about to eat, you are watching the heel of Yeshua getting bruised. Anytime a Jewish man follows a Halakhah, Takkanah, or Minhag that cancels, takes away, and/or contradicts something that Moses wrote, or makes them equal to what Moses wrote, the heel of Yeshua gets bruised. Anytime we see Messianic and/or Hebrew Roots leaders integrate Christian doctrines into the Torah Walk, you are seeing the heels of Yeshua getting bruised. When someone wants to replace Christmas with Chanukkah or Halloween with Purim, the heel of Yeshua gets bruised. Our obedience to Torah in truth and spirit is how we counteract the bruising of Yeshua's heel.

The bruising of Yeshua's heels is how the enemy tricks people into thinking they are following Yeshua, but they are far from the narrow road. Sadly, the enemy is effective at the bruising of Yeshua's heel and many around the world have fallen for it. If you think you are on the right path, you will not be looking for it. This is why we must continually pray that the Heavenly Father give people eyes to see and ears to hear (Deuteronomy 29:4).

From Genesis 1:1 to Revelation 21:27, our Heavenly Father displays grace, mercy, and forgiveness of sins; despite all this, the universal rule of sin and death is absolute. Once we have sinned, we can repent and ask for forgiveness, but that does not change our appointment with death. This is where Yeshua steps in and says, "*I am the way, the truth, and the life. No one comes to the Father, except through me* (John 14:6)."

When we guard Yeshua's words (John 14:23-24) and walk like he walks (1st John 2:6 & 1st Peter 2:21), that is when we truly believe in him. When we mature in the imitation of Yeshua and breathe our last breath, we will resurrect from the dead like he did. That is the summary of Romans chapter 6. Keeping Torah from within is how we connect to Yeshua (Matthew 5:17-19, Matthew 7:21-23, Luke 8:20-21, John 14:15-24, 1st John 2:6, Revelation 12:17, and Revelation 14:12). When we are connected to Yeshua, we have access to the Heavenly Father. That is the goal of Torah and why this book is written.

To The Messianic/Hebrew Roots Community:

We can do better. Yeshua said, "*By this everyone will know that you are my disciples, if you have love for one another.* (John 13:35)" Paul said, "*There should be no division in the body...* (1st Corinthians 12:25)" How can we show the world the love of Yeshua if we are so divided? Over the years, I've held certain jobs that allowed me to travel across the country and visit Messianic groups from Florida to California. It is hard to identify how many Messianic groups are out there. Some have a web presence, many do not. The main question I've asked for years is, "Why isn't there more unity within the Messianic community?"

Torah is supposed to unify us, Yeshua is supposed to unify us, and Paul wrote heavily about the unification of the body. We should not be as divided as we are today. There is so much division within the faith because far too many doctrines from mainstream theology are being woven into a walk that completely clash. Mainstream theology and Torah do not mix.

Let us throw away all the horrible mainstream doctrines that have become a cancer for the body of believers. On the opposite side, let us reject the teachings of Judaism that clash with the words written by Moses. Let us use the purity of Torah as the foundational platform to open dialogues and build unification within the faith. I suspect that one of the reasons why Yeshua has not returned yet is that the body is simply not ready for his return. If you are a Messianic leader reading this, I hope I was able to soften your heart to fight for unification under Torah!

Yeshua is our High Priest in the Order of Melchizedek! The Melchizedek priesthood is a ministry that teaches the righteousness of our Heavenly Father: Torah. Let us unite in following Yeshua's example and show people what it means to be Torah observant. Let us dive into the difficult subjects of Torah together. Through our dedication to Torah as Moses wrote it, let us move those within Judaism to jealousy as Paul said in Romans 11:11. Let us boldly tackle the hard questions whispered in the dark corners of our faith together! As we do so, let us love one another. I challenge all who believe themselves to be Torah observant. Let us remove the "messy" from Messianic to present a proper body of Messiah. A unified body of believers who love one another and are truly

Choose Life

Choose Life

passionate about Torah as Moses wrote it. This is what The Heavenly Father wants us to be, and what Yeshua desires for his followers.

I leave you all with the last chapter of Malachi. Thank you for reading this book, and to YHWH be all the glory!

> "For, behold, the day comes, it burns as a furnace; and all the proud, and all who work wickedness, will be stubble; and the day that comes will burn them up," says YHWH of Armies, "that it shall leave them neither root nor branch. But to you who fear my name shall the sun of righteousness arise with healing in its wings. You will go out and leap like calves of the stall. You shall tread down the wicked; for they will be ashes under the soles of your feet in the day that I make," says YHWH of Armies. "Remember the Torah of Moses, my servant, which I commanded him in Horeb for all Israel, even statutes and ordinances. Behold, I will send you Elijah the prophet before the great and terrible day of YHWH comes. He will turn the hearts of the fathers to the children, and the hearts of the children to their fathers, lest I come and strike the earth with a curse." - Malachi 4:1-6

www.ingramcontent.com/pod-product-compliance
Lightning Source LLC
Chambersburg PA
CBHW061546120626
46550CB00004B/1386